PENGUIN BOOKS

every
parent

Dr Matthew Sanders is a Professor of Clinical Psychology and Director of the Parenting and Family Support Centre at The University of Queensland. He conducts research in the areas of parenting, family psychology and the prevention of behavioural and emotional problems in children. He is the founder of the internationally recognised Triple P-Positive Parenting Program, which has won a National Violence Prevention Award from the Commonwealth Heads of Government in Australia. He has received an International Collaborative Prevention Research Award, is a fellow of the Australian Psychological Society and the Academy of Experimental Criminology. He is married with two adult children.

every
parent

a positive approach
to children's behaviour

Matthew R. Sanders PhD

PENGUIN BOOKS

PENGUIN BOOKS

Published by the Penguin Group
Penguin Group (Australia)
250 Camberwell Road, Camberwell, Victoria 3124, Australia
(a division of Pearson Australia Group Pty Ltd)
Penguin Group (USA) Inc.
375 Hudson Street, New York, New York 10014, USA
Penguin Group (Canada)
90 Eglinton Avenue East, Suite 700, Toronto, ONM4P 2Y3, Canada
(a division of Pearson Penguin Canada Inc.)
Penguin Books Ltd
80 Strand, London WC2R 0RL, England
Penguin Ireland
25 St Stephen's Green, Dublin 2, Ireland
(a division of Penguin Books Ltd)
Penguin Books India Pvt Ltd
11, Community Centre, Panchsheel Park, New Delhi-110 017, India
Penguin Group (NZ)
67 Apollo Drive, Rosedale, North Shore 0632, New Zealand
(a division of Pearson New Zealand Ltd)
Penguin Books (South Africa) (Pty) Ltd
24 Sturdee Avenue, Rosebank, Johannesburg 2196, South Africa

Penguin Books Ltd, Registered Offices: 80 Strand, London, WC2R 0RL, England

First published by Pearson Education Australia, 1992
This revised edition published by Penguin Group (Australia), 2004

10 9 8 7

Design by Gayna Murphy © Penguin Group (Australia)
Typeset in Bembo regular 12/14pt by Midland Typesetters, Maryborough, Victoria
Printed and bound in Australia by McPherson's Printing Group, Maryborough, Victoria

National Library of Australia
Cataloguing-in-Publication data:

Sanders, Matthew R.
Every parent: a positive approach to children's behaviour

Rev. ed.
Includes index.
ISBN 9780143002116.

1. Child psychology – Popular works. 2. Behavior disorders in children –
Treatment. 3. Child development. I. Title.

649.64

penguin.com.au

CONTENTS

Tables and figures

Tables

Figures

[*]Figures reproduced in Appendix 4 in reusable form.

PREFACE

It is difficult to think of a more challenging task than being a parent. For an undertaking for which no training is provided and is typically learned on the job, it is a big responsibility. It is little wonder that so many parents experience difficulties and times of uncertainty.

This new edition of *Every Parent* is about how to build positive relationships with children and to help children develop the skills, values and behaviours that enable them to do well in life. *Every Parent* provides plenty of no-nonsense, practical advice on how to deal with a wide range of common everyday parenting situations and behaviours to prevent children developing serious behavioural or emotional problems. Essentially, it tries to make the task of raising children a little easier. In my twenty-seven years' experience as a clinical psychologist working with parents and children, I have found that parents are generally looking for practical ideas that work and can readily be put into action with their children; this book aims to do just that.

Since the first edition of *Every Parent* was published, I have received a lot of feedback from parents and childcare professionals about things they would like to learn more about. Each chapter of *Every Parent* has been revised and updated to incorporate new findings from research on how to help parents raise their children. The successful core features of the first edition are preserved; namely, each chapter contains helpful advice on how to prevent or manage a wide variety of common behavioural and emotional problems. There is also a new chapter – 'The Foundations for Successful Parenthood' – that focuses on family survival skills and includes important parenting tips on developing better teamwork between parents, successfully balancing work and family roles, the importance of thinking positively about children, and ways of coping with the stress of parenthood. In this edition I have given greater attention to how parents can deal with children's feelings and emotional problems such as worry and anxiety. I have also introduced additional strategies for helping children make a successful transition to school, to become more independent and to develop healthy self-esteem.

The five core principles of positive parenting described in Chapter 1 remain the essential tools for promoting healthy adjustment in children. However, the term 'constructive parenting' better captures what this approach is really about. Constructive parenting is all about building competencies. It's about how parents can teach their children to develop the social, emotional, language and interpersonal skills they need to do well in life. This approach emphasises laying solid foundations early in life so that children have the social and emotional skills they need to succeed. It is about building alternatives for children rather than simply reducing or managing problem behaviour. The approach involves a fairly simple idea: for every problem a child experiences, there are skills and behaviours they can learn that will help them successfully deal with the situation that is causing concern. For example, when a parent gets annoyed because their child uses a whining voice when asking for something and then screams if the request is refused, the child needs to learn how to make requests using a pleasant voice, and if the answer is no, they need to learn to accept the 'bad news' without becoming upset and/or rude. Constructive parenting gives parents the skills they need to help children learn acceptable behaviour that enables them to get along well with others.

I hope that readers find this book useful in undertaking an important and potentially extremely rewarding job in our society: raising well-adjusted youngsters.

NOTES TO THE PRACTITIONER

This book was written primarily for parents and other carers look-ing for practical information and advice on the prevention and management of common behavioural and emotional problems in preadolescent children. Professional therapists may also find the book useful as a tool to complement individual or group work with parents of children with behavioural or emotional problems, or as a resource for parents with common everyday problems with their children. The material is likely to be of interest to any professional working with parents and/or children.

Every Parent strongly emphasises the importance of parents learning how to teach their children the behavioural and emotional skills they need to more effectively deal with situations that cause problems. The parenting information contained in this book is divided into three sections. Part 1 provides background information to help parents better understand the nature and causes of behavioural and emotional problems in children. It also introduces parents to five core principles of constructive parenting and eighteen specific strategies to prevent or manage difficult behaviour in children. Part 2 is a step-by-step parenting guide to dealing with common problems of infants, toddlers, preschoolers and primary-school-aged children. Part 3 provides guidelines on how parents can put a specific parenting plan into action.

The advice in *Every Parent* has been thoroughly evaluated in a series of randomised, controlled trials involving families who sought assistance through the Parenting and Family Support Centre at The University of Queensland. A list of publications relating to these trials can be accessed through our website at http://www.pfsc.uq.edu.au/01_about_us/publications.html.

This book can be very useful when used as a reading assignment for parents undergoing therapy or counselling. Specific management advice for a wide range of behavioural and emotional problems is provided in Chapters 5–7 and a guide to implementing the advice appears in Chapter 8.

Many parents can learn about these skills simply by reading the material in this book and then putting what they read into action. However, some parents require more focused support. This typically involves: providing specific guidance on how to tackle a specific problem, demonstration and modelling of the relevant skills through role play, and coaching for parents as they practise the skills while the therapist observes the family interaction and provides feedback. Feedback and support, particularly in the early stages, is needed for many families. The level of support provided to parents varies depending on the case.

PART ONE

constructive parenting

AN OVERVIEW

CHAPTER 1

What is constructive parenting?

The challenge

Being a parent is difficult. It is a demanding, challenging and, at times, frustrating experience. It can also be tremendously rewarding. It is a full-time, lifelong, unpaid and expensive endeavour. Most parents enter their parenting career unprepared for what lies ahead, and most complete their task with little recognition or thanks for their efforts. However, there is no occupation that is more important than raising the next generation. We are expected by society and by our families to nurture and care for our children in a way that promotes their development and emotional wellbeing. This basic task of raising children is a complex one. In the process of growing up, children need to develop a sense of their own personal worth and identity, and to learn to manage their emotions. They also need to learn a great many skills that will enable them to become responsible, independent, competent, self-disciplined and well-adjusted human beings. The fundamental challenge for every parent is to raise healthy, well-adjusted children who have the necessary skills and resources to enter adult life.

What can parents do to meet this challenge? In many ways the task revolves around understanding the factors that influence children's behaviour and development. It involves learning how to promote a healthy, positive parent–child relationship, and how to encourage desirable behaviour and to deal effectively with misbehaviour. Every parent must decide for themselves what behaviours, skills and values they wish to encourage in their children. They also must decide what behaviours they wish to discourage and how they will handle their child's misbehaviour, which usually begins to occur well before the child's second birthday. Most parents find that there are no simple answers.

Parents often ask themselves questions about how to tackle specific parenting tasks. Some of these questions concern how to promote certain traits or qualities they would like to see in their children: 'How can I encourage my child to be cooperative?', 'How can I encourage her to feel good about herself?' and 'How can I encourage him to be interested in music?'. At other times parents look for ideas about how to teach their children specific skills: 'What is the best way to toilet-train my two-year-old?', 'How can I teach my four-year-old to share and take turns?' or 'What can I do to get my kids into a good homework routine?'. Parents also want to know about how to get along well with their children. Questions such as, 'What can I do to ensure I have a good relationship with my children?' reflect this concern. Other questions focus on how to deal with misbehaviour: 'What should I do if my child bites or hurts another child?', 'What should I do when my kids fight and argue with each other?' or 'How do I get my child to stay in his own bed at night?'. These and many other issues are just some of the practical concerns of parents learning to raise children.

We all want our children to grow into well-adjusted youngsters, free from major emotional and behavioural problems, but few of us have any specific training in parenting skills to help us achieve this goal. We rely on our own commonsense and judgement, and our experience of being parented ourselves as children. Some parents read books about children's development or get advice from their parents or from friends who have children. Most of us, however, learn to parent on the job through much trial and error.

Fortunately, many common behavioural and emotional problems in children can be prevented. That is why this book focuses on how to prevent these problems in infants, toddlers, preschoolers and school-aged children. Much of the parenting advice given here is quite specific; you will find an easy-to-follow, step-by-step guide on ways of dealing with problems as varied as handling crying and whining in toddlers, to helping children learn to solve problems for themselves.

The material in this book is based on my experience over twenty-five years in researching and treating problems raised by parents who sought professional help for their children and themselves, and on my experience in raising two children of my own. Thousands of children and their families have used the parenting advice in this book, with excellent results. The parenting information has been tested in many studies involving parents experiencing behavioural problems with their children.

Getting the most out of this book

To get the most out of this book, I suggest you refer to the relevant section whenever you need suggestions for dealing with particular issues. Each problem discussed has a self-contained guide for preventing or overcoming the problem. You may be tempted to turn immediately to Part 2, which deals with solutions to the specific problems you may be having with your child, but you will find these specific advice sections more helpful if you read the material in Part 1 first. This section deals with different types of behavioural problems, the causes of these problems, and strategies that can be used to promote positive family relationships and thereby prevent many problems from arising. So, read the first section and then refer to the sections of particular interest to you. If you decide to try one or more of the suggested strategies for handling particular issues, refer to the final chapter, which deals with putting your plan into action. It is also a good idea to prepare yourself by reading the sections relating to problems that may be encountered in your child's next developmental phase.

You may have already sought professional help. If so, it's worth discussing your plans with your counsellor to ensure that you are not working at cross-purposes.

Parent traps

Do you frequently feel exasperated, ashamed or embarrassed by your child's behaviour? Do you find that your child often irritates you or that you have to threaten and shout a lot to get any cooperation? Do you ever feel that you dislike your child? Do you argue with your partner about how to handle your child's behaviour? Do you criticise yourself for being a less than perfect parent? If the answer to any of these questions is yes, you may have become caught in a parent trap.

Parent traps are self-defeating situations that parents find themselves caught up in and do not know how to get out of. Parent traps add to the level of stress that many parents experience, and make the job of raising children more difficult. Constructive parenting is a way to avoid these parent traps. It involves learning to change children's behaviour without resorting to yelling, and how to positively motivate children and work as a team with your partner on parenting issues. Following are the most common parent traps (see Chapters 3–8 for advice on how to deal with them).

The 'Criticism trap' involves the parent becoming locked into frequent and usually unnecessary power struggles with their child. It typically involves the parent reacting to the child's misbehaviour, such as fighting and arguing, with criticism ('Robert, leave your brother alone.'); threats ('If you do that one more time you're in big trouble, my boy.'); yelling ('Robert! Leave him alone!'); or hitting. This type of discipline, in which the parent's anger escalates rapidly, often backfires and can lead to resentment and further hostility between parent and child. If these kinds of battles take place frequently, family life can be stressful and it's time to try a new way of handling the situation.

The 'Leave them alone trap' occurs in combination with the criticism trap and involves the parent ignoring the child when they are behaving well or playing cooperatively. If good behaviour is taken for granted and ignored, it will occur less often in the future. A basic principle of positive parenting involves attending to and encouraging the behaviour you would like to see more often.

The 'For the sake of the children trap' involves parents in unhappy or high-conflict relationships staying together for the sake of their children rather than learning ways to resolve their disagreements. The assumption is that children need two stable parents; this ideal is challenged by research that shows that children who live in families where there is a lot of conflict and stress between the parents have more emotional and behavioural problems than children raised in stable one-parent families. Serious relationship problems should not be ignored. Conflict over parenting causes inconsistency, which in turn makes many behavioural problems worse.

The 'Perfect parent trap' is the result of our desire to be perfect rather than merely competent parents. Since there is no such thing as a perfect parent, aspiring to become one can lead to disappointment, resentment, and feelings of guilt and inadequacy.

The 'Martyr trap' occurs when parents become so over-involved in parenting that they neglect their own needs for fun, intimacy, companionship, recreation and privacy, only to find that their personal relationships suffer and they end up feeling dissatisfied and resentful. Quality parenting takes place when adults have their own lives in balance. Being a martyr does not produce quality parenting.

The 'It's all their fault trap' occurs when parents blame children for their misbehaviour. Parents can sometimes interpret the actions of their children as a deliberate attempt to upset the parent or make their life difficult. When parents believe there is a conspiracy against them, they are more likely to feel angry and irritated by their children and overreact when problems occur. Problem behaviour is rarely the result of children deliberately setting out to harm or upset their parents.

The 'It's all my fault trap' involves parents blaming themselves for everything their child does. Parents caught in this trap tend to criticise themselves whenever anything goes wrong. They can become anxious and feel depressed and exhausted. Most behavioural problems in children are the result of several different factors. Parenting is important but it is not the only thing that affects children. The influence of peers, schools and the wider community can all influence the types of behaviours children learn. The challenge for parents is to identify things they can do something about.

Common parenting problems

Let's look at some common behavioural and emotional problems and the difficulties they create for families. If you recognise your child, don't despair. Remember that solutions for each behaviour pattern are offered later.

The whiner

Whether we call it whining, whingeing, fussing or complaining, most parents are intimately acquainted with this problem. The tone of a child's voice that turns a request into a demand, especially when it occurs often, can drive a parent to distraction. Many parents report that from the first time she opened her mouth the whiner seemed to have a high-pitched, nasal tone. They go on to give endless examples: apart from whining for food before the evening meal, she will whine if a brother or sister touches anything of hers, she will whine during trips to the supermarket, trips in the car, and especially when the family visits her grandparents. In fact, the whiner seems to be whining all the time. Many parents of whiners pride themselves on being patient and tolerant. They try very hard not to get upset or angry, but the pressure of having a child who constantly whines takes its toll. The parents may be fuming inside, and begin to worry when they start to resent the time they devote to their children. Often this prompts them to seek professional help.

The tantrum thrower

Since perhaps the age of eighteen months this child has thrown incredible temper tantrums. The tantrum thrower's behaviour may become so unacceptable that his mother is requested to remove him from childcare, kindergarten or preschool. When he throws a tantrum – and that can be up to eight times a day – he can be heard at the end of the street. Some tantrum throwers' neighbours, convinced the child is being physically abused, call the police. A tantrum for this child consists of throwing himself to the floor, screaming at the top of his voice, hitting his hands and legs against the floor and, on occasions, holding his breath until he is blue in the face. The tantrums can last from thirty seconds to sixty minutes and are used as a way of controlling others and getting his own way. For example, he might throw a tantrum if refused something he wants. Many parents of tantrum throwers have reached desperation point when they seek professional help. They feel they have tried everything: pleading, bribing, spanking, trying to distract the child, and even ignoring the behaviour. Nothing has worked.

The bed refuser

This child doesn't really have a bed, or so it would seem. She sleeps on the floor in front of the television until her parents are ready for bed. Then she sleeps snuggled happily between the two of them. She simply refuses to go to bed in her own room and her parents have long since given up trying to make her stay in her own bed. They have also given up trying to put her to bed at anything like a reasonable hour. She usually decides when she goes to sleep. On most nights she falls asleep in front of the television somewhere between 9.30 and 10.30 p.m. She wakes when one of her parents picks her up to take her to bed. Unless she is put into her parents' bed, she screams at the top of her voice until her parents finally give in. She is capable of screaming continuously for over an hour. Children who refuse to go to bed, repeatedly get out of bed or frequently wake during the night can become a real handful for parents.

The bad sport

This child hates to lose. Ever since his parents can remember, he has had a competitive streak. In the beginning, one or both parents might have secretly admired the fact that the boy had spirit, but they did not actively encourage him to view every game or activity as something he had to win. He became a sore loser. When the bad sport starts school, the other children may not want to play with him. His teacher will often report that he tries to bully and dominate his classmates. This does not really surprise his parents, who will have witnessed a scene like the following often. Their child is playing 'Star Wars' with his neighbour. They play quite happily for about ten minutes while the bad sport tells his friend exactly what to do and repeatedly shoots down his space ship. However, as soon as it is the other child's turn, the bad sport refuses to 'die'. After being shot he immediately gets up, throws his space ship to the ground and storms off in a huff. Often he will then burst in the back door sobbing, telling his parents that his friend 'always shoots down my ship'. The bad sport's must-win attitude and competitive behaviour are his great undoing. If something isn't done to help him cope more effectively with his peers, he will end up being rejected by them.

The fussy eater

Some children with behavioural problems are not as noisy as the first two. A friendly, polite six-year-old who is liked by just about everyone she meets might be a fussy eater. At the dinner table she constantly plays with her food, eats very slowly and won't try a wide range of foods. She also refuses to use utensils properly, leaves the table frequently, complains about not being hungry and becomes quite upset if pressured to eat. However, within thirty minutes of leaving the table, usually with her evening meal barely touched, she often wants a snack, typically a sandwich. Parents of fussy eaters claim that they refuse to eat anything that is good for them, such as meat and vegetables. All that fussy eaters really want is bread, ice-cream and sweets, a diet that is not designed to build strong, healthy bones and muscles. When, where, what and how a child eats is a major worry for many parents of young children. Many conflicts with children are fought at the family dinner table. Some parents spend the whole meal prodding, threatening or pleading with their child to eat a small portion of carrot or broccoli. Others spend their time hassling their children about table manners, eating too slowly or gulping food. As we will find out, many of these problems can be avoided completely if the meal time is managed differently.

Improving children's behaviour through constructive parenting

Children who whine, throw tantrums, refuse to go to bed, are bad sports or are fussy eaters, all have one problem in common: their behaviour brings them into conflict with others, usually their parents but in some cases, with teachers and peers. Their parents often hope that the behaviour causing the trouble will just go away. Various people may have advised them that the problem is 'just a phase' and that the child will eventually grow out of it. In many cases, however, the opposite is true. The problem becomes worse.

Improvements begin when parents take action. This action involves the parents learning positive ways of reacting to the child's behaviour. It requires them to change their usual way of handling the behaviour. For many parents the solution is straightforward: it simply requires a decision to try a different way of dealing with the behaviour. For a few parents, other important changes are also needed. For example, parents who are preoccupied with their own interests, careers or other pursuits may neglect their child's needs for love, attention, affection and adequate supervision. These parents may need to change their priorities to allow more time for their child. For other parents, all that is required is a minor adjustment to the strategies or tactics they already use. Sometimes small changes can lead to big differences in a child's behaviour.

Values and constructive parenting

How parents raise a child is strongly influenced by their values and beliefs. What we see as being acceptable behaviour is influenced by the values we consider important. For example, parents who view total obedience as important to family life will interpret children's challenges to adult authority, such as a child becoming argumentative, as a threat, and this may lead to confrontation. Another parent may see the same argumentative behaviour as the child learning to express an opinion, to stand up for themselves and to be assertive. The same behaviour can therefore be viewed either as a problem or as quite healthy, depending on our values.

The skills children need to learn

Constructive parenting emphasises the importance of helping children become responsible, self-reliant and self-disciplined. It also focuses on helping children learn to become independent decision-makers and problem-solvers. At the same time, however, children need to become socially skilled human beings who get along with others. This involves children learning how to compromise and to respect the rights and opinions of others, including their parents. Self-discipline stems partly from having clear guidelines and ground rules. All parents ultimately have to decide what values are important to promote in their children. There are four sets of skills that are particularly important to children's development, and will enable children to succeed at school and beyond.

1. **Language, communication and social skills**
    It is through language that children learn to communicate their needs. The ability to speak and communicate well is also necessary for children to develop social and interpersonal skills. Children with well-developed social skills get along well with other children and adults in their lives. Some important social skills include sharing, taking turns, politely making requests and expressing ideas, opinions and feelings appropriately. Many parents want their children to have good manners, be respectful towards elders and to be helpful around the home.

2. **Managing emotions**

In the process of growing up, children gradually develop the ability to recognise, accept, express and manage their emotions. Children experience many different emotions including positive feelings of excitement, joy, love, acceptance and happiness, and negative feelings of frustration, disappointment, anxiety, anger, loss and sadness. The challenge for parents is to help children deal with these feelings and express them in appropriate ways. For example, it is normal and healthy for children to feel angry and disappointed about not getting their own way about something, but it is not okay for children to express their disappointment by lashing out and hurting others.

3. **Independence skills**

Children who learn to do things for themselves at an early age have an advantage over children who do not. There are many self-care skills children learn, such as getting dressed, using the toilet, brushing teeth and hair, using eating utensils, tidying away toys and doing homework. Parents who encourage children to do things for themselves from an early age help children learn to be responsible and show them that they can control their world and what happens to them through their own actions and initiative.

4. **Problem-solving skills**

Children who become good problem-solvers develop a basic belief in themselves. When confronted with an obstacle, such as not being able to put together a toy or make it work, they will try to solve the problem for themselves first, before seeking their parents' help. Good problem-solvers are optimistic and view difficulties as challenges rather than obstacles. Children living in homes where they see their parents solving problems (such as discussing a difficulty openly and generating solutions or reaching a compromise) grow up believing that problems do have solutions. They also come to realise that many solutions require their own personal effort. Children who grow up with good communication and social skills, and who are emotionally expressive, are more likely to become resourceful and independent problem-solvers who succeed in school and beyond.

What is constructive parenting?

Constructive parenting is an approach to raising children that helps children become socially and emotionally competent. It emphasises the importance of creating opportunities for children to learn the skills they need in order to do well in life. It involves treating children with respect and being positive towards them in our everyday dealings, and recognising the uniqueness and strengths of every child. As part of constructive parenting, parents must look for everyday opportunities for children to grow and to develop their potential in many areas of life. Constructive parents usually have a very positive outlook on life, and are pleasant to their children. Constructive parenting advocates five key principles of positive parenting that promote healthy adjustment in children.

1. **Create a safe, secure and engaging environment**
    When children grow up in a home that has plenty of interesting, age-appropriate activities available, they can spend much of their time amusing themselves, absorbed in purposeful activity. This is relevant to children of all ages. An interesting environment also needs to be a safe one.

2. **Foster a positive learning environment**
    Children growing up in a positive learning environment receive plenty of recognition, encouragement and acknowledgement for their efforts, and are more motivated to learn new skills and behaviours. There are many ways parents can show their approval, including praising children's efforts, giving attention such as a wink, smile or thumbs up, or simply spending time with their children.

3. **Use assertive discipline**
    All children misbehave at times. Constructive parents recognise that successful parenting involves dealing assertively, consistently, fairly and decisively with misbehaviour. They set rules and limits, and ensure that children know where they stand, what is acceptable behaviour and what their parents expect of them.

4. **Have reasonable expectations**
    Constructive parenting involves having reasonable expectations of children. This means that parents are neither too lenient nor too tough. They expect their children to succeed and to become capable. Children learn from an early age that their parents expect them to behave appropriately and to try their best when tackling challenging tasks.
5. **Look after yourself as a parent**
    Constructive parents know that their ability to parent is affected by many things in their lives. They look after themselves physically and emotionally. They do this by eating well, getting sufficient exercise and sleep, balancing work and family responsibilities, getting emotional and practical support as a parent, and taking care of their personal relationships with partners, family and workmates. Parents who look after their own needs have more time, energy and patience to parent well.

Above all, constructive parenting is concerned with equipping children with the life skills and values that enable children to participate in their community as emotionally healthy and greatly valued individuals.

Different types of behavioural and emotional problems

As children move from infancy to adolescence, they may behave in ways that cause concern to their parents. Behavioural and emotional problems come in many shapes and forms; some are short-lived and improve with age, while others are more persistent and can be related to more serious psychological disturbances in later life. Behavioural and emotional problems can be divided into two main types: the common, everyday behavioural problems of all children, and behaviours that are symptoms of more serious behavioural or emotional disturbances.

Common everyday behavioural 'problems' of children

All children behave at times in irritating, disruptive ways that may produce conflict within the family, such as making silly noises or pulling faces at the dinner table. While these kinds of behaviours are 'problems' in the sense that they may be a source of family friction or tension, they are quite normal and common in children of a similar age. These problems usually decrease as the child matures, providing the parents deal with them sensibly.

Examples of such behaviours in infants and preschool-age children include crying and fussing, whining and attention seeking, occasional fussy eating habits, fear of strangers, bedtime problems, thumb-sucking, disobedience and clingy, dependent behaviour. Other common problems include hassles in getting a child to cooperate with family routines such as getting dressed, having a bath, cleaning teeth, eating meals, going to bed at night or going shopping. Sibling conflict involving arguments and disagreements is also common. Effective handling of these normal family hassles can prevent more difficult problems from arising, while their mismanagement in young children can lead to the development of more serious problems in school-age children and teenagers.

More severe behavioural and emotional problems

Some children develop more serious problems, where the child's behaviour is clearly different from that of other children the same age. For example, many children have occasional fights or disagreements with their brothers or sisters, but a child with a serious conduct problem may have many more such fights, both at home and at school, may lose her temper frequently in a rage of uncontrollable anger and break and destroy her siblings' belongings, and then experience little guilt or remorse. The troublesome behaviour pattern tends to occur frequently, persists over time and may be associated with other symptoms of psychological disturbance.

The majority of children's behavioural and emotional problems can be divided into two groups.

1. **Externalising problems**

    These are generally conduct or 'acting out' problems that bring the child into conflict with others. Examples include behaviours such as disobedience, stealing, aggression, showing off, truancy, bullying, lying, being cheeky and disruptive at school, demanding attention, being selfish, being rude or throwing temper tantrums. These problems are often described as conduct disturbances. They range from mild to severe and occur more often in boys than in girls. Mild conduct problems typically include such behaviours as whining, non compliance, seeking attention, tantrums and being demanding.

More severe conduct problems can persist into adolescence and adulthood. These include aggressiveness, stealing, lying, threatening, destructive behaviour and truancy. Serious conduct disturbances often start out as mild problems at preschool age and get worse as the child moves through primary schooling. Children with severe conduct problems often have poor peer relationships, are more likely to drop out of school, and are at risk of developing antisocial personalities, alcohol and drug addiction problems, criminal behaviour or other emotional problems as adults. Conduct disorders are the most common reasons for referral to mental health clinics for children, and about a third of these children develop serious behavioural and emotional problems as adults.

2. **Internalising problems**
These tend to be distressing to the individual child, who is often anxious and has low self-esteem. Other problems can include phobias (intense irrational fears), anxiety and worrying, depression, sleeping problems, stomach aches, headaches, nausea, shyness, social withdrawal and obsessions (recurring irrational and unwanted thoughts). Internalising problems are more frequent in girls than in boys, and once again range from mild to severe.

Some children experience both internalising and externalising problems. Unfortunately, the majority of children with behavioural or emotional problems do not receive any professional help.

This book looks at ways of helping both groups of children: those with common behavioural problems, and those with more severe behavioural or emotional disturbances. In Chapter 3, we look more closely at some of the causes of behavioural problems, because before we can solve a child's problem, we must understand why children behave as they do.

Increasing self-confidence in parenting

Learning to parent well is about building self-confidence through experience and on-the-job learning. Parents these days are bombarded with lots of advice on how to raise children. This advice can be confusing and contradictory, and parents must remember that it is the job of each individual parent to decide for themselves how they wish to raise their child. As parents undertake new parenting tasks and skills, and learn through experience, most parents become more self-sufficient and eventually able to make most decisions without having to turn to anyone else for advice or help.

Successful parenting involves trusting your own judgement and believing in your parenting capabilities. One way to think about this is to write down all the tasks you have to do from the time your child wakes up in the morning until they finally fall asleep for the night (such as dressing, feeding, getting ready to go out and settling at night). For each task, rate your confidence in successfully managing the task on a 1–10 scale (1 = not confident at all; 10 = very confident). Add up your scores for each task and then divide by the number of tasks on your list. Parents who have high confidence scores between 8 and 10 are less likely to become annoyed with their children, and their children display fewer behavioural and emotional problems.

As a starting point, take the following parenting confidence quiz. Then, after reading *Every Parent*, take the quiz again to see what changes you have been able to make. To increase your confidence, follow the practical advice in Chapter 8, which shows you how to set clear, specific parenting goals and to keep track of whether you have been able to achieve them.

Conclusions

Learning to be a successful parent is one of the greatest challenges a person faces in adult life. Everyone has to learn parenting skills, and there are no simple answers. Parenting is about helping children learn

Table 1: Parenting confidence quiz

This quiz assesses your confidence in dealing with common parent-ing situations. Imagine that your child engages in the behaviours listed below. For each one, rate how confident you are that you could successfully deal with your child's behaviour in the situation.

Rating scale:

1. Not confident **2.** A little confident **3.** Somewhat confident **4.** Very confident

SPECIFIC PARENTING SITUATIONS	HOW CONFIDENT ARE YOU? 1–4
1. My child won't get out of bed in the morning	
2. My child shows a fear reaction to strangers	
3. My child refuses to get dressed	
4. My child refuses to eat breakfast, lunch or dinner	
5. My child misbehaves when we have visitors	
6. My child gets upset after being refused something	
7. My child wanders off or runs away when we are out	
8. My child whines or complains	
9. My child constantly seeks attention	
10. My child interrupts when I am on the telephone	
11. My child misbehaves while travelling in the car	
12. My child becomes upset when I leave them with a babysitter	

13. My child refuses to do what they have been told

14. My child misbehaves when we are out (for example, while shopping)

15. My child becomes anxious or tense

16. My child becomes self-conscious or easily embarrassed when watched by others

17. My child becomes unhappy, sad or depressed

18. My child is aggressive towards other children

19. My child throws temper tantrums

20. My child spends too much time watching television or playing computer games

21. My child refuses to do their chores

22. My child swears

23. My child runs themselves down (for example, 'Nobody likes me')

24. My child lies to me

25. My child tells me about being bullied by another child at school

Total score

Scores:
80–100   High level of parenting confidence
61–79   Moderate level of parenting confidence
25–60   Low level of parenting confidence

the social and emotional skills they need in order to do well in life. It also involves avoiding common parent traps that can lead children to develop behavioural and emotional problems. Constructive parenting involves five key principles of positive parenting.

1. Create a safe, secure and engaging environment.
2. Foster a positive learning environment.
3. Use assertive discipline.
4. Have reasonable expectations.
5. Look after yourself as a parent.

These principles ensure that children will grow up in a stable, loving home that provides a solid foundation for them to develop emotionally and physically.

CHAPTER 2

The foundations for successful parenthood

Parenthood is a life-changing experience. With the arrival of children come the added responsibilities of taking care of them both emotionally and financially. Most new parents find that some important adjustments to their lifestyle are required. Parenting involves making a lifelong commitment to our children to provide the love, care and emotional support they need. Being a good parent is not something that just comes naturally, and a lot of time and energy goes into learning the skills. However, being a parent is easier and much less stressful when there are solid foundations or building blocks to work from. Adults, like children, do better when solid foundations are laid. These foundations or building blocks for adults concern relationships and support systems. Getting along well with those around them, particularly their child's other parent, is an important foundation for successful parenthood and affects whether or not parents feel competent, valued and supported in their role. Good relationships provide all parents, regardless of their circumstances, with the basic social and emotional support they need. Many parents look to their child's other parent for that support. However, support can also come from others such as extended family members (grandparents, uncles and aunts, cousins), close friends, neighbours, workmates and even employers. In this chapter we look at how parents can build solid foundations of support so that parenting can be a more rewarding and enjoyable experience.

Working as a parenting team

There are many different parenting arrangements that can be made to work well. The most common is for a child to be raised by both biological parents in the same household. However, if parents separate or divorce, the child may be raised by one parent and have varying amounts of contact with the other. If one or both of the child's biological parents re-partner, the child may be raised in a step-family, where they may have step-brothers or sisters from earlier relationships, or new siblings from the current relationship. Regardless of the circumstances, adults involved in the care of children need to work together.

Successful parenthood is about working as a parenting team. Usually this involves the child's parents supporting each other by sharing the daily tasks involved in raising their child. At times, working together can lead to conflict, particularly if parents disagree on how the job should be handled. Some disagreement is inevitable. After all, each person brings different life experiences to their parenting role, and these shape their views on how to raise children. For example, one parent may come from a family where eating meals at the dinner table was accepted and expected; the other parent may have been used to eating in front of the television. Couples need to communicate with each other to resolve differences of opinion, so that conflict and tension is avoided. Here are some ideas about how parents can support each other and develop good teamwork. The term 'parenting partner' is used here to refer to any person who has some regular contact with and responsibility for caring for a child. It may include a spouse, grandparents, aunts, uncles, nannies or friends.

Communicate openly with your partner about parenting

Discuss openly and honestly your views and ideas about raising children. It is inevitable that parents will have differences of opinion, and it is normal to disagree about some things. After all, each partner brings to parenthood behaviour patterns, attitudes and beliefs based on their own family experiences as a child and relationships with their own parents. Communicating openly means being prepared to discuss your ideas, beliefs, hopes, disappointments and dreams. It also involves discussing basic issues such as how children should be disciplined, the types of behaviours considered to be misbehaviour, and how household chores and parenting responsibilities can be shared. A lot of resentment can be avoided when parents are open about the things that worry them.

Discuss the basic values, skills and behaviours you wish to encourage

Every parent needs to decide for themselves the values, skills and behaviours they wish to encourage in their children. The specific skills and behaviours children will learn stem from the values parents consider important and promote. For example, when a parent wants their child to be respectful towards others, they need to encourage respectful behaviour, such as being polite and courteous when making requests rather than being demanding and rude. It usually means the parent modelling or showing the child the behaviour. Children learn by receiving encouragement when they behave respectfully and by being corrected when unacceptable behaviour occurs. Other values such as being responsible, tolerant, patient, honest, fair, generous and humble all translate into specific behaviours and skills children can learn. Being self-disciplined, a self-starter, and having the ability to set and pursue goals over time can also be encouraged in this way.

Talk often about your daily experiences with your children

Supporting your partner means showing an interest in their everyday experiences with your child. Simply asking how the children have been, and inquiring about what they have been doing while you were at work or away, conveys an interest in the effort your partner devotes to parenting. It will also mean that you can share important information about your child's needs. For example, being told that

24

a toddler has missed their usual afternoon nap will help a parent prepare themselves better to deal with the child's needs. As many children spend more time with their mother than their father, their mother ends up knowing more about their activities. For example, many fathers do not spend enough time with their children and find it difficult to answer questions such as the name of the child's teacher, times of parent–teacher meetings and so on. By having frequent brief conversations about children, parents can share important information and keep each other up to date. If couples take care to keep each other informed about their daily parenting experiences, each parent will have a better understanding of their child's and partner's needs.

Support your partner when they are under stress

When your partner is dealing with a child who is causing a problem (such as throwing a temper tantrum), step in and help out with any demands or needs of your other children. For example, if one parent is dealing with a child who is upset by something that happened at school, and the second child is calling for attention or help with homework, step in and deal with the needs of the second child. This will allow your partner to deal more effectively with the first child.

Listen to your partner's point of view

When your partner tells you about their day, listen carefully to what they have to say. If a problem occurred (such as the child demanded a toy while shopping), avoid the temptation to come to the rescue by giving your partner advice on what they should have done differently. Such advice, even if it is meant to be helpful, can make a parent feel that they are not being listened to and that they are being criticised. Sometimes parents simply want to tell someone what happened. Offers to share your ideas or to help are more likely to work and be accepted if advice has been asked for. Even then, your partner may not agree with everything you say. It is normal to occasionally disagree. Being a good listener means trying to understand what your partner has been through and how they might be feeling. It also involves trying to 'read' how they would like you to support them. Being critical of their handling of the child will usually make them defensive.

Set aside time to discuss the issue

Sometimes problems do not go away; they require both parents to discuss the issue more fully to work out a solution. This works best when the couple discusses the issues without distractions (such as television and loud music), and it is best to wait until children are in bed. Decide together what you want to talk about in advance – only discuss one or two problems at any one time – and limit the discussion time to twenty minutes or less, thus avoiding long, drawn-out conversations. Take turns in stating your view about the nature of the problem. Next, brainstorm possible answers to the problem by thinking of as many solutions as possible. Write all the solutions down, and decide which ones you wish to try. Implement the chosen solutions and then review the problem a week or so later. Revise the solution if needed. If the problem continues, have another discussion to try a different approach. The most important thing to remember is to keep communicating about the issue and avoid blaming each other.

Coping with the stress of parenting

At times, parenting can be a very stressful experience. Parents' feelings and moods affect their everyday relationship with their child. Our capacity to be patient, sensitive, caring, forgiving, organised, and to think clearly and make good decisions are all affected by our mood. When parents are worried, anxious, depressed, agitated, angry or upset, they find it more difficult to be positive, consistent and patient, and their children can suffer. For example, when parents are depressed they have less energy, feel exhausted, are more irritable and feel like spending less time with their children. When children sense their parents are avoiding or withdrawing from them, they may feel rejected and confused and may misbehave just to get attention.

Stress is a natural response to a threat or challenge. It is our mind's and body's way of preparing us for action. When we are stressed, our bodies may feel tense, and worrying thoughts may go through our minds. A certain amount of stress is helpful and creates energy for the things we need to do. However, too much stress is unhelpful and can lead to negative feelings such as anger, frustration and irritability.

How we feel depends greatly on how we interpret the events around us. Many things affect our emotional wellbeing, including our inherited genetic make-up, temperament and coping skills.

Being an effective parent means taking care of your own emotional needs. A parent's capacity to be calm, consistent and patient with their child is greater when their own needs for intimacy, support, privacy and a break from children are being met.

The good news is that there are many positive things that parents can do to deal with these problems. Here are some ideas about looking after yourself as a parent.

Acknowledge the problem

If you feel upset or unhappy, the first step in dealing with the problem is to accept that you do feel upset and that there is a problem. Sometimes, simply talking about your feelings or situation with someone you trust can really help. You might be surprised to discover how many of your friends have experienced similar problems. Speaking to another parent, friend, relative or even neighbour is a good starting point.

Make necessary changes to your lifestyle

If stress results from having too many commitments, consider reducing them. Make a list of all your commitments and note which are essential and therefore cannot be avoided, and those that are optional and could be reduced. Be prepared to cut back on optional commitments. Politely say no to new requests or demands from others that lead to extra commitments. If you feel you have to do more of the family chores than your partner, be prepared to discuss with them a fairer division of tasks and responsibilities. Energy levels can be improved and mood swings reduced by eating a balanced diet and taking regular exercise (for twenty minutes at least three times a week).

Be aware of negative or irrational thoughts

Negative thoughts can be quite distressing. It is often helpful to write down the things you say to yourself about a situation that is upsetting you. Negative thoughts – 'He's crying deliberately to upset me', 'I can't cope with this screaming; I'm going to kill him', 'I know he's going to turn into a drug addict just like his father', 'I can't do this; I'm useless as a parent', 'Peter has everything, and I have nothing; I'm worthless', 'I can't cope with this pressure' – can lead a person to feel inadequate and demoralised. Being aware of when these kinds of negative thoughts occur is an important step in beating negative thinking. Write them down in a notebook as they occur to you during the day.

Talk sense to yourself by challenging and talking back to negative thoughts

When unhelpful thoughts occur, don't just accept them as true. Learn to interrupt and 'talk back' to them. If you accept they are true, it can prevent you from taking the action needed to deal effectively with a problem. Learning how to talk back to negative thoughts involves interrupting and then challenging or disputing what you have just told yourself. Ask yourself questions about your negative thoughts – 'Is this really true?', 'How do I know that it is true?', 'What's the evidence to support this thought?', 'Is there another way of explaining his behaviour?' – then tell yourself something more positive and realistic about the situation. For example, if you tell yourself that 'Rowan deliberately tries to embarrass me when we are out', say something like, 'No. That's not helpful. He is only three, maybe he's bored when we go shopping and I need to find something to keep him busy.' This will prevent you from becoming angry and saying something hurtful to your child. Developing a more rational and helpful way of thinking about life takes practice. Use the following form to talk back to negative thinking.

Table 2: Talking back to negative thoughts

WHAT HAPPENED	UNHELPFUL THOUGHT	MORE-HELPFUL THOUGHT	HELPFUL ACTION
Toddler spills a glass of milk on a newly cleaned floor.	*I am sick of this. I just cleaned this floor. Why can't she be more careful? She's so clumsy. She did that on purpose.*	*No. She's not doing it on purpose. She is only two; toddlers have accidents. It's not a big deal.*	Keep calm. Three deep breaths. Clean up the spilt milk.
A nine-year-old tells his mother he has no homework and asks to have more time playing on the computer. The parent later finds out the child has a project due the next day.	*Joel can't be trusted. He deliberately lied to me to get out of doing that project. He's getting more like his hopeless father every day.*	*Joel is a bit disorganised with his homework, and this time he needed to get right into his project. I need to help him get into a better routine with his homework each day. He is not getting like his father; he is only starting to look more like him.*	Have a discussion with Joel about a new homework routine involving an hour of computer or TV a night only after all homework is completed.

Getting support

Raising a child is a lot easier when parents have a good support network to call upon. Apart from having the support of their child's other parent, some parents are fortunate enough to also have grandparents, siblings and other relatives, friends and neighbours that may be a source of practical or emotional support during difficult times, including emergency situations (for example, when a sick child needs to be taken to hospital). Lack of emotional support at times such as when parents move to a new area (or country) can make parents feel lonely and isolated. However, parents cannot rely on others to always be available when they might be needed. Parents should try to build up a good support network that will work for different purposes.

Make a list of people you trust and can rely on for support.

Write down their names and contact details (address, telephone number and email), and the type of emergency in which you could call them. For example, if you were ill or your child-minding arrangements fell through, who could you call on?

Also write down the names and contact details of your family members who should be contacted in an emergency. Write down the name and number of your family doctor, child health nurse, paediatrician, local hospital, police and fire services, in case of an emergency.

Have your support list in a handy place so you can see it at a glance.

Balancing work and family

Increasingly, mothers are spending less time at home with their babies before returning to work. The traditional role of the male breadwinner and female homemaker has been largely replaced by both parents being in the paid workforce and children being looked after by others at least some of the time. Balancing the competing demands and responsibilities of being a parent and a worker can be a stressful and challenging task.

Many parents have mixed feelings about returning to work; they may feel relieved that their child is old enough to cope without them for part of the day but may lack confidence in being able to complete their duties at work or earn enough money to support their family. Some parents find the very nature of work stressful, and this inevitably affects the family. Worrying a lot about work can make parents irritable and exhausted. Parents can also find that the periods just before and after work can be times of conflict with children, which adds to the stress of work. Here are some ideas on how to balance work and family responsibilities.

Plan and prepare

Preventing your home life from disrupting your work requires preparation and planning. Being rushed and running late is a major reason for extra stress at the start of the working day. You can reduce early-morning stress by being organised. This will also make for a more pleasant start for children at school or childcare. It helps a lot to teach children to do things for themselves in the morning, because the more things children are able to do for themselves, the more time a parent will have to get themselves ready. Use praise and encouragement to help children become independent in skills such as dressing, eating, making their bed and packing their school bag. Children are easier to manage in the morning if they can follow a basic routine every day, so develop a leaving-home routine and set some basic ground rules for the morning. They should be woken up at the same time each day, and know how to get dressed, eat breakfast, get ready for school, play quietly (if there is time), then be ready to leave. Keep to the same order, and offer praise and encouragement if they cooperate with the morning rules. Spending lots of time searching for something you need can waste precious time, so have a place for everything you use regularly, and keep everything in its proper place.

Manage your relationship with your partner

Try to avoid unnecessary conflict before work. Arguments and disagreements with children or partners before work can make getting ready to leave a difficult part of the day. If your child is misbehaving, you will need to follow through with your normal discipline routine. A home runs more smoothly when the work is divided fairly, so make sure you and your partner work together as a team so that one partner does not have to carry all the responsibility for the children. Write a list of daily, weekly and occasional tasks that need to be done around the home. Divide the tasks among the family members, including all adults and the children who are old enough to contribute. If your budget allows it, having paid help with housework can make a big difference.

Get proper support

Choose your childcare arrangements carefully. Parents have greater peace of mind at work when they know that their child is being well looked after. Visit the childcare centre, speak to other parents, check it out for yourself. Do the children look happy, busy and safe? Do staff spend a lot of their time talking with the children? Is the environment safe and clean? Do the children look well looked after?

Make your family your priority

When you are at home with your children try to avoid spending a lot of time thinking or worrying about work. This is your family time, so enjoy it. If you are preoccupied with work, it usually means you are less available to spend time with your children. You will be more productive and successful at work if you can relax and enjoy your children when you are with them.

Do not allow work stress to affect your home life

If possible, avoid arranging important meetings or stressful tasks first thing in the morning; these can add unnecessary extra pressure to be on time. Sometimes with children, even the best-laid plans can come unstuck, and stress can be reduced by being realistic. Some parents have very high expectations of themselves in terms of what can be accomplished at work. By setting more realistic and achievable work goals, daily stress can be reduced. To do this, be prepared to sit down with your employer and discuss and negotiate expectations that are realistic and achievable. Bottling up the problem and suffering the consequences may lead to loss of enjoyment and reduced performance at work.

When you are at work, let work be your priority. Although there will be times at work when you cannot help thinking about your children (such as when they are sick, in trouble or involved in special events at school), try to avoid letting family matters disrupt your concentration. Worrying about family problems while you are at work does little to solve them.

Try to complete difficult or stressful tasks early in the day, so that when it is time to leave you are less likely to carry forward stress and worries into the home.

Be assertive in letting your family and childcare needs be known to employers and supervisors at work. Be prepared to request time off work to deal with important family business. Providing such requests do not happen often, many employers are quite prepared to allow time off to attend to important family matters.

Many employers have developed work-and-life-balance programmes. Find out about your workplace entitlements. Make it your business to know what you are entitled to in the way of carers leave, family leave, flexible working hours and childcare.

Try to use commuting time to unwind. Switch off work and review the next challenges that lie ahead when you get home. Listening to relaxing music or an audio book as you travel can be helpful. Everyone needs contrast to have a balanced life, so ensure you have alternating periods of work and play, and it is essential that you take holiday breaks when they are due. Make sure you switch off work when on holidays. Family time can be ruined if parents work during family holidays. Get involved in recreational activities you enjoy outside work, such as playing sport, joining a choir or craft group or book club, or making regular dates to see films with friends.

Develop a proper coming-home ritual. Much family conflict can be avoided by ensuring that the first hour after your arrival from work is pleasant. Greet your partner and children in a loving and caring manner; hug or kiss them and ask about their day and show an interest in what they say. Get changed out of work clothes and then switch to helping out with the necessary tasks.

Parenting classes

Parenting classes are becoming very popular and are helping many parents. I strongly support the idea of all parents undertaking some kind of parenting course to prepare them for the task of raising children. There are many benefits in doing a well-run parenting course with a professionally competent facilitator. These benefits include getting to know other parents, sharing ideas, concerns and solutions with other parents, and gaining valuable information about children's behaviour and development. However, be an informed consumer. Be prepared to ask the course organiser the following questions:

- Is the course leader properly qualified to run the course?
- What are the person's professional qualifications and have they had any specialist training in parent education?
- Has the programme been evaluated and if so what were the results? What benefits to children were found?
- Can you speak to other parents who have completed the course?
- Does the course provide clear information and advice on handling specific problem situations or behaviours?

If the course organiser answers these questions without getting defensive, you can feel reasonably confident that the course is worth at least checking out. If you like what you see and hear at the first session, then commit to completing the course.

However, no parenting course can prepare you for all the challenges that will come. All children are different, and so are parents. Parenting is about being open-minded and willing to learn on the job. By being prepared to learn with your child, you will be more flexible and can make adjustments according to your child's individual needs.

Conclusions

Most parents do a fine job raising their children. However, parenting is never easy. Becoming a parent is a big responsibility and requires some thought about how you intend to look after your own needs for emotional and practical support, right from the beginning. When parenting responsibilities are shared, as they so often are today, all those involved should work towards a common approach to raising children. Although children can cope with some differences in the parenting styles of the adults in their lives (such as parents, grandparents, childcare staff and teachers), it is much less confusing for children when parents agree about basic values, skills and behaviours they wish to encourage and the methods of parenting to use. Working parents must learn to balance the competing demands of work and home. Neither can work well when parents are under too much stress from either source.

CHAPTER 3

Understanding children's behaviour

Why do children behave the way they do? How can children from the same family be so similar in some ways but so different in others? Why do some children develop behavioural problems while some do not? What is the role of heredity and that of the child's family in influencing children's behaviour? To understand children's behaviour we need to consider that, from the moment of conception, children's growth and development are influenced by four main factors: their inherited genetic make-up, the family in which they are raised, the community where the family resides, and the broader culture within which the family lives. Heredity and environment play joint roles in shaping children's behaviour and development. Together they determine what particular behaviours, skills, attitudes and abilities each child develops. They also influence whether the child develops behavioural or emotional problems.

Heredity: the child's temperament

Each child inherits a unique genetic make-up from both parents. This make-up gives the child the biological equipment needed for survival and for all subsequent development. Children inherit many of their physical characteristics from their parents, including eye colour, skin colour, hair texture, certain physical diseases and a tendency to develop others. Some researchers believe that some psychological and behavioural characteristics are also largely inherited. These include intelligence, basic temperament (a biologically based tendency to behave in certain ways) and a vulnerability to psychological disturbance. The following three basic personality attributes emerge early in a child's life and appear to be both inherited and related to the development of behavioural problems:

- EMOTIONALITY is measured by an infant's arousal in response to events in their environment. Highly emotional infants fuss and cry a lot, and often respond negatively to stimulation and show fearful or angry reactions to sudden changes in stimulation, such as being spoken to by an unfamiliar person.
- ACTIVITY LEVEL refers to energy expenditure and the amount of vigorous movement and activity that children display. Active infants who have begun crawling or walking are often very busy. They are excitement-seekers and have high activity levels. They have good gross motor movement, explore their environment energetically, and enjoy vigorous play. Children with a high activity level are often headstrong, persistent and difficult to control.
- SOCIABILITY refers to an infant's preference for interaction with people. Sociable infants show a marked interest in human faces. They enjoy and are responsive to the attention of others. They often initiate contact with a wide range of people, not just their parents. If an infant is high on sociability but the mother is low, the mother may find the child's demands for attention irritating and exhausting. This in turn can affect the quality of the mother's interactions with her baby.

From very early in life, about 10 per cent of children appear to be particularly difficult to rear. These children appear to inherit a difficult temperament that places them at risk of developing behavioural problems later on. As babies, they fuss and cry a lot, are difficult to settle as they often have sleeping and feeding disturbances, and are difficult to get into predictable routines. Such problems usually arise within the first six months. Parents who have been through the ordeal of trying to settle a baby who cries frequently and will not settle at night know the frustrations, tensions and anxiety these children can create. In other words, some children, because of their own temperamental characteristics, are more likely than others to create parenting problems that can in turn lead to further behavioural and adjustment problems. Many physically abused children have difficult temperaments. However, there are no hard and fast rules; not all temperamentally difficult infants develop behavioural or adjustment difficulties, and some easy-to-manage infants go on to develop problems later in life. The outcome depends not only on the child's temperament but on how parents deal with their child's behaviour and on their general child-rearing patterns.

A child's genetic make-up can also be influenced by changes that occur by chance in the egg or sperm or in the newly fertilised egg. These changes can result in some of the physical, behavioural or emotional characteristics of a child. Certain disabilities, such as Down's Syndrome, occur this way. A number of syndromes or disabilities increase the chance that a child will develop behavioural problems.

Children's health and behaviour

Children's physical and emotional health are closely linked. Whenever a child's behaviour is causing a serious problem for parents, it is important to identify whether there is anything physically wrong with the child that may explain the problem. Many things other than genes can affect children's health. These include the kind of early environment children experience before birth and in the early years of development when their brains are developing. For example, during pregnancy the health of the mother has a big effect on the child. If during pregnancy the mother was malnourished, had an infection such as rubella, or used excessive amounts of alcohol, tobacco, cocaine, mercury and other drugs, the child would be at greater risk of not only poor health but also developmental and behavioural problems. If a child is born prematurely or has low birth weight, they will be more vulnerable to illness as infants and more likely to develop behavioural and developmental problems.

Chronic health problems can also contribute to behavioural problems. For example, problems such as being underweight, obese, malnourished, asthmatic, diabetic, epileptic or prone to convulsions, or when children suffer head injuries as a result of accidents or abuse, can increase the chances that children will develop behavioural or emotional problems.

Even everyday minor illnesses affect children's behaviour. When children are irritable and grumpy, the challenge for parents is to figure out whether the child's symptoms result from a minor illness such as a cold or tiredness, or are a sign of something more serious. In the early stages of illness, this can be difficult to tell. If in doubt, take your children to your doctor.

When children feel unwell, their play, exploration and cheerfulness are reduced. Other behavioural changes often associated with illness include fussing, crying, complaining, altered sleep patterns, decreased energy and activity levels, and reduced appetite. There are usually other signs that indicate a child is unwell and requires medical attention, such as drowsiness, lethargy, breathing difficulty, poor circulation, poor feeding, vomiting, high fever, and complaining about feeling sick or in pain.

However, it is important to remember that children's behaviour not only depends on their genetic make-up, temperament and physical health but also the ways parents respond to their behaviour. We will turn to the important role of the environment next.

The importance of family

No two children are raised in identical environments, even if they are part of the same family. In the early years of a child's life, the family has the responsibility for the child's socialisation, but once the child enters kindergarten or school, peers and teachers also start to play an important role. Parents still have the main responsibility to help children learn the many skills and behaviours they need if they are to grow into well-adjusted and responsible members of the community. As parents, we play a major role in helping children learn a great many things: to walk, to talk, to use the potty or toilet correctly, to dress and undress, to tie shoelaces and to respect the property of others. We help our children learn to follow directions, ask politely when making requests and, of course, to deal with frustrations, successes, disappointments and conflicts with others.

Even with children whose genetic make-up and temperament predispose them to psychological problems, the way we handle the problems affects whether difficulties continue, worsen or improve. Biology and genetics provide the boundaries within which development takes place, but the child's family and life experience help a child develop into a social being.

Focusing on the role of the environment is important for one very basic reason: while you cannot change your child's genetic make-up, you can change their environment. As parents, we decide how our child is raised and therefore the kind of environment our child experiences, at least at home. Fortunately, this means there are usually many concrete actions we can take to prevent or overcome common behavioural and emotional problems.

Learning through experience

Many common behavioural problems in children are concerned with social interaction, which means the ways children relate to other people in their lives and how others relate to them. Many problem behaviours are also learned in the process of interacting with others. Even if children are biologically predisposed to developing problems, they are not born knowing how to steal, lie, cheat, throw temper tantrums, or be violent or cruel. These behaviours usually develop gradually over months or years, and may eventually become part of the child's usual behaviour. Understanding how children learn is very useful in deciding how to deal with problems. Figure 1 (page 41) summarises the ways family relationships can contribute to behavioural and emotional problems. If you are concerned about some aspect of your child's behaviour, it might be useful to ask yourself which (if any) of the influences apply to your child. Make a list of those factors you consider important to understanding your child's difficulty. This will provide important clues about what can be changed to modify a problem behaviour.

Let's begin by discussing the idea that problem behaviours produce consequences that help to maintain them.

Accidental rewards for misbehaviour

From the very beginning, a child's behaviour produces results or outcomes. For example, babies soon learn that crying is a very effective way of signalling that they are in distress. Parents quickly learn to change a wet nappy or to feed their infant when she cries. Hence, crying leads to the consequence of being fed. A smile often results in an adult smiling back, cooing or cuddling the baby. Children learn that their behaviour matters. They quickly learn that it can be an effective way of controlling the actions of others.

Both desirable and undesirable behaviour are influenced by the consequences they produce. Careful observation of children's behaviour often shows that it has hidden pay-offs. The reactions of parents and siblings can accidentally reward misbehaviour, as the following case study illustrates.

Carl is three-and-a-half years old. His parents, Mary and Robert, have had problems with him since he was about eight months old. They both describe him as aggressive, disobedient and constantly demanding of their attention.

During an initial interview with this family, I was particularly interested in observing whether Carl would engage in any of the behaviours Mary had complained of and, if so, how his parents handled them. Carl, both parents and I were in a large playroom equipped with a variety of appropriate toys and four chairs, one for each adult and one for Carl if he wanted to be seated. From the moment our discussion started, Carl wanted his parents' attention. During the first ten minutes of the interview, he interrupted his mother twelve times. An interruption usually consisted of his calling out, 'Mum, come and look at this,' or 'I want you to play with me, *now*!' During this ten-minute period, Carl climbed on his

FIGURE 1: REASONS CHILDREN DEVELOP BEHAVIOURAL PROBLEMS

Reason	Example	What the child may learn	What the parent may learn
Accidental rewards	Child calls out to mother loudly after being put to bed. Mother goes into the child's bedroom to settle the child down.	When I am put to bed, I can call out to get Mum's attention.	When my child won't fall asleep I need to soothe him to sleep. (The parent is rewarded for giving attention because it is followed by the child calming down.)
Escalation trap – child's view	Child asks for a drink. Parent says, 'No. Your dinner will be ready soon.' Child screams. Parent ignores this screaming. Child screams more loudly and throws themselves on the floor. Parent says, 'Okay, have it, but stop that noise.'	When Mum says no, if I become really upset and loud, I will get what I want.	To stop my child getting upset, I have to give in to him. (The parent's compliance is rewarded because it stops the child protesting.)
Escalation trap – parent's view	Parent asks the child to turn off the TV and have a bath. Child ignores the request. Parent raises their voice and again tells the child to turn off the TV. Child protests, 'These are my favourite ads.' Parent threatens to hit the child if they do not move. Child says, 'I'm coming. I'm coming.'	When my parents ask me to do something calmly, the instruction can be ignored. I only need to comply when they threaten me, to avoid getting hit.	He never listens to me. I have to threaten to hit him to get him to do as he's told. Threatening and hitting work!

Reason	Example	What the child may learn	What the parent may learn
Learning through watching	One parent shouts abuse at the other parent for not paying the bills on time. The other parent storms out of the room in a temper, slamming the door.	It's okay to slam the door and shout during disagreements with others. (The child is more likely to use similar behaviour in dealing with conflict in the future.)	Children copy or imitate my behaviour.
Ignoring desirable behaviour	Child asks in a very pleasant voice if his parent can help him open a container. Parent ignores the request, and says, 'Just wait a minute, will you.'	If I ask nicely for things I am ignored; maybe if I whine it will work.	My child is demanding and whines a lot.
Vague instructions	Parent looks at the mess on the floor and says, 'Damian' with a stern look on her face.	Mum is upset with me over something, but I don't know what it is.	My child does not do what he's told.
Poorly timed instructions	Child is watching her favourite TV show. Parent asks the child to have a bath. Child complains loudly.	I have to do as I am told except when I want to watch my favourite show, then I should complain a lot.	My child will not cooperate unless it suits her.
Emotional messages	Child spills a glass of milk and parent says angrily, 'You are so clumsy. Be careful, will you.'	Mum thinks I can't do anything right, and she hates me.	My child is careless and creates more work for me.
Hitting	Parent spanks child for lying about where they went after school. Child pleads not to be hit.	Hitting others is okay if they do something I don't like. Also, if I am dishonest, I should try not to get caught.	I have to be strict and must punish my child firmly to eliminate dishonesty.

mother's lap three times and poked his tongue out at her about 3 cm from her face. During this brief encounter, Carl's mother gave him four instructions not to interrupt and his father gave three instructions to 'go and play'. After the twelfth interruption, Robert excused himself and attempted to settle Carl down; this consisted of sitting down next to Carl on the floor and watching intently as Carl proudly showed his father how to work the crane on a large truck. For the next twenty minutes Carl was the perfect child. He had what he wanted: the complete and undivided attention of his parent. So long as he had it he was fine. However, problems arose immediately whenever he was required to play on his own.

Carl's behaviour in the playroom was fairly typical of his behaviour at home whenever his parents attempted to talk to each other. It was also typical of his behaviour when he visited his grandparents or Mary's friends. In other words, his reaction was not an isolated response in an unusual clinical situation. Later observation of Carl, and his parents' reaction to him, showed a sequence of attention-gaining behaviour followed by adult attention that was played out many times each day.

Let us look closely at what happened and try to pinpoint some of the hidden pay-offs for Carl. Firstly, it is quite clear that his interruptions and demands were very successful in gaining attention from his parents. Some of the attention was negative, of course, but in terms of the sheer amount of reaction, Carl was clearly finding quite an audience in his parents. Secondly, Carl's behaviour was successful in temporarily interrupting the conversation of the adults in the room. Each time he whined for his mum to come and play, Mary paused and turned towards him, gave him eye contact, and then explained she was busy. Thirdly, Carl's constant demands eventually produced a very powerful consequence: Robert sat down and played with him just to 'shut him up'. Having what he wanted, Carl was quite happy and behaved himself for the rest of the session.

The hidden pay-offs for misbehaviour are not always as obvious as they are in Carl's case, but careful observation of children's behaviour often reveals social consequences that accidentally or unintentionally encourage misbehaviour. Five main types of consequences can reward difficult behaviour: social attention, material rewards, accidental activity rewards, sensory rewards and food rewards.

- **Social attention**
  Parents and children attend to each other in a variety of ways. They look, smile, hug, frown, grimace, talk, yell, threaten, spank, and so on. Some children unfortunately learn that the surest way to get a reaction from their parents is to misbehave. When misbehaviour results in a lot of social attention, the attention can reward the behaviour, as in Carl's case. Parental attention is the most common hidden pay-off for bad behaviour. You might ask, 'What are we supposed to do? Simply ignore the behaviour?' Unfortunately, the answer is not simple. Ignoring, as we will find out, does not always work.
- **Material rewards**
  Most parents occasionally have to deal with their child's demands to be bought something, such as toys, sweets or other items of interest. However, there are dangers in giving in to demands like those illustrated below.

  'Mum, can you buy me this?' [*pointing to a toy in a store*]

  'No, Jamie, I said you weren't to ask for things in the store today.'

  'Mum, buy me this. I want it. *Pleeassse!*' [*getting agitated*]

  'Jamie, don't carry on like that.'

  'I want it. I want it. Buy it for me.'

  'All right, but this is the last time. Don't you dare ask for anything else.' [*slightly embarrassed and irritated*]

  'Gee, thanks, Mum.'

  Jamie is now much more likely to ask his parents to buy him things on future shopping trips. When demanding behaviour produces results, it is more likely to happen again.
- **Accidental activity rewards**
  Another way parents can accidentally reward misbehaviour is to provide an activity the child likes as a consequence of misbehaviour. For example, many parents of young children use distraction to deal with conflict over toys. If one toddler makes a direct line towards a toy truck another child is playing with,

his mother might intervene just as he strikes and grabs the toy, and says, 'Darling, look at what Mummy's got,' holding up another toy. Often such distraction is followed by the parent giving the child a lot of attention while trying to interest him in the new toy or activity. One of the potential dangers of this approach is that the child is denied the opportunity to learn that they should not snatch other children's toys. Furthermore, the parent may have accidentally rewarded the behaviour by giving the child a lot of positive attention and an interesting alternative activity. Another example of an activity reward is a situation where a parent waits until a child is bored or whining and then, concerned that the child has been ignored, sits down and plays a game with her. Providing an activity reward for bored behaviour can cause problems, and it is better to deal with the whining first and then look for an opportunity to engage the child in a new activity.

- **Sensory rewards**
  Some behavioural problems such as repetitious or self-stimulatory behaviours are related to the physical sensations they produce. For example, behaviours a child repeats over and over – such as rocking back and forth, flapping hands and poking their eyes – can produce physical sensations children enjoy, and they allow them to control the level of stimulation they receive. Some children learn to repeat certain noises over and over, such as *daddaddaddadadda*, to block out confusing or distressing stimulation.

- **Food rewards**
  Many conflicts with children are over food. Parents can very easily accidentally reward their child for behaviour such as complaining or demanding by giving him a drink or food. Unfortunately, not only does this action reward the child for complaining, it also rewards snacking between meals, with the consequence that the child may not eat properly at mealtimes. He may also learn to rely on food as a way of reducing boredom or tension and therefore risk becoming overweight. Handling children's requests for food is a real problem for parents. It is important that parents respond predictably and immediately to a baby's hunger cries, but as a child develops (particularly by the age of two), parents need to become

more careful in responding to food requests. Children have to learn that meals are eaten at certain times, and that unlimited access to food outside these times is not acceptable. In essence, parents must change their way of dealing with food requests during infancy to avoid children using food as an escape.

Escalation traps

In an escalation trap, a child learns to escalate or 'turn up' the intensity of his behaviour to force his parent or another child to back down or give in. The child becomes more and more unpleasant until the adult either gives in or threatens (or actually carries out) some punishment. Here is a typical example:

> 'Mum, can I go over to Tommy's house?'
> 'No, Jason, dinner will be ready in about ten minutes and I want you to tidy the mess in your room before dinner.'
> 'But I want to go out and play. I'm not hungry anyway.' [*in a whining voice*]
> 'No. Dinner will be ready shortly. Come on. Go and do your room.'
> 'You're mean. I'm going anyway. Get out of my way.'
> 'Now listen, you. Just stop that noise. The whole neighbourhood can hear you carrying on. Well, I suppose you can go for a little while but you must come back when I call you. Not like last night when I had to come looking for you.'
> 'All right. Bye.'

You will notice that his mother's initial refusal sparked noisy and insistent behaviour. Just at the point where his behaviour became quite unpleasant, his mother backed down and let him have his own way. This parent has just accidentally rewarded the child for escalating in the face of the parent's resistance. What Jason may have learnt is that when he doesn't get his own way, all he has to do is complain louder and he will get what he wants. He in fact received a double reward: his mother agreed to his demands and he was allowed to play with Tommy.

Many parents find this kind of escalation hard to deal with, particularly when it happens in public, but if children are rewarded for escalating, they can become very difficult to manage.

Unfortunately, parents themselves are accidentally rewarded for giving in to the child because the child stops the screaming or yelling, at least for the moment. When parent *and* child are both being rewarded, the pattern of interaction pays off and is likely to occur again. Consider the following situation:

'Paul, go and put away your bike and skateboard. Now, please.'

'Dad, I'm watching my favourite show.'

'Go and do it now. Your mother can't get the car in the garage with all that mess in the driveway.'

'No. Wait till the next ads.'

'Get moving or it's the belt for you.' [*reaching for his leather belt*]

'I'm going. I'm going. Why are you always yelling at me?'

By complying, Paul has just accidentally rewarded his father for making threats. Dad is now more likely to threaten and yell when Paul disobeys. 'What's wrong with that?', you might ask. 'After all, Paul did what he was told.' What is wrong is that Paul will probably learn to comply only when he is threatened, and will ignore requests that are put more calmly. There are also some emotional side effects to this kind of approach, such as the child becoming anxious, fearful or angry. These will be discussed later.

It is important to remember that parents and children can train each other to escalate as a way of dealing with problems. Such escalation, particularly when it occurs often, is very unpleasant. When parents find themselves continually having to escalate to get their child to cooperate, it is time to look for another way of handling the problem. The child may be out of control. Aggressive children with more severe behavioural problems often show this pattern of escalation in their dealings with others.

Learning through watching

Children learn a great deal through observation. They will often try to imitate our actions and are delighted when they learn to do things just like Mum or Dad. Through observation, children learn many important things about their world. Every day parents provide children with a model of how to behave in certain situations. Because there is no such thing as a perfect parent, this modelling is sometimes of behaviours they do not wish their child to learn, such as swearing or using abusive language when annoyed about something. Many parents spank their child for being aggressive towards other children. When some parents see their child being violent towards others, they will say something like, 'I'll teach you to hit . . .', whack, whack. Children observe their parents closely at times like this. What they notice is that when something happens that Dad doesn't like, it is okay to become angry, yell and hit. Rather than decreasing the child's tendency to hit, this model may increase the chances that the child will learn to hit. Parents who hit often are likely to have children who hit a lot as well, particularly when they become parents themselves.

Many behavioural problems can be learned through modelling. Examples include swearing, cheating, lying, aggression and disobedience. These behaviours can all be learned through observation, particularly if the child notices that the behaviour leads to the person getting their own way. Children also model themselves on the behaviour of siblings, peers and other high-status people such as rock stars and television characters. This is well understood by the shocked parent who discovers her six-year-old using words the child has never heard at home but picked up shortly after starting school or after a weekend visit from cousins. If older brothers and sisters are disruptive, noisy or disobedient, younger siblings are more likely to learn the same behaviour.

Ignoring desirable behaviour

Some children develop behavioural problems because they rarely receive positive attention for good behaviour. Feedback about the things we do right is important in developing a positive view of ourselves. One mother in our research project was observed interacting with her child at home on five different days, for about thirty minutes each time. The child was causing considerable problems for her, as he seemed to be withdrawn, sulked a lot, and would explode occasionally and lose his temper. Every twenty-five seconds, a trained observer noted what the child was doing and how his mother responded to him. The observer noted, for example, whether the parent praised, ignored, punished, threatened, asked the child a question, and so forth. The results of these observations were enlightening: 85 per cent of the total attention the child received followed some negative behaviour, such as whining or sulking. Only 15 per cent of the attention the child received was for positive behaviour, yet he was actually behaving appropriately about 52 per cent of the time. Not once over the five days was he praised for good behaviour. This parent was very surprised to learn that the child had been good for over half the time he was observed; she thought he had been naughty for about three-quarters of the time.

For this child, there was little pay-off for good behaviour. The message is clear: when you ignore good behaviour, don't be surprised if it doesn't happen very often.

How parents give instructions to their children

All parents ask children to do things, and children learn to respond appropriately. Requests that require the child to initiate an action ('Come to the dinner table.' 'Begin your homework.' 'Put your toys away.' 'Wash your hands.') are called start instructions; requests that require the child to cease doing something ('Don't pull kitty's tail.') are called 'stop' instructions and are often followed by a 'start' instruction ('Stroke kitty gently, like this.')

Sometimes children simply refuse to comply with parental requests of either kind. Children who are very disobedient may be described by their parents as stubborn, headstrong, selfish or determined, and a lot of conflict between parent and child can result. Every bath, mealtime, bedtime, family outing, shopping trip or ride in the car can turn into a battle of wills. The parent wants one thing, the child wants another. When such battlelines are drawn, the child often wins.

Some of these problems are related to the way parents give instructions. Few stop to consider carefully how the timing and type of request, as well as the way it is made, can affect children's behaviour. We will discuss in a later chapter how to make your instructions and requests more effective, but for the moment, let's look at some of the problems that can arise when giving instructions to children.

- **Giving too many instructions**

  Every instruction we give or rule we make creates an opportunity for a child not to comply. There is a simple but basic rule relating to giving instructions to children: the more instructions given, the more opportunities to disobey. During a thirty-minute home observation, one parent in our research programme gave her three-year-old ninety instructions, such as 'Don't do that', 'Get down from there', 'Leave it alone', 'Don't whinge', 'Come over here'. In thirty minutes, the child had ninety opportunities to disobey. This could have been halved by halving the number of instructions. Apart from making the child feel 'picked on', giving too many instructions is also exhausting for parents.

- **Giving too few instructions**

  Just as giving too many instructions can create problems, so too can the opposite. Children are more likely to learn what is expected of them and how to behave if their parents take the time to explain rules they would like to operate in specific situations. For example, some children develop poor table manners because no one has taken the time to give them proper instructions in the appropriate use of their knife and fork.

- **Giving instructions that are too difficult**

  What we can reasonably expect of children depends greatly on their age and developmental level. For example, a nine-year-old can reasonably be expected to make their own bed, but it is probably a task beyond most four-year-olds (although the latter can often help). Parents who expect too much too soon will experience resistance and sometimes resentment. For example, expecting a three-year-old to tidy up a very messy room without any help is asking for problems. On the other hand, some parents don't ask their children to do enough for fear they will make a mess or not complete the task satisfactorily. Older children should be encouraged to take some responsibility around the home, including helping with dishes, tidying their bedrooms, cleaning the yard, and so on. A home in which adults and children pitch in to complete necessary chores are best for children in the long run because with practice and encouragement they learn what to do and how to do it efficiently. It is simply not acceptable for fourteen- and fifteen-year-olds to expect their parents to do everything around the house while they watch television, play computer games or listen to music for hours.

- **Giving rapid-fire instructions**
  Sometimes a parent gives a string of instructions all at once, before the child has had a chance to comply with the first request. For example, they may say to a nine-year-old, 'I want you to finish your maths homework, rake up the leaves on the path, tidy your room, and then set the dinner table.' Children often feel bombarded with demands and are more likely to comply if each instruction is given separately.

- **Giving poorly timed instructions**
  Poor timing on a parent's part can lead to problems. If a child is doing something interesting, such as watching a favourite television show, a request that interferes with that is less likely to be obeyed. There needs to be some give and take here. Adults don't immediately jump to it if they are busy or already completing another task, and we need to take children's interests and activities into account before we ask them to do something else. You can avoid a storm by simply waiting until the television programme has finished. However, it is important to recognise that some children will always say they are doing something interesting as a way of avoiding helping out at home. If this happens it is better to insist that the child complies with the instruction. Also, it is entirely reasonable to interrupt an activity and ask for something to be done, such as removing rollerblades from the stairs, if there is a risk or danger involved, or it has already been requested.

- **Giving vague instructions**

  Children are more likely to ignore requests that are expressed as questions than those that are clear, specific instructions. For example, a parent might say to a child, 'Would you like to have a bath now, Jamie?', which implies that the child has a choice. The choice is more apparent than real, however, because if the child doesn't respond, the parent becomes insistent. Another example is the parent who wants to stop her three-year-old from monopolising a backyard swing and says, 'Why don't you let Mary have a turn now?' These kinds of 'questions' are instructions in disguise. If parents really want to give their children a choice, they should be prepared for a response like, 'No thanks, Mum' or 'No, I don't want to share'.

  Some parents, when they see their child doing something inappropriate, will say, 'Daniel!', then pause and frown. If Daniel has just done three inappropriate things such as jumped on the couch, teased his sister and hit his brother, it is unclear which behaviour the parent considers a problem. The parent should have said, 'Daniel, don't jump on the couch. The couch is for sitting on.' Other examples of vague instructions include things like, 'Don't be silly', 'For heaven's sake' or 'Watch your step, boy'. In general, vague instructions are more likely than clear, specific ones to be disobeyed.

- **Instructions and body language**

  The effectiveness of a request depends not only on the words used but also on the accompanying body language, such as our facial expression, whether we directly face the child, how close we are to the child, and our posture and tone of voice. Some parents learn quickly that before they ask their child to do something it is better to move to within arm's length, to gain eye contact and to avoid yelling out from a distance. Long-distance instructions are easier for a child to ignore.

Emotional messages

Children's behaviour is affected by the emotional tone of what adults say to them. When children are difficult to handle, their behaviour often produces emotions that are conveyed to the child through the parents' words, actions or body language. Some of the ways parents communicate their emotional reactions can create further problems for the child.

Frequent angry messages

All parents get angry with their children at times. As mentioned in 'Escalation traps' on page 46, children can accidentally reward parents for yelling and shouting by complying with the angry request. Unfortunately, in these cases, children may not learn to comply with calmly delivered, softly spoken requests. Instructions and other statements made when a parent is intensely angry ('You really are a horrible child sometimes!') can indicate that the parent is angry with the child rather than with their behaviour. An alternative is, 'I don't like that behaviour'. There is an important difference between the two messages. The first reflects on the child as a person, the second on what they are doing.

One of a parent's hardest tasks is to keep calm when disciplining or correcting a child. When we become extremely angry we lose our objectivity, overreact and can punish the child unnecessarily severely. When a parent frequently becomes angry with a child, it is often time to learn a new way of handling the problem.

Making a child feel guilty

Some parents try to shame their child into cooperating. 'What would your teacher think of you now, if she could see you carrying on like that?' 'Why don't you think about someone other than yourself for once? I'm tired too but I still have to cook dinner.' 'I think you're being selfish and rude.' This is trying to control the child by making her feel guilty, ashamed or embarrassed. However, she may not understand specifically what she has done to cause problems. Parents who frequently moralise in order to get their children to comply with their wishes can create much resentment and hostility. In many situations it simply doesn't work. Children may internalise these messages over time, start seeing themselves as mean, selfish, uncaring and insensitive, and then act accordingly. Children who receive a lot of personal attacks like this can also become very self-critical, worried and anxious. Some even become depressed.

If the child's behaviour is the problem, make sure you focus on the behaviour rather than on the child's supposed underlying motive.

Putdowns and rejections

Emotional and behavioural problems in children can also arise when their parents call them names. Children are often very sensitive to being called names such as 'stupid' or 'idiot'. These words are sometimes used as part of a general putdown or criticism of the child but occasionally can be used in isolation. They may reflect the parent's exasperation with the child but they usually make the situation worse rather than better.

Use of corporal punishment

Few topics create more confusion and concern for parents than the issue of corporal punishment. To smack or not to smack? Most parents answer this question well before the child's second birthday. On the one hand, parents hear that to 'spare the rod is to spoil the child', while on the other, they are told that corporal punishment is cruel and psychologically damaging. Experts disagree on the use of corporal punishment. Let me explain my view on the issue.

First of all, a firm smack on the bottom can be an effective deterrent, particularly when the child is doing something dangerous. However, this kind of punishment does not work for all behaviours, nor for all parents. At best it works some of the time, with some behaviours, for some children. Even then it will only work if used correctly. I do not recommend it.

Secondly, many behavioural problems are related to ineffective and inconsistent use of punishment. Many children referred to our parenting programme have received a lot of corporal punishment. Not enough punishment is not the problem; the way in which discipline is used frequently is. Any discipline technique works best when it occurs immediately after the offending behaviour, every time the behaviour occurs and in sufficient intensity to serve as a deterrent. Many parents, however, do not use spanking in this way. Here are some examples of how punishment can contribute to children's behavioural and emotional problems.

- **Threats but no action**

  'Andrew, if you do that to Robert one more time, you'll cop it.' 'Timothy, if I've told you once I've told you a thousand times, *don't* throw sand. One more time and that's it. It's the belt for you.' 'You wait until your father gets home.' When a child hears many threats but rarely receives any consequence, threatening punishment becomes an ineffective way for a parent to control their child's behaviour. Sometimes, threats of punishment can even serve as a dare to a child, who will then test the parent to the limit.

- **Punishment given in anger**

  Parents often use spankings and other punishments when they are angry with a child. When parents become extremely angry there is always a risk of losing control and physically hurting the child. I have worked with children who have been so severely beaten that they have had to be hospitalised. Angry, out-of-control adults can inflict terrible, sometimes permanently damaging injuries on their children. Children have been killed by their parents in a rage that has spiralled out of control.

  When a parent becomes angry, their anger can signal to the child that the adult has lost control. As mentioned earlier, an angry parent will often criticise the child – 'You horrible brat!' – rather than the behaviour that is causing the problem. Such rage-filled outbursts can make a child feel unloved, resentful and insecure. Many parents who seek help for children with behavioural problems fall into this trap of reacting to irritating behaviour with explosive outbursts. While feeling angry is normal, it is not helpful to act in openly hostile ways when children misbehave.

- **Punishment as a crisis reaction**

  Problems can arise if punishment is used as a crisis reaction. I recall one parent who was constantly harassed with complaints and protests from her ten-year-old son about where he wanted to spend a long weekend. Several times she had tried to reason with him and explain why it wasn't possible to do what he wanted (he wanted to go skiing and the family simply couldn't afford it). However, the child went on and on and on and on, with one complaint after another. Finally, the mother exploded, screamed at the boy and sent him to his room. You may feel that you would do exactly the same, and that the parent's reaction was quite justified. However, this mother only punished the boy when his behaviour became absolutely intolerable to her. She was exhausted from the constant demands, and when she finally broke she reacted in a fiercely emotional way. It might have been better to react earlier, and to use whatever discipline she felt appropriate *before* the boy's behaviour became intolerable.

We often lose our capacity to think clearly in a crisis and end up overreacting. In this case, after the explosion, the mother felt tremendously guilty and spent the next hour trying to calm her son down and to reassure him that she really did love him and was sorry. Part of this family's treatment involved teaching the mother to respond more quickly to difficult behaviour.

- **Inconsistent use of consequences**
Many children learn to break rules and disobey instructions because they are not consistently enforced. Being consistent in our reactions to children is a difficult thing, because our mood, feelings and behaviour are all influenced by a variety of other factors, such as our relationship, work pressure and health. These make being perfectly consistent almost impossible. However, when parents become very inconsistent in their use of consequences, it is almost guaranteed to fail. If a child is punished for refusing to do chores on one day but not the next, she will not learn to complete her chores. Here is an example of the kind of thing I mean.

Shirley and Martin both had full-time jobs in a city bank. Brad, their seven-year-old son, was in Grade 2 at school, where he was polite and well behaved. At home it was a different story. According to Shirley, one of their main problems was that Brad used to swear and abuse both parents when he didn't get his own way. One clear difficulty the couple had was that they couldn't agree on how to deal with the problem. Shirley, who was on the receiving end of most of the outbursts, thought it was best to ignore the behaviour. Martin insisted that any swearing should be severely punished by using his belt to hit the child and sending him to his room, where he would stay sulking, often for up to two hours. The parents' inability to agree meant that Brad got away with swearing on some occasions, while on others he was severely punished. Such inconsistent use of punishment actually resulted in the behaviour getting worse over time.

Children cannot be expected to learn acceptable patterns of behaviour if their parents' reactions are unpredictable. The child gets a double message: sometimes swearing is okay, at other times it is not. This can be quite confusing to children.

The negative effects of punishment

While punishment can be made to work, any parent who relies heavily on negative tactics to deal with misbehaviour should be aware of some of the dangers in this approach.

One of the most important effects is that every time parents scream, shout, rave or hit their child, they are modelling the very behaviour they want their child to avoid. Children can easily learn that losing your cool and becoming aggressive is an acceptable way of dealing with frustration. Many abused children grow up to abuse their own children. In the long term, it is more useful to a child to learn alternative, successful and non-violent means of dealing with conflict. Here, of course, parents can serve as positive models, teaching their children reasonable ways of handling disagreements.

Children who are about to be punished often become anxious and fearful. A child who is sent to his bedroom to wait for his father to punish him often experiences negative emotions. He may cry, shake or plead with his parents not to hit him. Good behaviour that is motivated solely by fear is unpleasant for children. When this fear happens often, the child may become timid or withdrawn. He may also experience suppressed hostility and rage, and can become quite unmanageable when his parents are not around.

Children who are punished frequently may try to avoid or escape from the situation where punishment occurs. For example, many children who steal learn to lie to avoid punishment. Runaways have often experienced a lot of punishment at home. When I made a home visit to a family in our programme, I arrived at about 4.30 p.m. to witness a major battle taking place. The mother was chasing her ten-year-old boy around the house with a belt, trying desperately to catch him and to administer 'what he deserves'. Fortunately, the child could run faster than the mother and finally disappeared down the street, yelling obscenities that I am sure could be heard several blocks away.

If punishment seems likely, it is a natural response for the child to escape. Many older children become runaways under just these circumstances. Something similar occurs when speeding motorists slow down when they see a police car. It also partly explains why criminals try to escape from prison.

One of the main difficulties of using punishment to control behaviour is that the effects are short-lived. Research has shown that punishment may lead to a temporary reduction in a problem behaviour, but it does not produce lasting change. I can recall one parent who was a very strong advocate of the wooden spoon for her two boys when they were fighting. Every time they fought she would bring out the wooden spoon as a threat. Miraculously, she reported, they stopped every time. I asked the mother to keep a record of how often the boys fought and how often she threatened and actually used the wooden spoon. After one week the following results came back: fights 7; spoon threats 3; use of spoon 4. Clearly, her strategy had not led to a permanent reduction in the fighting. The boys had not learned to play cooperatively. The spoon only stopped the fight once it had started, and for lasting and meaningful behaviour change, other strategies were needed.

While punishment has disadvantages from the child's viewpoint, it has some problems for parents as well. Firstly, parents can be accidentally rewarded for using punishment because it produces a temporary reduction in the misbehaviour. Unfortunately, parents may be more likely to use this approach in the future because of this pay-off. Secondly, parents can easily be misled into thinking that the punishment has been effective. One way to check out whether your approach is working is to count how often you have to use it. If from one week to the next you have to smack or threaten your child for the same behaviour at about the same rate, say twice a day, and this remains fairly constant, it is unlikely that the approach is working. Effective discipline methods need to be used less and less often because the child is learning the correct behaviour. Thirdly, many parents find punishing an upset child a difficult, unpleasant chore, and some feel extremely guilty and distressed after the event. For some parents, these emotional reactions can last long after the punishment is handed out.

When punishment is misused, used very inconsistently or is harsh, it can make a behavioural or emotional problem worse. One parent I interviewed claimed that she lined each of her four children up every morning to give them a whack. She told them, 'That is for all the times you do something rotten today.'

The parents' relationship

Commonsense tells us that when a parent is unhappy with their partner, children are affected. However, the connection between a couple's relationship problems and difficulties with children is quite complex. The day-to-day demands of raising children can place a strain on any relationship, particularly when parents are living with an extremely difficult child. However, with difficult children, a couple's relationship can also be strained because each disagrees with the other on basic childrearing issues, such as which behaviours should be disciplined; what type of discipline should be used, how often, by whom; supervision of children; or how much time the parents spend with the child. Sometimes these conflicts are resolved in a straightforward way when both parents learn new parenting skills. When a couple can reach agreement on a basic workable strategy for dealing with the problem, the relationship conflict often partially disappears.

When a couple's relationship is strained in a number of other areas and there is a lot of open hostility between the parents, children often suffer. Relationships with high levels of open conflict, involving arguments and shouting, appear to produce different effects on boys and girls. Boys may develop antisocial behaviours such as aggression, whereas girls may become anxious, withdrawn and depressed.

Unhappy relationships affect children both directly and indirectly. Children are affected directly when they observe their parents engaged in conflict. This can be distressing to children, who want their parents to be happy. Indirectly, they can be affected because a parent may be worried about the relationship and may become depressed, spend less time with the children, and become inconsistent or irritable.

Children thrive in a positive, warm, loving family environment where two parents work as a team in matters of childrearing. Where this is simply not possible, due to serious differences between parents, the couple needs to seek marital counselling. Children who are emotionally unstable in a high-conflict home often improve following a marital separation. Keeping together for the sake of the children can sometimes do more harm than good.

Peer and school influences

Children's behaviour is also influenced by factors outside the home. The two most important outside influences related to the development of behavioural problems are the child's relationships with other children and their academic success at school. Children with behavioural problems are often unpopular. Aggressive and negative children are often rejected by their peers, who simply don't want to play with children who bully, boss or hurt others. These children often have poor social skills and find it difficult to make new friends. Such rejection increases the chances that they will align themselves with other disruptive and difficult children. Once a child is part of a peer group or gang that encourages antisocial behaviour such as stealing, lying and truancy, the difficult behaviour may worsen, both at home and at school.

There is little doubt that a child's academic progress also has an important impact on behaviour and self-esteem. Children who make slow progress at school, find the work difficult, have learning difficulties, or rarely receive any positive feedback or rewards, are more likely to drop out of school. This in turn increases the chances that the child will come under the influence of a peer group consisting of other disillusioned youngsters. When children are unpopular, are failing at school and are very disruptive, they are more likely to become involved in delinquent behaviours including drug and alcohol abuse. The further down the path towards delinquency a child has progressed, the more difficult it is to reverse the process.

Parents' emotions

Most parents are aware that their moods affect the way they relate to their children. Our children's behaviour can also affect the way we feel about ourselves as parents and as people. It is not surprising, therefore, that parents' emotional problems can affect their child's behaviour.

Parental depression is the most common of the emotional problems that can affect children. It is estimated that up to one in five adults will suffer from a serious bout of depression at some time in their lives. At any given time, up to 7 per cent of women are clinically depressed. While most adults experience occasional bad moods, perhaps following a disappointment or upsetting experience, most of these 'down' periods are short-lived and will often respond to such simple solutions as a break from children, a chat with a close friend or getting out of the house. Clinical depression is much more severe and persistent, affecting many aspects of a person's life, including parenting. Symptoms of depression include feeling sad or miserable, loss of interest in usual activities, sleep disturbance, weight loss, suicidal thoughts, and feelings of helplessness, hopelessness and being unworthy. When parents are depressed, they often interact with their children less frequently, provide less supervision, and are more irritable and impatient. This can lead to explosive outbursts over trivial things that normally wouldn't worry them. Depressed parents also find it hard to be consistent and positive with their children when they themselves are feeling miserable.

Families where one of the parents suffers from depression are more likely to have children with behavioural and emotional problems, particularly conduct disturbances. Exactly why this might be so is unclear, but it is probably due to the child inheriting a vulnerability towards emotional disturbance, and the fact that the parent's depression disrupts the normal parent–child relationship.

Whatever the cause of depression, parents suffering from depression should consider seeking professional help to combat their condition so as to reduce the risks to their children. Many cases of depression respond well to modern treatment, and once the parent's depression has lifted somewhat, the children's problems can be tackled more effectively.

Stress can also have a negative impact on our ability to parent well. Modern parents are confronted with a variety of day-to-day stresses that can affect family relationships. These include financial, housing or transport problems; work-related stress and pressure; problems with neighbours or interfering relatives; and stress associated with frequent moves, the death of a parent, lack of intimacy, divorce and returning to work after the birth of a baby. Most families learn to cope with these stresses pretty well, and children are not adversely affected. However, anything that disrupts the normal family routine can be upsetting to children, who like security and predictability. In such circumstances, children may become unsettled and more difficult to manage.

Perhaps the most common stress for parents is money. Families with few financial resources can find it hard to cater for children's needs.

Parents' beliefs and expectations

Parenting is a complex task. The way we raise our children is affected by our attitudes, beliefs and expectations about children and childrearing. Parents' views are strongly influenced by the models their parents provided when they were children, their own experience with children, the opinions of partners and the media. Some beliefs parents commonly hold about children make the task of raising children difficult, including the following.

• **'It's just a phase.'**
  Parents sometimes explain away their children's behaviour, particularly misbehaviour, as a 'passing phase'. For example, parents of two-year-olds who throw temper tantrums often comfort

themselves by seeing the behaviour as part of the 'terrible twos' syndrome. It is important to remember that not all two-year-olds throw tantrums, and that those who do do not always grow out of the habit. While there are differences between children of different ages, and parents' expectations of them need to be adjusted accordingly, many behavioural problems are not a necessary part of normal development.

As an example, I can recall a parent at a playgroup meeting insisting that her three-year-old's aggressive behaviour towards other children was 'just a phase' and therefore nothing to worry about. Unfortunately, the other parents in the group were not quite as tolerant, and the child had become very unpopular with other children because of his aggression. This parent eventually sought help when her child was five. His behaviour had become so difficult that the director of the kindergarten asked her to remove him from the group. This child's behaviour was not a passing phase, and his problem could have been dealt with much earlier if his mother had recognised that his behaviour was unacceptable and needed to change.

- **'He's doing it deliberately, just to annoy me.'**
When I meet with parents requesting assistance with their children, I routinely ask the parents what they believe to be the cause of the problem. Some blame themselves; others believe that their children deliberately set out to upset, annoy or irritate them. Sometimes a parent feels that their child has an inbuilt personality flaw, or even an evil or mean streak. Few children with behavioural problems are able to explain the reasons for their actions. Most simply do not know, and certainly all would have difficulty putting their reasons into words. Parents who are convinced that the problem is simply the result of a character flaw can often ignore some of their own actions that might contribute to the problem.

- **'It's all my fault.'**
Some parents blame themselves for almost everything their child does. I have interviewed many guilt-ridden and worried parents; many have become depressed, and in severe cases may become immobilised and incapable of making even minor changes to

their daily routine. It is important to remember that some children are much more difficult to raise than others. Children who have feeding problems, cry excessively as infants and have sleeping difficulties are hard for almost all parents to deal with. The characteristics of the child, the child's peer group, the health of the child, and the degree of support parents can provide one another can all influence the way a child develops. It is not helpful for parents to blame themselves for everything that happens to their children. Feeling guilty and depressed only makes it harder to make the necessary adjustments and changes. Some things that happen to our children are simply out of our control. We can't control who our children like in their peer group, what happens in the classroom or playground, which television programmes or computer games are made for children, the advertising that is directed towards children or the actions of our spouse towards the child. Self-blame is destructive and never solves anything.

Parents' expectations

The behaviour parents encourage, reward or discourage very much depends on what they consider normal for children at different ages. Some behavioural problems can arise because the parent expects too much too soon. For example, parents who try to toilet-train infants of six to eight months of age will often find the task more difficult than if they had waited until the child was two years old. By two, children have sufficient physical maturity and understanding of language to learn to use a potty with little difficulty. Parents who expect their children to be perfect – for example, to always be polite and well mannered, to always be tidy and helpful and to never become angry – are setting themselves up for a life of disappointment and constant battles. This is a particular problem for parents who are extremely houseproud. Children need space to play in and explore. Children's games are often messy and disorganised by adults' standards. Trying to make a child's bedroom the only place they can make a mess creates more problems than it solves. Some behavioural problems are the direct result of parents being overly fussy and rigid.

Wider community influences

Behavioural and emotional problems are more likely to occur when children live in neighbourhoods that lack basic community amenities such as safe playgrounds, recreational space or supervised activities for children of different ages. Communities where there is high crime, unemployment, drug abuse and little civic pride are more likely to produce children and teenagers who develop problems. When children grow up not feeling part of or proud of their community, social problems are more common.

Children are also influenced by what they see and hear through the media, computers, video games and the Internet. In a world where children are continually confronted with violent images in films, television and games, and have access to pornography through the Internet, parents need to do what they can to restrict children's exposure to these potentially harmful influences.

Cultural influences

Parents are raising their children at a time when broader cultural influences can undermine the stability of the family. Children are growing up in a world where violence is common, and where war, terrorism, torture, natural disaster, racial hatred, bigotry and intolerance are common. Children see and hear things through the media that can be very distressing and confusing to them, and the challenge for parents is to help children feel safe and secure in a world of uncertainty and change. This is not an easy task.

Now that we have explored the reasons for children's behavioural and emotional difficulties, we will turn to what parents can do about these problems.

Conclusions

The causes of behavioural and emotional problems in children are complex. They involve a mixture of genetic and biological factors that parents cannot do much about, and environmental factors created by the everyday interactions that take place between children and their parents. Children learn many behaviours that come to be regarded by parents and others as problems. This learning takes place largely through social interactions in the home, interactions that feed and maintain the behaviours. The key issue for parents is to identify the factors that appear relevant to your child and that you can actually do something to change. Fortunately, the majority of common behavioural and emotional problems can be either prevented or significantly improved through adopting positive parenting strategies that target the causes of problems.

CHAPTER 4

Promoting healthy relationships
with children

Constructive parenting is concerned with the way we educate, nurture and care for children. There are five goals that parents should aim to achieve if their children are to develop in a psychologically healthy way.

1. To help children communicate well and become socially competent.
2. To help children express and manage their emotions.
3. To help children master important developmental skills and tasks.
4. To help children become good problem-solvers.
5. To encourage children to develop positive feelings about themselves.

Parents who achieve these goals are more likely to produce happy, healthy and well-adjusted children.

Helping children to become more socially skilled is much easier when parents know how to help children learn new skills and behaviours. This chapter introduces strategies for encouraging children to learn appropriate ways of behaving and getting along with others.

Many children who are difficult to manage lack the social skills they need to deal with the situations they confront. For example, children who are aggressive or demanding, or show off, boast, tease, hurt or bully other children may lack the skills they need to make and keep friends. Children who rudely demand attention when their parents have visitors often lack the skills of being able to wait or ask politely for what they want. Other children have the skills but don't use them. For example they know how to ask civilly if they want to borrow something from a sibling, but they simply don't do it very often, preferring to whine and complain. We need to know how to teach our children the skills they require in their dealings with others, and to motivate them to use those skills.

Many common behavioural problems can be solved by simply helping children to learn a better way of handling a situation. For example, when a mother tells her toddler who has just pulled her hair, 'No, don't pull hair. Stroke my hair like this,' she is demonstrating a better, alternative way of behaving.

The next two sections outline basic strategies that can be used to promote healthy adjustment in children.

Strategies for promoting good relationships with children

This section deals with ways of encouraging good communication between parent and child, and provides ideas for helping children learn socially appropriate behaviours and important developmental skills and tasks. The approximate ages where different strategies are most useful are highlighted, but these should be used as a rough guide only, as children of the same age can develop at different rates.

Spending brief, quality time with your child

RECOMMENDED AGE RANGE: ALL AGES

One of the most important things you can give your child is your time. Children of all ages need their parents' time and attention if they are to develop normally. This means more than simply being with your child and providing food, clothing, shelter and supervision. It is possible for an adult to spend an entire week with a child, yet spend no quality time with them at all.

Children need to grow up feeling that they are cared for and loved by their parents. Ideally, both parents have to spend time with their children to accomplish this goal. The key to having a good relationship with a child is to spend frequent, small amounts of time doing things the child likes to do. For example, children often want to show an adult something they have made, or talk to them about a discovery or experience. Your son might arrive home from preschool bursting to tell you about his trip to the fire station. This is the time to provide quality attention, when he is ready and interested in telling you about what happened. At that time, make yourself available. Interrupt what you are doing and give your child your undivided attention for a short while. Often it takes only a few seconds.

Brief (between thirty seconds and two minutes) periods of individual attention can do much to strengthen your relationship with your child. It is during these times that children learn that parents are accessible, approachable, interested and caring. Remember, quality parenting takes time. Listening patiently to a child's make-believe story, learning about what happened at preschool or school, helping a child with a difficult toy, playing a game and answering hundreds of questions are all part of developing a child's sense of being cared for and loved. These activities can be tiring. Nevertheless, parents need to be accessible to children, whether they are babies or teenagers. Brief, frequent encounters are generally better than longer but less-frequent ones.

Failure to show an interest in the child's day-to-date activities can make her feel that Mum or Dad doesn't care. Some parents get into the habit of frequently requiring the child to wait – 'I'm busy. I'll be there in a minute.' 'Wait until I've finished the washing up.' Requiring children to wait is something both appropriate and necessary, for example if you are speaking on the telephone. However, when children always have to wait or are required to wait for too long, their parents miss out on the spontaneous joy and excitement at the point of discovery. Don't be surprised in this case if your child stops wanting to talk to you about things, or learns to demand very loudly to get your attention.

For older children, brief, quality time with parents is still important. Even though school-age children need attention from parents less often than toddlers and preschoolers, the crucial point is that parents must be accessible when they are required. Parents can't provide guidance and support to their child if they are inaccessible.

Talking with children

RECOMMENDED AGE RANGE: ALL AGES

Children learn a great deal through conversations with adults. Showing an interest in what a child has to say is not only a way of giving positive attention for desirable behaviour, it also provides an opportunity for a child to practise conversational and other social skills, for example describing their experiences and events at school, or asking questions as a way of obtaining information. Conversational skills are important because it is through language that children learn to relate to others.

1. **Wait until the child is engaged in an activity**
   Take notice of when your child is busy and engaged in an activity. Approach him and move within conversational range.
2. **Pause and observe the child's activity**
   Find out what the child is doing. Take notice of the purpose of the child's activity. For example, sit on the couch and watch as your daughter tackles a new game on the family computer, or sit next to your son as he works on his school science project.
3. **Respond to your child's comments**
   Make yourself available and ready to respond to any requests, questions or comments that your child might make. 'Dad, look at how many battleships I have shot down!' Respond with an interested comment or answer. 'What's your highest score so far?'
4. **Withdraw if there is a negative reaction**
   Remove yourself if your child seems uncomfortable with your presence. If she becomes embarrassed, or in some way shows she would rather be alone, simply withdraw. There will be many other opportunities.
5. **Offer an additional comment**
   Give a brief, interested comment or question about the child's activity. 'That was a good kick.' 'How's your project coming

along?' 'You've nearly finished that puzzle.' 'What's Superman doing now?' 'Why did Mrs Smith become angry with Steven?' 'Can you show me how to play that later?'

6. **Continue the conversation**
   If the child responds or asks you another question, continue the discussion.

7. **Share information**
   Communication is a two-way process. Avoid getting trapped into asking a whole series of questions. Volunteer information about your experiences, the highlights of your day, ideas, opinions and feelings so that a two-way discussion can occur. This kind of interaction fosters the child's conversational skills.

8. **Keep the interactions relatively brief**
   These sorts of interactions are best when they are fairly brief, say thirty to sixty seconds. Children can often converse better in short bursts. Their interest in discussing something can quickly change, particularly if another activity captures their attention.

Giving your child plenty of physical affection

RECOMMENDED AGE RANGE: ALL AGES

Another way of caring for and communicating your interest in a child is to provide plenty of physical contact. Frequent holding, touching, cuddling, tickling, kissing and hugging are important if children are to grow up feeling cared for and comfortable with giving and receiving affection. Physical affection is very important in the first few years of a child's life and will allow the child to form secure attachments with his parents. As a strategy for encouraging desired behaviour, physical affection is best provided either while the child is engaged in some desirable activity, or immediately following it. Physical affection is not advised while the child is shrieking, crying or throwing a tantrum. It may calm them temporarily, but also may encourage these behaviours to occur more often.

1. **Have plenty of physical contact**
   Try to have some positive physical contact every day. If you want your child to be physically expressive, lots of practice helps.

2. **Vary your contact**

   Children enjoy variety as much as adults do. Holding hands, cuddles, kisses, tickles, hugs, pats, strokes, back rubs and foot tickles are all ways of communicating affection and having fun with your child. Experiment to find out what your child likes.

3. **Be careful**

   Avoid being rough. Accidents can easily happen when physical fun becomes too boisterous or the child gets over-excited, for example when parents throw their kids in the air.

4. **Be spontaneous**

   While most of the time it is okay to give your child physical contact when you feel like it, avoid doing so while the child is misbehaving, or as a way of calming an agitated child. Don't always expect your child to respond affectionately, particularly if she is absorbed in an activity.

5. **Tell your child you care**

   When you are close to your child, it's a good time to let him know in words that you love him. Children need to hear that they are loved.

6. **Do not force physical affection**

   Some parents become upset if their child rejects physical affection. Children differ quite a lot in how much physical affection they seek from their parents. Not all babies like being cuddled; some may even struggle and resist. As these infants grow older, they may continue to resist or avoid physical contact with their parents. One way of helping such a child become more comfortable with physical contact is to start with the level of contact she feels comfortable with, and then gradually increase the amount and type of contact. Begin with a pat or by touching the child lightly when you praise her, but don't expect her to do likewise. Let her first become comfortable with gentle contact. If she seeks out contact, be prepared to reciprocate at the same level. For example, she may want to hold your hand as you walk down the street. Simply allow this to happen. Don't demand any more than she is prepared to give. Gradually she will become used to more and more frequent contact, and then other types of contact, such as a cuddle, may be possible. Forcing the child will not work and may make the situation worse.

Providing engaging activities for children

RECOMMENDED AGE RANGE: ALL AGES

Children can become difficult because they are bored and have very little to amuse themselves with apart from watching television. The best activities for children are those where they can actively participate rather than passively observe. An environment that is rich in interesting things for children stimulates their curiosity as well as their language and intellectual development. It also keeps children active and busy and thereby reduces the chance of behavioural problems developing. Many parents soon discover that some of the most difficult times with children are when there is nothing for them to do, such as when visiting a grandparent who has lots of breakables on low tables, but no toys or other things of interest to children. Children quickly become bored, tired and irritable in these situations.

Another important advantage of providing an interesting play environment is that incidental teaching becomes easier. Children will have more things to attract their attention and to talk about, which means more opportunities to start conversations with adults and therefore more opportunities to learn.

A play environment also needs to be a safe environment. Accidents in the home are a common source of injuries in children, and are a particular problem with infants, toddlers and preschool children. Try to ensure that your home is as safe as possible. Some tips on safety-proofing the home are covered on pages 115–18 in Chapter 5.

There is no need to spend a lot of money on expensive toys that often have a very limited life. There are some simple rules on selecting toys for children: toys should be robust, capable of being used in a variety of ways, and able to be used by children of different ages. They should not have too many small moveable parts. These sorts of toys can easily be swallowed by young children, are hard to clean up and have parts that can easily be lost.

Some of the best activities for children involve them participating as a member of a group or team. Through such group contact, children can learn a variety of skills: about being a team member, sportsmanship, how to relate to other children, how to take turns, how to win and lose gracefully, how to work together with other children and, in sporting activities, how to improve coordination and learn rules.

Children in most modern communities have access to a wide variety of activities outside school and on weekends. Examples include Cubs, Brownies, Girl Guides, Boy Scouts, gymnastics, tennis, swimming, football, hiking, rowing and so on. Letting children participate in two or three out-of-school activities is a good idea. However, some of these activities can be time-consuming for parents, who can end up feeling like taxi drivers, ferrying their children to one activity after another. Some parents try to involve their children in too many activities on too many days of the week. Kids need time to relax at home, and as a child moves through school some activities may need to be curtailed so he can complete homework, study and other school-related projects.

Sometimes the choice of activities can be a source of friction between parents. How much choice should children have? Once they start an activity, should they be made to continue if they don't like it? What should parents do if children want to play contact team sports?

Many a child has been forced to participate in a sport simply because a parent likes the game. This is often a mistake. The child's own interests and natural aptitude should be taken into account. However, once a child makes a commitment to play a particular sport or to join an activity, she should be encouraged to see it through at least for the season, particularly if the parents have had to pay for expensive uniforms or equipment. Some children need a bit of encouragement to continue in an activity. If they are simply allowed to drop out, they may do so with the next new activity they try and end up not participating in anything at all.

It is important to remember that organised activities for children are also social events where children can meet other kids and make new friends.

Strategies for encouraging desirable behaviour

Tuning in to desirable behaviour

RECOMMENDED AGE RANGE: ALL AGES

Another important skill in developing good relationships with children involves giving positive attention or feedback when a child is behaving well. Attention can be a very powerful motivator. When your children are doing something you like, let them know you appreciate it. Catch your child being good, and desirable behaviour will occur more often. Positive attention can be given in many different ways, for example a comment, touch, smile, wink or hug. They all communicate to your child that you care, that you are interested in her and that you approve of what she is doing. You will also be setting a good example for your child about how to relate positively to others. By encouraging good behaviour, you will help your child learn more quickly what is expected of her. Here are some guidelines.

1. **Watch carefully**

   Before you say anything, watch your child as she plays, moves around the house or completes an activity. Identify anything she is doing that you would like to occur more often. In other words, ask yourself what specific behaviour of hers you like.

2. **Be clear**

   Praise your child enthusiastically by describing the behaviour you like. 'That's terrific, Andy. You went to the bathroom all by yourself. Well done.' 'Thank you, Mandy, for taking out the rubbish today.' 'What a beautifully set table, Ben.' 'I like the way you and Andrea are sharing.' Describe the behaviour rather than the child. Rather than saying 'Kevin, you're wonderful,' say, 'Kevin, that was very thoughtful the way you included Jamie in your game with Boris.' A specific description is more informative for the child.

3. **Initially, respond immediately and often**

   At first it is better to respond to the child's desirable behaviour as quickly as possible. For some children, particularly those who are disruptive, an immediate response is necessary because the good behaviour may not occur very frequently. Initially praise your child often. Later on, when the new behaviour is occurring more often, the praise can be given less frequently. For example, you might decide you want to encourage your child to put her dirty school clothes in the washing basket at the end of each day. For the first week, praise her every time she remembers to put her clothes in the washing basket, but once she is putting her clothes in the right place each day, praise her only occasionally.

4. **Take an interest in what your child is doing**

    Watch with interest what your child is doing. Just knowing that a parent is watching a game or activity can serve as a powerful motivator. Children also want parents to watch when they have mastered a new skill, for example standing up on skates, catching a ball or swimming the length of a pool.

5. **Comment enthusiastically on your child's activity or game**

    Describe warmly your child's action or achievement. With toddlers, comments such as the following can work well: 'That block tower is really terrific.' 'That puzzle has lots of pieces. How did you ever work that out?' 'That bulldozer looks as though it could easily push those blocks away.' Older children also like positive comments about their activities.

6. **Comment on your child's toy**

    Children love to share their toys with an interested adult. 'Hasn't Dolly got beautiful yellow hair?' 'Has Teddy broken his leg? It must be very sore for him.'

7. **Help out with difficult toys or games**

    Offer help if your child is having difficulty with a toy. 'Peter, if you turn the blue one up the other way, the red one will fit on top.' 'If you turn the nut the other way it will go on.'

8. **Be sincere**

    Praise works best when you mean what you say and are genuinely interested in what the child is doing. This can be hard at times, particularly if you are tired or busy. However, praise that is given reluctantly, unenthusiastically or in a flat, emotionless tone of voice is not as effective as sincere praise.

9. **Use other forms of attention**

   Positive attention can include more than words. Sitting or standing near a child, touching, smiling or simply joining in a game for a while all communicate your interest and show that you are pleased with what's going on.

10. **Share your positive feelings**

    When you praise your child, use 'I' statements such as, 'I liked the way you stayed close to me when we went shopping today.' 'I' statements communicate that your child's behaviour affects you positively. Other examples of 'I' statements include: 'I really think that was a tremendous effort to get your marks in maths up this term. Well done.' 'I really appreciate it when you offer to help wash up the dishes without being asked.'

11. **Attend to small improvements**

    In general, look for small and gradual improvements in behaviour rather than expecting your child to be perfect straightaway. A child can be helped to learn a new skill if you attend to gradual improvements. For example, to teach a child to catch a ball, her parent could first stand close and show her how to cup her hands, then gently throw the ball so it lands in the right place. If the child succeeds with her first 'catch', the parent could move slightly further back and repeat the action. Each catch can be praised. Over time, the throws can be harder and from further back. This kind of shaping of a new skill is a very effective way of teaching children to do a variety of complex tasks.

Tuning in to desirable behaviour is a very effective way of changing behaviour. Children often feel good about themselves and respond with delight when parents are positive and encouraging. However, children who have received very little praise for good behaviour may at first react in an embarrassed or even silly way. Be prepared to persist if you get this kind of reaction from your child. It usually disappears once the child becomes more experienced in receiving praise. Sometimes, though not always, older children can become embarrassed by being praised in front of friends. With teenagers and older children it is better not to make too much of a fuss in front of peers. A quiet word in the child's ear works just as well. Praise can work with both younger and older children, providing it is genuine and done in such a way that the child feels comfortable.

Parents may also feel a bit awkward when they shift from reacting mainly to misbehaviour to responding to good behaviour. Some come from homes where they received very little positive attention themselves and they feel embarrassed or self-conscious when they start to relate to their child in a different way. Praising, like most skills, requires practice.

Using incidental teaching

RECOMMENDED AGE RANGE: TEN MONTHS TO TWELVE YEARS
There are tremendous learning opportunities in the home for children of all ages. Day-to-day interactions between children and parents provide a context for many exciting discoveries. Children, through their interactions with others, not only learn their native language, but important social skills and the many basic self-care skills – such as brushing teeth, dressing and toileting – that are needed for independent living.

Many of these basic skills can be developed through a process of incidental teaching. This involves using interactions that children initiate as an opportunity for teaching a new skill. Good teachers have used incidental teaching for centuries. When children initiate contact with adults, they usually want help, want to show the adult something, want attention or want information. Under these circumstances, they are often ready to learn. They are motivated to acquire new knowledge or skills because their attention is focused on the issue at hand and they are interested. In fact, their request usually identifies the thing they want ('Can you show me how this works?'). The parent is now in a powerful teaching situation. They might simply answer the child's question or might invite the child to think of the answer herself ('See if you can figure it out. What do you think those screws are used for?'). In other words, the parent can delay giving the child what she wants so that she has the opportunity to solve the problem, think of the word or practise the skill.

Incidental teaching occurs when the parent responds to the child's request ('Mum, can you tie my shoelaces?') by requesting a more advanced, sophisticated or mature response ('Well, what's the first thing you have to do with the two laces?'). Incidental teaching can be used in many daily situations to develop a variety of new skills, such as when the child is getting dressed, during play, while talking to him about his day at school, while helping him with homework, while reading to him or hearing him read to you, or when he asks for help. Incidental teaching works best when the parent has time to listen and is not rushed or hassled.

It is important to be able to work out the topic the child is referring to. For example, when an eighteen-month-old points to an object but can't name it, the adult has to be able to work out the focus of the child's interest, such as whether he wants the cup or ball on the shelf. The child's topic or request should relate to something the parent is prepared and able to give, such as help with a toy or activity, attention or permission, and the parent should be able to identify a potential learning goal for the child, for example to name the object she has just pointed to, to prac- tise a skill or to acquire some new knowledge. If you intend to refuse the request, then say no immediately and do not attempt to use incidental teaching. From the age of about ten months, chil- dren make numerous approaches to their caregivers which present ideal opportunities for incidental teaching. Here are some steps to follow.

1. **Set the scene**
   Incidental teaching can be used anywhere that there are interest- ing and engaging things for the child to look at, touch, explore or experience, or that are likely to promote conversation. Most homes have numerous objects or materials that can promote discussion.
2. **Wait for the child to begin**
   You should simply wait for the child to initiate conversation. Don't hover over him, just be close by.
3. **Respond to the initiation**
   You should show an interest in what your child is saying by look- ing at her, smiling and directing your full attention to what she is trying to communicate.

4. **Check that you understand what the child is saying**

    If you are not sure what your child means, check. 'What are you pointing to? Do you mean the fire engine?'

5. **Ask the child to say more**

    Ask the child to elaborate, expand, explain or clarify. 'What colour is that car?' 'What do you want me to do with this train carriage?' 'Tell me where this one goes.' 'What happened when the settlers first arrived in this country?' When children are requested to elaborate on something they are interested in, it is an ideal time for them to acquire new knowledge and concepts about a topic. For example, when an eight-year-old is watching Dad check the tyres of the car before going on a long trip, the child might ask, 'Why are you doing that?' This is an excellent time to teach the child something about inflation of tyres for safe driving. If the child had not asked the question, she would have been far less receptive to Dad's explanation.

6. **If necessary, prompt a better response**

    If the child cannot or does not answer, the parent can prompt her. 'Remember how we made the pattern last time? One piece goes here and this piece goes where?' 'Six times two equals twelve, so six times three equals?'

7. **Provide a model**

    If the child still does not answer, or answers incorrectly, tell him the answer and ask him to repeat it. 'Six times three equals eighteen. What does it equal?' 'W-O-O-D spells wood. Can you spell that?'

8. **Give positive feedback**

    This involves confirming the answer given by the child so that she knows the answer is correct. 'Blue, that's right. Your shirt is blue, the same colour as your bike.'

Incidental teaching is most effective when it is brief and enjoyable for both parent and child. If you feel angry or irritated during incidental teaching, stop the procedure immediately. As soon as the child indicates she has lost interest in the activity or game, stop.

Setting a good example through modelling

RECOMMENDED AGE RANGE: THREE TO TWELVE YEARS

Children have a marvellous capacity for learning through observation. Modelling is a strategy parents can use in day-to-day dealings with children to encourage a wide variety of desirable behaviours and skills. At a general level, modelling is quite straightforward. It involves setting a good example for your child, showing your child through your own actions what is appropriate or desirable behaviour. Remember that while your children learn a great deal through watching others, you are the most important model in their life. Here are some ideas on how modelling can be used to encourage desirable behaviour in children.

1. **Identify the behaviours you wish to encourage**
   The first step is to become aware of the behaviours you wish to encourage through modelling. Examples may include skills such as learning to use the toilet, setting the table, using a knife and fork, kicking a football, mowing the lawn (for older children), sewing and needlework. Other things include how to take care of pets, interact with family and friends, make a bed, tend a garden, use a hammer and iron clothes. The particular skills a child can learn will depend largely on the child's age and interests.

2. **Let your child watch**
   Children's natural curiosity will often lead to their observing your actions. Watch for signs of your child showing an interest in what you are doing.

3. **Describe what you are doing**
   Children learn a lot by having the adult explain or describe the steps involved in carrying out a task.

4. **Answer your child's questions**
   Using words the child understands, answer any questions he may have.

5. **Allow the child to copy your actions**
   If the activity is safe, encourage the child to try it for herself.

6. **Help your child when necessary**
   Children often need help when they try something for the first time. Offer assistance, and then let him try again on his own.

7. **Give positive feedback**
   Praise your child's efforts by describing her accomplishments. 'That's great. You've sewn your first stitch.'

8. **Avoid modelling undesirable behaviour**
   Try to avoid setting a bad example, for example smoking, alcohol abuse, foul language, careless use or storage of power tools, not wearing your seatbelt or not cleaning up after making a mess.

9. **Do not force your child**
   Don't force your child to copy a particular behaviour if he is not interested or is bored. Wait until he shows an interest.

Encouraging independence through 'Ask, Say, Do'

RECOMMENDED AGE RANGE: THREE TO SEVEN YEARS

Many parents try to encourage their children to do things for themselves from an early age. For example, children need to learn how to dress and undress themselves, how to play independently for short periods, how to wash themselves, clean their teeth and use the toilet. Children should be encouraged to learn these skills as soon as they are ready.

Unfortunately, not all children seem motivated to learn these skills, and our attempts to help them can be quite frustrating. They may demand that we dress them, or refuse to try to do things for themselves. As a result they can become overly dependent on their parents.

'Ask, Say, Do' is a way of helping children become independent in self-care skills. This strategy can easily be used in your daily dealings with children and can be used as soon as children have some basic understanding of language (from twelve months). Follow these steps.

1. **Get everything ready**
   Gather together everything you need — such as all items of clothing, toothbrush and toothpaste — in advance. This ensures that the child does not have to wait while you search for missing items.

2. **Gain your child's attention**

   Look into your child's eyes, smile and try to be cheerful and relaxed. If you are flustered or running late the child will sense this pressure. The whole idea is to make learning fun.

3. **ASK**

   Ask your child what needs to be done first. 'When we brush our teeth, what do we do first?' 'When we get undressed, what shall we take off first?' 'Okay, we'll tidy up together. What should be picked up first?' The child has to think about the correct sequence of events and so feels in control of the task. You may feel that your child will not know, or will become uncooperative, but don't give up. Children eventually learn not only what to do but also the words related to the step.

4. **If your child gives the correct answer, repeat it**

   Repeating what the child says is a way of giving positive feedback and encouraging language development. 'Yes, that's right. You take off your shoes. Well done.'

5. **SAY**

   If the child does not give the correct answer, cheerfully tell him what to do. 'First you take off your shoes. You show me how to take off your shoes.'

6. **If your child complies, offer praise for completing the task**

   Remember that feedback for correct performance is important. 'Good girl. You did that all by yourself.'

7. **DO**

   If the child still does not perform the task, describe what is required by guiding him through the motions. For example, put your hands on his and guide him through the task. Use the smallest amount of physical pressure necessary to help him get started. Once the child has started, reduce the pressure so the remaining tasks can be completed independently.

8. **Give positive feedback**

   As the action is completed, speak up and praise the child by describing what has been accomplished. 'That's great. You took your shoes off all by yourself.'

9. **Repeat the last six steps for each part of the task until it is completed**

   For example, when teaching a child how to undress, go through these steps for the shoes, then the shirt, the pants, and so on.

10. **Phase out your help**

    Once your child has mastered all the steps involved, you can reduce the amount of help you give. One way of doing this is to require the child to perform several of the steps before giving praise and attention. Then wait until all the steps can be performed before giving attention.

Your child will find it easier to learn a skill if you describe the actions involved. Don't expect your child to learn complex tasks all at once. It takes time and patience. Your child will not learn at all if you continue to do everything yourself for the sake of speed and convenience. If necessary, organise your morning routine to allow extra time with your child.

This basic strategy can be used for teaching children a wide variety of skills, including tidying a bedroom, riding a bike, taking care of animals, learning to cook and sew, using a computer, and repairing a puncture on a bike tyre.

Strategies for dealing with difficult behaviour

So far we have dealt with ways of encouraging appropriate behaviour and helping children learn new skills. However, there is more to producing well-adjusted children than rewarding desirable behaviour. An important part of socialising children involves helping them learn to control their own behaviour by regulating impulsive actions, curbing inappropriate behaviours and managing anger and other negative emotions. In this section we turn to the issue of how to discipline and set limits for children's behaviour. Each strategy has its uses under certain circumstances, as well as its advantages and disadvantages.

The way parents speak to children when disciplining them is important. The idea is to remain firm, calm and to treat children with respect and kindness. Avoid the temptation to become angry, yell, shout or say hurtful things to your child. Never threaten to withdraw your love or to reject your child. Children need to know that even when they misbehave and are being disciplined, they are still loved.

Diversion

RECOMMENDED AGE RANGE: ALL AGES

Sometimes the simplest way to deal with a problem is to divert the child to another activity. If you know the early warning signs that a problem is about to begin (such as a child showing agitated movements or going red in the face), you can attract the child's attention and direct them to another activity that is appropriate for the situation. For example, if a crawling infant is approaching a three-year-old's block tower and you can see the older child is concerned that the tower is going to be knocked over, you could tell the older child a way of distracting the younger child. 'Warren, give Stephen the car to hold.' When the older child cooperates, praise them for doing as you suggest. 'Warren, that was very good how you found something for Stephen to do.' In this way the older child is diverted from hurting the younger child, and the younger child is given something else to do that does not involve knocking over the tower.

To be effective, diversion needs to occur *before* any misbehaviour begins, otherwise you can accidentally reward the misbehaviour.

Establishing clear ground rules

RECOMMENDED AGE RANGE: FOUR TO TWELVE YEARS

Children cannot be expected to behave appropriately unless they know what to do. They need some limits to be set for them. Rules help children learn what is expected of them. Families with no rules can live in chaos; those with too many can be so strict and rigid that children have no freedom to express themselves. When making and using rules for children, remember the following guides. Also, where possible, children should contribute to decisions about family rules.

1. **Have a small number of rules**

   The more rules there are, the more opportunities children have for breaking them, which in turn means more problems with enforcement. Each family has to decide on the rules appropriate for them, but here are some examples of important rules for all children to observe.
   - Children should always let their parents know where they are.
   - Children should always return home by the agreed time.
   - Children should respect and look after other people's property.
   - Children should speak to other family members in a reasonable manner.

2. **Rules should be fair**

   Rules should apply to all children in the family. For example, rules relating to the granting of independence, such as when children are allowed to do certain things on their own, should be the same for all children in the family. If Andrea is allowed to catch the bus to the movies with friends at age thirteen, the same rule should apply to James when he is thirteen. Parents need to use their own judgement when deciding which rules to insist on. Don't be manipulated by children who claim that 'everyone else in our class is allowed to'. If you don't believe it is a good idea, stand your ground. Children will respect you more if they see you being fair and consistent.

3. **Rules should be easy to follow**

   Children are more likely to follow rules that are simply stated and that they understand. They should be able to state a rule themselves and show you exactly what they should do in a particular situation. Parents can check on children's understanding of the rule by asking them, 'What is the thing to do when you first get into the car?' They should be able to answer, 'Put on your safety belt.'

4. **Rules should be enforceable**

   There is no point in having rules if you are unprepared or unable to enforce them. Enforcement should involve praise when the child obeys the rule and consistent consequences if the rule is broken. (Consequences for breaking important family rules will be discussed in more detail later in this chapter.) They include withdrawing privileges for a set period, grounding children, requiring extra duties or chores, or withdrawing pocket money. Both parents must enforce the rules consistently, otherwise children will not learn to follow them consistently.

5. **Rules should be positively stated**
   Rather than having a huge list of don't's, state the rules in terms of do's. Here are some examples. 'Walk when you are by the pool' rather than 'Don't run by the pool'; 'Always let Mum or Dad know where you are going before you leave the house' rather than 'Don't leave the house without telling Mum and Dad where you are going'; 'Pick up your clothes and towels after having a bath' rather than 'Don't make a mess in the bathroom'.

   Do rules are specific in the sense that they describe exactly what is expected of the child. Avoid vague phrases such as 'Be careful when you —' or 'Show respect to your elders'. As well as sounding preachy, they don't tell the child what to do.

Rules for particular situations

Sometimes it is very useful to lay down ground rules before going to particular places, such as on shopping trips, visits to relatives, excursions into unfamiliar cities, or trips on planes or boats. These are rules that apply to specific situations, and they do not operate after the outing has finished. First ask yourself whether the proposed rule is really necessary. If it is, proceed as follows.

1. **Set the scene**
   Call a meeting of all family members. Turn off the television or any other distractions. Choose a time that does not interfere with favourite television shows or other important activities.
2. **State the reason for the meeting**
   Let the children know why they are there. 'Kids, Mum and I want to talk to you about this camping trip on the weekend. There are a couple of rules we would like you to remember about camp

safety, to avoid the problems we had the last time we had a week-end away. Remember, Ben, you got lost in the bush, and Sandy, you nearly burnt yourself on the gas cooker when you were cooking the toast. This will take about five minutes. Okay?'

3. **State each rule clearly**

   'There are three things we would like you to remember at all times. The first thing is to always wear something on your feet. There can be broken glass in the grass, not to mention the ants that can bite.'

4. **Seek your child's opinion on the rule**

   If kids have strong feelings about the fairness or otherwise of the rule, it is better to discuss this in advance and, if necessary, work out a compromise. Sometimes children have very good ideas about how to make the rule workable. Ask, 'What do you think about that? Is that fair enough? Does it make sense to you?' Sometimes difficult children will not participate sensibly in these discussions. If so, state the rule clearly and end the discussion. Debating and arguing serve no useful purpose.

5. **Ask the child to repeat the rule**

   This helps the child remember what is required. 'So, what do you have to remember?'

6. **Repeat steps 4 and 5 for each additional rule**

   'The second thing to remember is, stay near to the campsite unless an adult is with you. We don't want anyone to get lost this time.'

7. **Summarise the rules**

   Ask the child to state all the rules covered. 'Let's see if you can remember them all.'

8. **If necessary, write the rules down**

   Some parents find it helpful to write basic house rules down on a piece of paper and then stick them to the fridge so everyone can see them.

9. **Decide on specific consequences for complying with and breaking a rule**

   Rules are more likely to be followed if they lead to consequences, particularly after a new rule is introduced. Children should be praised for remembering the rules and, if they have been par-ticularly good, some appropriate reward, such as an activity they enjoy, can be used to recognise their effort. If they break the rule, there should also be appropriate consequences. (We will deal with choosing suitable consequences for misbehaviour later in this chapter.)

10. **Wind up the discussion**

   Close the discussion by making a quick summary of the key issues covered and agreed upon.

Dealing with rule-breaking through directed discussion

RECOMMENDED AGE RANGE: FOUR TO TEN YEARS

Directed discussion is a way of promoting alternative behaviour when a child has done something wrong. It is useful with house rules such as not coming indoors with muddy shoes or boots, leaving school bags or dirty clothing in the wrong place, and running through the house instead of walking. It is best used when the child's behaviour has been a slip-up rather than a frequently occurring event. Follow these steps.

1. **Gain your child's attention**

   Obtain the child's attention by using their name and requesting a chat or giving a direct instruction. 'Tim, come here, please. I'd like to talk to you about what happened just then.'

2. **State the problem briefly, simply and calmly**

   For example, if your child walks in the back door with muddy gumboots, say, 'Do not come inside with your gumboots on.'

3. **Explain why the behaviour is a problem**

   'It makes a mess on the floor and then someone has to clean it up.'

4. **Describe, or get the child to suggest, the correct alternative behaviour**

   'What's the right thing to do? Where should your boots go?'

5. **Practise the desired behaviour**

   If there is a chance for the child to practise the correct way to behave, get him to do so immediately. 'Now you show me the right way to come indoors when you're dirty. Go right back to the back door and start again.'

6. End the discussion by thanking the child for doing the right thing

When you use directed discussion, try to avoid becoming annoyed. Keep your cool and speak in a matter-of-fact way. Avoid statements such as 'you silly boy' or 'what a grub'. Simply thank the child for completing the correct behaviour.

Using good behaviour charts

RECOMMENDED AGE RANGE: TWO–AND–A–HALF TO NINE YEARS

Another very effective way of encouraging better behaviour is the use of a behaviour chart, also called 'happy faces' or star chart. (See page 93 for an example.) A happy faces chart can be made out of cardboard or paper and displayed in a prominent and convenient place such as the refrigerator. The chart consists of a number of squares, about 2 cm, large enough to draw in or stick on smiley faces, stars or stickers. The basic idea is that the child can earn smileys for good behaviour. This strategy is often useful for children between the ages of about two–and–a–half and nine. With older children, say between the ages of ten and thirteen, points or ticks can be used instead.

A behaviour chart is probably best used when a specific problem has arisen. For example, Rupert's mother decided to use a star chart when she was having trouble putting Rupert to bed. She gave him a star each time he got into his own bed without protesting. Rupert had a chart beside his bed with fourteen squares, one for each day for two weeks. At bedtime, Rupert's mother would ask him to get into bed. If he did so without a fuss, she praised him and put a gold star on his chart. When Rupert had earned three stars in a row he received a special treat the next day. Rupert decided his reward would be to choose his favourite dessert.

These charts are particularly useful for helping children learn daily routines in the home, such as completing set chores including drying dishes, keeping the bedroom tidy, completing homework, and so on. The chart can take the heat out of a situation where the parent otherwise has to nag to get a child to cooperate. The chart works best when the stars or faces can be exchanged for a back-up reward. Some of the best (and cheapest) back-up rewards involve activities rather than things, for example being able to stay up a bit later to watch a favourite television show, going on a family picnic, being read to in bed even though the child can read for herself, being able to invite a friend over to play or to stay the night, or playing a board game with Dad after dinner.

How to set up a behaviour chart

1. **Get ready**
   Get everything ready: the chart, gold stars, stickers, or felt pens if you intend drawing happy faces or small pictures.

2. **Hold a discussion with your child**
   Tell your child what is going to happen. Get her attention either through a simple request for a chat or by a direct instruction. 'Jane, come here, please. I'd like to talk to you about something.'

3. **Describe the problem simply, briefly and calmly**
   'Over the past week we have had a lot of hassles over keeping the bathroom tidy. I have had to remind you each night to hang up the towels and put your dirty clothes in the washing basket.'

4. **Say why the behaviour concerns you**
   'When you leave your mess on the floor someone else has to pick it up, and it's usually me. This makes me annoyed, and I don't like getting annoyed. I think you're old enough to do this on your own.'

5. **Describe how the behaviour chart works**
   'We're going to play a little game to help you remember. See this chart? It has seven squares on it. One for each day of the week. You can earn a special sticker like this, which we will put on here if you leave the bathroom tidy each night. When you earn seven of these stars you can have a little treat for your good work. Okay?'

6. **Describe how often the child can earn the stars, happy faces, or stickers**
   This will vary depending on how often the behaviour occurs: every half-hour, hour, two hours, once a day. At first, behaviours that occur only once or twice a day – such as making a

bed – can earn stars each time. If the behaviour occurs very frequently – such as whining – say, at least twice an hour, it is better to use a system where the child earns a reward for each half-hour that he speaks properly without whining. You must make this decision about timing. In other words, you reward the absence of the problem behaviour. In general, it is better to reward a new behaviour frequently when you start. Once the desired behaviour is learned, rewards can become less frequent. For instance, in the whining example, you can start with short time periods then increase to one-, two- or three-hour time blocks.

7. **Describe what back-up rewards can be earned for a certain number of stars**
Make sure a back-up reward – such as inviting a friend over – is available within the first two days so that the child does not have to wait too long. Then, if all goes well, the reward can occur less often, maybe only at the end of the week.

8. **Ask the child to state the rules for earning stars and back-up rewards**
Praise the child for stating the rules correctly. If she does not appear to understand, or gets the rules wrong, state the correct ones and simply proceed. Children will learn what it all means by experiencing the plan in operation.

9. **Decide what to do if the child breaks the rules**
Few children manage to correct their behaviour without the occasional slip-up, so decide how you will deal with break-downs. There are several possibilities here. One is simply to withhold the reward. If the child forgets, he doesn't receive the star. Sometimes this is enough. For other children something more powerful is required. (We will discuss some strategies in detail later in this chapter.)

10. **Explain to your child the consequence of breaking the rules**
Ask the child to tell you what will happen if he breaks the rules.

11. **If possible, have a practice run**
Pretend first of all that the child has done the correct thing, and place a star on the chart. Then pretend the child has forgotten

the rule, and take her through exactly what you plan for dealing with disobedience.

Here is a sample behaviour chart.

FIGURE 2: A BEHAVIOUR/HAPPY FACES CHART

Each time the desired behaviour occurs, place a smiley face, star or a sticker in a square.

Managing the programme

Once you have developed your plan, the programme can be put into action. Follow the steps below each day to ensure that your plan is successful.

1. **Watch your child's behaviour closely**
    There is no point in starting a behaviour chart unless you know whether your child has kept to the rules or completed the required task.
2. **Catch your child being good**
    When you notice the desired behaviour occurring, give enthusiastic praise. Let your child know that you are pleased with his efforts.
3. **Describe the problem behaviour and the consequences**
    When the problem behaviour occurs, state firmly and calmly what has been done, and then put the consequences into action. 'Jimmy, Sandra, you've been fighting over the computer. Now the computer will be turned off for ten minutes.'
4. **Fill in the chart at the required time**
    If no problems have occurred during the selected time, gain your child's attention and let her know that you are pleased with her efforts. Suggest that she might like to put a sticker on the chart. If she doesn't want to, simply put it on yourself. Use a timer set to the required time period to remind yourself when the time is up.

    If an undesired behaviour occurs, describe that behaviour and ask your child to suggest what he should have done instead. Of course, no stars go on the chart. Do not use black marks on the chart or unhappy faces to indicate bad performance; this kind of negative feedback doesn't help.
5. **Give the back-up reward**
    When your child has earned the agreed number of stars, provide the back-up reward for his efforts.

Concerns about using rewards with children

Some parents are concerned that using rewards for good behaviour might cause problems. Some of these concerns are quite real, but problems can largely be avoided if the plan is set up properly.

'Is it bribery?'

A bribe is an inducement to do something wrong, illegal or immoral. Parents sometimes feel that rewards are bribes, and that their children should comply with instructions simply because they are supposed to. It is better to think of the reward as an encouragement or incentive for the child to try a bit harder at correcting a problem. Children who develop problems often need their parents' support and recognition in tangible ways.

'Won't he become dependent on rewards?'

Will the child learn to rely on getting rewards and so do nothing unless there is a pay-off? This is a reasonable concern, but the danger can largely be avoided if the parent follows a few simple rules. First, always pair the reward with some other form of attention such as praise so that the reward can be phased out. Second, use activity rewards rather than things you have to buy. Third, give the reward when the child has earned it rather than when she asks for it. Fourth, use the behaviour chart sparingly, for brief periods of time, and for specific behaviours. Most parents find behaviour charts most useful during the first two or three weeks when the child is learning a new behaviour. Once the new behaviour is established, the child can gradually be weaned off the chart. Positive attention is often enough incentive to keep the improved behaviour going.

'Won't it discourage self-motivation?'

Strategies such as smiley faces charts, giving children stamps in their school books for good work, merit awards, and praising children for desirable behaviour, are all based on the idea that good behaviour deserves to be recognised and rewarded.

Nevertheless, some psychologists and parents believe that giving external rewards to children for improved behaviour is bad for them. They believe that it is disrespectful to the child, weakens his self-motivation and natural interest in the activity he is rewarded for and, because the adult controls the reward, takes away the child's responsibility for his own behaviour.

I disagree with most of these criticisms, for several reasons. First, the children who benefit most from programmes that involve rewarding good behaviour are often not motivated to change and do not enjoy the tasks they need to perform. Such children may never have experienced the satisfaction of completing a task, and rewards can help them start to experience success. Second, there is nothing disrespectful about wanting to show appreciation or encouragement for a child who has behaved well. Rewards can be used to strengthen rather than weaken self-discipline. Third, rewards can be used to enhance rather than restrict responsibility. Children can be rewarded for responsible behaviour, such as taking care of a younger sibling when crossing the road. Fourth, children can be encouraged to self-evaluate and reward their own performance. Comments from parents, such as 'What do you like about your painting?' or 'Tell me what you found interesting in the story' can be combined with praise and other forms of positive attention to encourage self-reflection in children. Finally, rewarding desirable behaviour is one of the most effective methods of motivating children. Sensible parents learn how to use such strategies to their child's and their own advantage.

'How will other children in the family react to one child getting special treatment?'

The concern here is that if one child is on a special programme that involves rewards, other children in the family may resent it and misbehave themselves. This occasionally happens, but in my experience it is relatively rare. Other children often respond to a simple explanation as to why the child concerned needs special help. Usually there are advantages for all family members if a difficult youngster's behaviour improves. Of course, it is still important not to neglect the other children if one is put on a behaviour chart. Where several children have the same kind of problem, a separate behaviour chart can be used for each.

Giving clear, calm instructions

RECOMMENDED AGE RANGE: TWO TO TWELVE YEARS

In Chapter 2 we discussed how the kind of request we make of children influences whether or not they cooperate. Here are some ideas about how to give children instructions that work. If you really want a child to do something, then always be prepared to back up the instruction. If you are not prepared to do this, then don't follow this procedure. If you give the child a choice, be prepared for them to say no.

1. **Get close**
    Move to within arm's reach of your child so that she is sure to hear and will find it difficult to ignore what you say. Being close also makes it easier to follow through if she disobeys.
2. **Gain your child's attention**
    Call your child's name. 'Paul, listen.' Don't require him to look at you, just be sure he can hear.
3. **Use positive body language**
    Turn your body towards your child, get down to her eye level, stop whatever else you are doing and look at her.
4. **State what you would like your child to do**
    Describe exactly what you want your child to do. 'Paul, it's bathtime now. I would like you to pack up the game and hop into the bath, straightaway, please.' Do not always insist on instant obedience. Allow him to finish what he is doing. Finding out where he is up to in a game or activity can help because a natural break will occur at the end of a turn, set or game.
5. **Give your child time to comply**
    After the instruction, pause for five seconds and say nothing. Children need time to get started.

6. **Give positive feedback if your child complies**
   Praise your child for complying with an instruction. 'Thank you, Linda, for doing as I asked straightaway. Well done.'

7. **Repeat the instruction if the child does not obey**
   State the request again in a firm, calm, matter-of-fact way. 'Paul, I asked you to do something. Pack up and get into the bath, please.'

8. **Wait another five seconds if necessary**
   Once again, give the child time to comply. Remain close at hand and say nothing else. No debating, arguing the point or losing your cool. Just pause.

9. **Praise your child for complying**
   If your child complies with the second request, offer praise.

10. **If your child still doesn't comply, back up your request with a consequence**
    If your child continues to be defiant, use an immediate, decisive consequence such as quiet time or time out (see pages 100–105).

11. **After the time-out period, return your child to the place where the problem started, and repeat the instruction**
    Repeat steps as many times as required until your child does what she is told. You must be sure that you are asking her to do something she can accomplish. The aim is to break the cycle of yelling, hassling and repeated nagging. It requires you to be firm and consistent and to keep your cool. It is a way of getting out of the escalation trap described in Chapter 3.

Backing up requests with logical consequences

RECOMMENDED AGE RANGE: FOUR TO TWELVE YEARS

Janice put Damian's bike away in the shed for two days because he rode without his crash helmet and on the wrong side of the road. Daniel removed a troublesome toy after Henry grabbed it from Lucy while she was playing with it. Nora refused to buy any icy poles the next time she went shopping because the kids continually took them from the freezer at home without asking. Bill was grounded for four days for arriving home late from football training without any explanation. These are all examples of logical consequences for misbehaviour. Each parent chose a consequence that fitted the situation in an effort to discourage further problems. Here are some ideas for using logical consequences. It is a very useful strategy for behaviour that is mild and doesn't occur often. This approach is most useful with basically well-adjusted kids who have a few specific problem behaviours that cause family conflict.

1. **Describe the problem behaviour**
    When you observe the undesirable behaviour, gain your child's attention and clearly state the nature of the problem. 'Johnny, you know you must not grab toys from your sister while it's her turn.' Try not to get angry or wound up.

2. **Withdraw the activity**
    If possible, remove the activity, such as a troublesome toy, bike or ball, or take the child from the activity by, for example, turning off the television or sending the child to another room.

3. **Give an explanation**
    Tell the child why you are doing this and how long the consequence will last. 'Since you won't play nicely with your sister, these games will be put away for ten minutes. Then you can try again to play without grabbing.'

4. **Keep to the conditions**
    Allow the child access to the activity once the time is up.

5. **Be reasonable in the amount of time the activity is withdrawn**
    Banning a child from playing with something such as a bike for three weeks is excessive when two hours might have worked just as well. In general, long periods are no more effective than shorter ones.

6. **Avoid arguments**
    Don't debate or argue the point with your child.

7. **Be decisive**
    When the problem occurs, act immediately and decisively. If you discover the problem after the fact, act as soon as the opportunity arises.

Using quiet time to handle disruptions

RECOMMENDED AGE RANGE: ONE–AND–A–HALF TO NINE YEARS

Quiet time is a mild but effective strategy for helping children learn more acceptable behaviour. Quiet time is useful for children who will obey their parents' instructions to stay in the quiet-time place for the allotted time. It involves removing a child who is misbehaving or being disruptive from an activity and making her sit quietly on the edge of the activity or in a quiet-time chair. This chair can be in the same room where the disruption took place. Quiet time is particularly useful for mild disruptions that involve a child disturbing the games or activities of other children. For example, Sheila decided to use quiet time to help David learn to take turns on the family trampoline when other children were visiting. When she saw David push in or refuse to get off after his time was up, she walked up to him and told him he must remember to let the other kids have a turn. She then led him to the edge of the activity and told him to sit quietly for two minutes. He was allowed to watch but could not join in. When Sheila first heard about quiet time she was convinced it would not work. However, David quickly learnt to sit quietly if he wanted to return to the activity, and it only took three quiet times before he was taking turns like everyone else. When introducing quiet time, follow these guidelines.

1. **Before you begin, explain how quiet time works**
    Tell your child which behaviours will earn quiet time. Explain calmly why you will be using it. Rehearse the routine by showing your child exactly what will happen the next time the problem behaviour occurs. Children under the age of four often have to experience the routine a few times before they understand what is involved.

2. **When the problem occurs, give a 'stop' instruction**
    When you notice the behaviour occurring, gain the child's attention and calmly but firmly tell him to stop the problem behaviour. 'Peter, stop pushing your sister right now.' Act quickly whenever you see the behaviour occurring.

3. **Praise your child for compliance**
    If the behaviour stops, thank the child for doing as he's told, and suggest another activity.

4. **Back up your instruction with quiet time**
    If the behaviour continues or occurs again within the next hour, tell the child what he is doing wrong ('I have asked you to stop pushing your sister') and the consequence of disobeying ('Now go to quiet time').

5. **Do not lecture, nag or threaten quiet time**
    Act, don't threaten. Make sure the child is taken to the quiet-time place. Protests should be ignored. If the child protests or refuses, firmly but calmly guide her to the quiet-time area.

6. **Before you leave, let your child know the rules**
    'After you have sat there quietly for two minutes, you can come out.'

7. **Withdraw all attention while your child is in quiet time**
    Once the child is in quiet time, do not speak to him, and ensure that he receives no attention from anyone else.

8. **After quiet time, help your child get involved in an activity**
    When quiet time is over, do not mention the incident. Encourage the child to find something to do, such as rejoining the activity, then look for an opportunity to catch him being good.

Parents often have questions about quiet time.

*   'How old should a child be?' Quiet time can be used with children from about the age of eighteen months to nine years. Younger children will learn what quiet time is about by experiencing what happens when they are disruptive. A toddler's cot or playpen can be used as a quiet-time area.
*   'Shouldn't I also be encouraging good behaviour rather than just disciplining her when she's naughty?' Yes, indeed. Quiet time, like all discipline techniques, works more effectively if you praise your child when she does the right thing.

- 'What should I do if my child won't sit quietly in quiet time?' Allow your child to make a noise for up to ten seconds before you take action. Unless your child is particularly difficult he will soon get the idea that by sitting quietly for a short time he can rejoin the activity more quickly. If the activity is something the child likes to do, this often happens after three to five quiet times, sometimes more quickly. If your child simply refuses to stay in quiet time or continues to make a noise after ten seconds, then you can back it up with time out, which is explained below.
- 'What should I do if my child sits but is not quiet?' Some children will sit in a quiet-time chair but will cry, sob or call out. Quiet time starts when the child is quiet. It stops when the child has been quiet for two to three minutes. Some parents make the mistake of letting the child out of quiet time while she is still upset. If this happens, the child will not learn to be quiet in quiet time. If she becomes disruptive and throws a temper tantrum, it is better to use time out.

Using time out to deal with disruptions

RECOMMENDED AGE RANGE: TWO TO TEN YEARS

In time out, the child is removed from the situation where a problem has occurred. It usually lasts for two to three minutes, and is used immediately after the child demonstrates a problem behaviour. It can be a back-up to quiet time or the consequence of very disruptive behaviour such as aggression, temper outbursts or disobedience. It works in much the same way as quiet time, except the child is typically put in another room such as a laundry, bathroom or hallway. Time out is an alternative to shouting, threatening or smacking a child who has misbehaved. When it is used correctly it can be an extremely effective way of helping children learn more acceptable behaviour. Its main advantage is that it requires the adult to remain calm. Becoming angry when a child is upset often leads to more anger on the child's part, causing the spiralling escalation referred to in Chapter 3.

Sending a child to her bedroom is a variation of time out. The main problem in using the child's bedroom as a time-out area is that it often contains toys and other things the child can play with during the time-out period. The best time-out areas are rooms that are fairly dull and uninteresting, but well-ventilated, safe, with good lighting and able to be closed off if necessary.

Parents who have tried a version of time out may have found that it hasn't worked for one of the following reasons. First, the child has been allowed to decide when to come out. For example, the parent may say, 'Amanda, don't speak like that in this house. Go to your room and come out when you're ready to behave yourself.' The child may simply walk into the room and come straight out again. Second, it has been used inconsistently. Time out works best when it is used every time a problem behaviour occurs. Third, the child comes out of time out while he is still upset. This is a major problem because he learns that if he yells loudly and long enough he will eventually get out. Getting out of time out should depend on the child actually being quiet for two to three minutes rather than promising to be good, or simply being there for the set time. Time out starts when the disruption stops.

Many parents I have worked with choose the laundry area for time out, having first safety-proofed it by placing harmful products out of reach and tightening taps.

The guidelines for using time out are similar to those for quiet time.

1. **Explain the time-out routine to your child**
   Before you begin using time out, explain the procedure. Tell your child which behaviours will earn time out, and rehearse the entire routine with him. The rehearsal is a practice run of what will happen the next time your child, for example, throws a temper tantrum.
2. **When the problem behaviour occurs, gain your child's attention, describe the problem behaviour and the correct alternative behaviour**
   Give a clear instruction. 'Jane, stop that fighting immediately.' Respond quickly, as soon as you see the behaviour

occurring. Be sure to respond each and every time the behaviour occurs.

3. **Praise your child for cooperating**

   If the instruction works, praise the child for complying. If the behaviour continues, tell him what he's done wrong ('I've asked you to stop fighting') and the consequence for disobeying ('You haven't stopped. Now go to time out for three minutes.')

4. **Back up with time out**

   Make sure the child actually goes to time out, but do not lecture, nag, threaten or argue the point. If the child refuses or struggles, firmly but calmly guide her to the time-out area and leave her there. Use the minimum force necessary to get the child to move towards the area, and reduce this physical assistance as soon as the child begins to walk without struggling.

5. **Remind your child of the rules**

   Once you have taken the child to the time-out area, tell him he can come out after a few minutes, providing he is quiet. Short time outs are just as effective as longer ones. With toddlers, a thirty-second quiet period can be sufficient. With children aged three to five, one to two minutes can be used. With children from five to ten years, three to eight minutes can be used. Time-out periods longer than these do not add to the effectiveness of the strategy. Leave the door open, but close it immediately if the child tries to leave the room.

6. **Ignore disruptions in time out**

   If the child becomes disruptive in time out (screaming, calling out or kicking the door or walls), ignore it. She is trying to get your attention, and being successful will defeat the purpose of the exercise. If she attempts to escape by opening the door or climbing out the window, be prepared to return her to the time-out area immediately. If necessary, stand by the door until the time-out period is over. Once the child is in time out do not speak to her, enter the time-out area or give her any attention until the time-out period is over. Some children will try to escalate their behaviour, particularly if they have learnt to do this to get their own way, so you must be prepared to put up with the storm.

7. **After time out, try to catch your child being good**

   When time out is over, don't mention the incident. Encourage the child to play or amuse herself and then look for a chance to praise her for behaving correctly. However, if the child received time out for disobeying an instruction, such as 'come to the dinner table', take her to the spot where the original instruction was given, then repeat it. If she complies, offer praise. If she continues to defy you, return her to time out for a further two to three minutes.

8. **If the problem occurs again, use time out again**

   If there is a repeat of disruptive behaviour that has earned time out in the previous hour, tell the child what they have done wrong and immediately put him back into time out.

Time out can be used for a wide range of behavioural problems, including refusing to comply with requests, teasing, fighting, temper tantrums, swearing and destructive behaviour such as throwing or breaking objects. It can be used with children up to the age of nine or ten. It can also be used as a back-up to other forms of discipline such as logical consequences and quiet time, both of which are discussed earlier in this chapter. Once a child becomes too strong to put into time out, other strategies should be considered. (These strategies are discussed in Chapter 7.)

Using planned ignoring to deal with problem behaviour

RECOMMENDED AGE RANGE: ONE TO TEN YEARS

Not all difficult behaviour needs to be specifically corrected. Sometimes it is sufficient simply to ignore it. Planned ignoring involves withholding attention from the child while the behaviour is in progress. It is most effective for minor problems such as complaining after being refused something, making a mess while playing and accidents such as breaking glassware. It works best when all attention is withheld from the child, including reactions from siblings, peers and extended family. Sometimes parents say they have tried ignoring a behaviour and it hasn't worked. One parent I worked with said that she ignored her son when he was cheeky to her – what she actually meant was that she had not hit him. She still looked at him, stopped what she was doing and often told him off. It is not surprising that 'ignoring' failed to work. The child still received quite a lot of attention for being cheeky. Use the following as a guide to dealing with planned ignoring.

1. **When you observe the undesirable behaviour, decide whether you should ignore it**
   If you decide to ignore a problem behaviour, make sure you ignore it every time.

2. **Withdraw all attention**
   Turn away from the child and, if necessary, walk away. Make no response at all. Avoid eye contact with your child.

3. **Continue to ignore the child if the behaviour worsens**
   Be prepared for the behaviour to become worse before it improves. Children don't like being ignored and may become noisy and demanding before they finally realise that you mean business.

4. **Attend to your child when the behaviour ceases**
   When the undesirable behaviour stops, wait a few seconds and then attend to the child. Praise her for behaving correctly once again. 'Thank you for being quiet. What was it you wanted to ask me?'

5. **If the problem starts again, remove all attention while it continues**
   You must consistently ignore the child each time the behaviour occurs.

6. **As soon as the child is busy and behaving well, give praise and positive attention**
   Catch your child doing the right thing.

Planning activities to prevent behavioural problems

RECOMMENDED AGE RANGE: ONE TO TEN YEARS

Many behavioural problems can be avoided completely if adults take steps to ensure that children have interesting and engaging activities available. Bored children are often disruptive. Helen and Mark understand this principle. Whenever they go visiting with Daniel, their two-year-old, they always take toys and games that Daniel can play with. Mary and Cameron also know what can happen when they take their three boys, aged seven, nine and ten, for picnics in the country if they don't take something for the kids to do on the way. This family decided to set aside some special activities that are only allowed to be used in the car. They included two hand-held computer games and a variety of cassettes that the children chose. Most of the time car trips are no hassle because the kids have something to do other than look out the window.

1. **Pinpoint high-risk situations**

   Think of situations where children have been disruptive or naughty in the past because there was very little for them to do.

2. **Identify suitable activities for each situation**

   In each situation, ask yourself how you might keep your child amused for at least some of the time. For example, on shopping trips children can be involved in finding the cheapest washing powder, locating goods of different colours or shapes or helping find Dad's favourite shaving cream or aftershave. In a bank, children can be given a deposit slip and can practise filling out their own while the parent waits to be served.

3. **Discuss the ground rules in advance**

   Discuss new ground rules in advance and encourage your children to select something they would like to take that will keep them amused, for example colouring books, picture books or a Rubik's cube.

4. **Generate an activity list**

   Involve children in the planning of activities for school holidays. Some parents have found that an activity list can help reduce boredom during holiday periods or bad weather. Ask your child to try to think of all the activities he would like to do during the holidays. Encourage him to generate a list of about twenty or thirty items, including many things he can do on his own and don't cost anything. This list can be stuck to the refrigerator. Whenever he complains of having nothing to do, simply refer him to the activity list and ask him to choose something he would like to do.

5. **Help your child get started if necessary**

Sometimes you will need to help your child get started. For example, if she wants to play with playdough, you may need to place newspaper on the table and get the necessary materials ready. If she won't get started, give her a gentle prompt. 'How about rolling the dough out until it's really smooth, and I will come back to see how you're getting on?'

6. **Attend to your child periodically**

Give your child attention for brief moments periodically while he is busy. The child is more likely to continue if you do this. Don't wait for him to finish the activity before providing attention. Offer snacks and drinks while he is busy rather than waiting until he is bored and whinges for food.

General guidelines for coping with children's misbehaviour

Here are some general guidelines for dealing with children's misbehaviour. If you follow these general ideas, many headaches over children's behaviour can be avoided.

- Do set limits to your child's behaviour.
- Do praise your child for behaving appropriately.
- Do respond to misbehaviour immediately, consistently and decisively.
- Do respond to misbehaviour by describing what the child has done wrong.
- Do respond to misbehaviour by telling the child what would have been more acceptable.
- Do back up your instructions or reasonable requests by using logical consequences, quiet time or time out.
- Do remain calm when speaking to a child who is upset or has misbehaved.
- Do speak calmly but firmly to your child when she misbehaves.
- Do act quickly. Don't threaten to act.
- Do deal with the problem yourself rather than threatening someone else's action.

- Do try to prevent problems by ensuring that your child has plenty of interesting and engaging things to do.
- Do discuss rules with your child in advance and give him a chance to be involved in deciding on family rules.
- Do expect reasonable behaviour from your child but don't expect perfection.

Many problems with children can be avoided altogether if parents remember four other basic ideas.
- Do give children positive feedback when they do the right thing.
- Do encourage children to share their experiences with you.
- Do create lots of opportunities for children to be involved with engaging and interesting activities.
- Do show a genuine interest in what they are doing.

When to seek professional advice

Parents who experience several different problems with their child need to decide whether to tackle the problems on their own using the suggestions in this book, or to seek the help of a professional counsellor or therapist. Child psychologists can often be very helpful to families who have children with several different problems and are uncertain about where to begin. In Chapter 8, beginning on page 305, there is a list of the behavioural and emotional problems that probably require professional advice before you begin a behaviour-change programme. While much of the material in this book can assist children with serious behavioural or emotional problems, you may find professional guidance helpful in deciding which parts apply to your child. Your family doctor should be able to refer you to professionals in your area who specialise in working with children who have behavioural and emotional problems.

Be an informed consumer. Before entering counselling or therapy, ask some specific questions. What kind of approach does the person take in dealing with problems such as your child's? In particular, select a therapist who actively involves parents in the therapy process and who offers concrete, specific advice on ways you can assist your child. Ask how many sessions are typically involved and the cost per session. The majority of child behavioural problems can be addressed within six to ten sessions. What qualifications and training in dealing with children with problems does the professional have? Are after-hours appointments possible so that working parents can attend? Are drugs used as part of the treatment? If your therapist refuses to answer these sorts of questions or uses confusing psychological, medical or psychiatric jargon, seek an alternative referral. Expect to be fully informed, that both you and your child will be treated with respect, and that you will receive treatment tailored to meet your needs.

Conclusions

Positive parenting strategies give parents a remarkably wide range of practical options for helping children learn the skills and behaviours they need in order to do well and to effectively deal with a wide range of behavioural and emotional problems. However, a parent's success in using these strategies will often depend on achieving the right combination of things. For example, quiet time and time out are only useful when the child lives in a positive world containing interesting things for the child to do. The time-in place has to be a rewarding, enjoyable place the child wants to be involved in, before removing the child will act as a deterrent. Parents are more likely to use positive parenting strategies when they feel comfortable with their use and believe that the strategies will be effective with their child.

Some strategies, such as giving positive attention to children, can be surprisingly hard for parents when they themselves have experienced little in the way of positive encouragement as a child. The parent might feel awkward and embarrassed about telling a child what they like about their behaviour. For parents in this kind of situation, it is important not to abandon the strategy too easily. Often persistence leads to parents feeling more comfortable and, when children start to respond positively, parents really experience the benefits of being more positive.

PART TWO

applying constructive parenting

CHAPTER 5

Infants and toddlers

The first three years of a child's life are of special importance because it is during this time that the foundations for all subsequent development are laid. Children's physical, cognitive, language, social and emotional development can all be dramatically affected by their early experiences. It is during these earliest years that a child's brain develops rapidly. What is now clear is that the care and stimulation parents give to their infants actually affect the 'wiring' of nerve pathways in the brain. The experiences of children in the first three years are very important for the wiring of the brain's billions of neurons. The effects of this early brain development can last a lifetime.

In the first year of life, infants develop a basic sense of trust in their caregivers and environment. This means that the child should experience a positive, warm and predictable world where pain and discomfort are minimised. Four aspects of childcare contribute to this developing sense of security during the first year of life: whether the child's basic needs for food and nourishment are met, whether the child receives sufficient physical contact and nurturing, whether the child forms a close emotional attachment or bond with the primary caregiver and whether the child receives adequate stimulation.

Infants who are fed when they are hungry and have their other physical needs met; who receive plenty of positive, warm physical contact through cuddling, holding, rocking and being talked to; and who form an emotional bond with a caregiver, usually the mother, experience a positive and non-threatening world. Children's development progresses much more smoothly in such a climate.

Children's development proceeds through a series of fairly predictable phases from birth to adolescence. New behaviours, skills and capabilities, such as crawling, walking and talking, emerge in a fairly orderly and predictable pattern for most children during the first two years of life. Newborns begin life equipped with a number of basic reflexes. For example, if a baby is stroked on the cheek, it will automatically turn its face in that direction. This reflex has survival value because it helps the baby locate the nipple for feeding. Despite such reflexes, the human infant depends on the care and supervision of adults for survival. During the first eight to ten months of life, much of a baby's time is spent sleeping, feeding, mastering basic motor skills such as kicking, and exploring the environment.

In the second half of the first year, the child becomes a true social being. It is an exciting period for parents because their child becomes far more responsive to people and things around them. They recognise their parents' faces and voices, and begin to smile, babble and communicate. They make many exciting discoveries, including learning to crawl and explore, and they develop a curiosity about the world around them. This world consists of people, sounds, lights, smells and objects that differ in shape, size and texture. Babies gradually become less dependent on their parents and occupy themselves for longer periods, even though most of their day is still spent close to a parent.

The first two years involve rapid changes in the child's capabilities. Simple reflexes such as sucking are gradually replaced by more complex goal-directed ones such as crawling, walking, feeding and talking. Through their daily interactions with family members, children also learn a variety of social behaviours, such as smiling, cooing and laughing. It is also a time where the basic foundations of human intelligence and problem-solving are laid down, as children learn to explore objects in their environment through tracking (watching and following), mouthing and touching.

This chapter is not intended to provide an in-depth coverage of development during infancy and toddlerhood, nor to cover all possible problems that might arise in caring for children of this age. Rather, I have selected some of the most common difficulties parents experience.

Specific issues and problems in infancy

During infancy, the main difficulties parents encounter involve adjusting to the day-to-day demands and responsibilities of taking care of a child whose very survival depends on the parents' attentiveness and capacity to provide loving care. In addition, three specific problems can be a source of considerable anxiety to parents during the child's first year. These include accidental injuries to the infant, crying and fussing, and fear reactions. Strategies for dealing with each difficulty are discussed below.

Creating a safe play space

As infants and toddlers spend most of their time at home, it is important that this environment is as safe as possible, particularly after the child starts to crawl, probably around eight to ten months. This will allow exploration to occur with as little restriction as possible as soon as the child is ready. Having a safe environment also frees parents from worry about a child getting hurt or injured. Accidents are a leading cause of injury and death in young children, so it is important to recognise some of the dangers in the home and to take action to ensure that the environment is as safe as possible for your young child.

Each room in the house should be checked to make sure it is safe. Have a first aid kit in your house and make a list of emergency numbers for your family doctor, nearest hospital, ambulance, fire brigade, police and poisons information service.

- **The kitchen and living areas**
  Young children spend most of their waking hours in the kitchen and living areas, so ensure that breakables, cleaning materials

and sharp utensils are removed to high or lockable cupboards. Anything that may cause harm, such as sharp objects, household cleaners, bleaches, chemicals, medicines or glassware should be well out of reach of young children. Be particularly careful to ensure that potentially harmful objects are removed from low areas, especially those below 1 metre.

Electrical plugs and cords and power points can be a particular problem for toddlers. When power points are not in use, make sure they are covered (plastic covers that fit into the socket are available from department and hardware stores). Ensure that all cords are well insulated and not in need of repair. Keep all appliance cords well out of reach so a child cannot accidentally pull an appliance down on top of himself. Turn pot handles towards the rear of the stove. Use the front elements or burners for low-heat cooking and simmering, and the rear ones for high-heat cooking. Keep children away from unstable or fragile furniture until they are coordinated enough to not need to grab for objects to hold themselves upright. Keep the dishwasher firmly closed, and empty it when your child is not around (dishwashing powder can cause burns and poisoning). Make sure that television and stereo knobs cannot be removed and swallowed. Objects less than 3–4 cm wide can be swallowed by curious infants. Ensure that pot plants are not poisonous.

- **Bathrooms**
The bathroom can be a hazardous place for babies and toddlers. Water fascinates children, and from the age of about eight months many try to pull themselves into the bath or, occasionally, up onto the sink to turn on taps, or even onto the bench to get to the medicine cupboard. These exploration attempts can result in serious accidents such as falling into the bath, getting scalded, drowning or swallowing medicines. Never leave an infant or toddler unattended in the bath – children can drown in just 5 centimetres of water. Always check to make sure the bath water is the correct temperature (38°C or less) before putting your child in, and turn off all taps tightly so that she can't turn them on. Keep all cleaning agents, cosmetics and medicines out of

reach. Some parents decide to make the bathroom out of bounds for babies and toddlers unless they are supervised.

- **Stairs**
  Children from nine or ten months on are fascinated by stairs and inevitably want to climb them, which is a natural desire. Falling down stairs can cause nasty injuries, including head injuries, so supervise your child's attempts to climb stairs. Rather than making them completely out of bounds, put a safety gate on the third or fourth stair until the child can climb up and down safely.

- **Doorways**
  Use doorstops or latches to keep doors open to prevent fingers being jammed or injured.

- **Dangerous toys**
  Some toys are unsafe for young children. A toddler can easily put Lego, marbles, small cars and toys with small, removable parts into his mouth and choke. Indeed, any object smaller than 3–4 cm in diameter is potentially dangerous. Problems can arise when older children play with these kinds of toys and younger children are attracted to them. Older children should be encouraged to play with such toys in their bedrooms, outside the house or only if the younger child is closely supervised by an adult, and should be warned of the potential danger of the toy to their younger sibling.

- **Pools**
  Swimming pools should be fenced and child-proof safety catches fitted. Swimming activities should always be supervised and parents should insist that children walk rather than run near the pool. Young children should always wear flotation aids and be taught to swim as early as possible. Diving should be banned when several children are in the pool; too many head injuries, even in good swimmers, are caused by children misjudging a dive and hitting the bottom. Pool chemicals and pool filtration equipment should be locked away.

- **Play equipment**
  Outdoor play equipment should be kept in good condition and checked regularly for sharp edges and splintered wood. Infants and toddlers can easily crawl or walk into the path of older children on swings, so always supervise younger children.

- **Barbecue areas**
  Barbecues are extremely dangerous places for young children, particularly because children are fascinated by fire and will often try to touch an open flame. An open fire should never be left unattended, and young children should be kept well away from the cooking area. Gas barbecues should have knobs firmly tightened when not in use. Children should not be allowed to play with matches at any time.
- **Pets**
  Children need to be taught to be gentle with animals and to care for pets. Animals can seriously hurt children. Always supervise your child around dogs. Keep children away from strange dogs, particularly at feeding time or when there are puppies.

Fear of strangers

At around seven or eight months of age, most infants show a fear reaction to strangers. This reaction can include fretting or crying, or clinging to and refusing to separate from the parent in the presence of an unfamiliar person. Stranger anxiety is quite normal and usually disappears by the time the child is two. The intensity of the reaction varies from child to child; some appear very fearful, while others show hardly any reaction at all. The reaction tends to be most intense in unfamiliar surroundings rather than in the child's home environment.

Infants also differ in how they reunite with their parents after temporary separations. Some want to be picked up and held but are not distressed, others snub or avoid their parents, and others show angry, resistant behaviour even though they want to be held by their parents. The fear reaction can be triggered by a variety of events, including unfamiliar adults looking at, speaking to or trying to hold or interact with the child. It also can occur when the parent moves out of the child's sight, when there are strange, loud noises or if the parent attempts to leave the child with unfamiliar babysitters.

The way a child reacts to a strange situation is believed to be related to the quality of the mother–infant relationship and the degree of attachment or emotional bonding between them. Children who show minimal distress on separation, but who want to establish contact with their mothers on reunion, are more likely to have a secure attachment to their mothers. They feel safe and secure and are used to good things happening in their lives. Their mothers are sensitive to their needs and can accurately interpret signs of distress. Feedings are harmonious, there is frequent and pleasurable face-to-face contact between parent and child, crying is responded to quickly and effectively, and the child is likely to have experienced tender and affectionate holding.

Fear of strangers gradually diminishes during the child's second year, and many children come to enjoy the attention and company of friends and relatives. Parents have an important role to play in helping their infant cope and adjust to new experiences. Here are some ideas for dealing with stranger anxiety.

1. **Spend quality time with your infant**
   A child will cope best with new challenges if she has many warm, caring and enjoyable experiences with her parents at other times. Look at, talk to, smile at, affectionately hold and be responsive to your child's attempts to communicate with you, particularly her vocalisations and babbling sounds. Be prepared to interrupt what you are doing to respond to your child's signals.

2. **Give your child time to become familiar with new surroundings**
   When your child meets someone new, keep close to him until he indicates that he is ready to explore, move around the room or be held by someone else. Bring some familiar things into strange surroundings, for example a toy, teddy, doll, cuddly blanket or music box, to help your child feel secure.

3. **Take action if your child becomes upset by extra attention**
   Be prepared to come to your child's aid if she becomes distressed. For example, if she starts to cry while being held or spoken to by another adult, hold her yourself for a while until she is calm.

4. **Soothe and reassure your upset child**
   You can often settle your distressed infant by simply picking him up and cuddling and speaking calmly and warmly to him.

5. **Do not force an infant to be nursed by someone they are afraid of**
    This can make the situation worse by heightening the child's fear reaction and uncertainty.
6. **Keep calm when your child shows fear**
    When a child is upset, avoid becoming uptight and anxious. Your infant needs calm, confident, relaxed parenting when she is afraid. Hold her and demonstrate through your own relaxed actions that there is nothing to fear.
7. **Do not criticise your child for being shy**
    Even though you might like your child to be held by a good friend or relative, you should never berate or criticise him for not wanting to go to another adult.
8. **Respond warmly when your child smiles or reacts positively to new people**
    When your child responds positively to the attention of others, pay warm, caring attention to her when she is returned to you.
9. **Let friends and other trusted adults interact with your infant**
    Try not to become overprotective when stranger anxiety surfaces. The more opportunities your child has to meet and interact with others on familiar ground, the more quickly he will overcome his fear. Experience will teach your child that you are still there and accessible, even if he is temporarily with someone else.

Crying

Crying has a survival value for babies. It is a signal to parents that the child needs care. Infants cry when they are hungry, wet and uncomfortable, cold, distressed or want attention. Children soon learn that crying can control what happens to them. Because most parents find their child's crying distressing, most will seek ways of pacifying the distressed baby, including picking up, rocking, patting, stroking, singing to, walking around with or taking the child on trips in the car. During the first year of a child's life and during toddlerhood, crying tends to decrease, much to parents' relief.

During the first nine months of a child's life, crying often peaks in the late afternoon and evening. After the first three months, the amount and pattern of crying begins to change. There is a gradual decline in evening crying and over the course of the first year the nature of the crying changes. It becomes less a response to hunger or discomfort and is more readily influenced by learning experiences. For example, a child learns that they can cry to gain attention.

In the first three months of a child's life, parents often differ a great deal in how frequently and quickly they respond to crying. Most parents take between two and nine minutes to attend to the baby. Parents who frequently ignore a young baby's distress tend to have children who cry more often and more persistently in the nine-to-twelve-month age group. The key, therefore, in dealing with an infant's crying is to respond promptly. If the parent attends to an infant's distress signals, they will be more secure, and less demanding or impatient. Here are some steps to follow to effectively deal with your infant's crying.

1. **When you child is alert and happy, give them plenty of attention and things to look at**
    Infants cry less often if they receive plenty of loving attention, physical contact and visual stimulation when they are awake and not fussing.

2. **Respond quickly to crying**
    When your child cries in situations such as after waking from a nap or when hungry, do not ignore him for a long period. It is better to attend to the child within the first minute, before he becomes really distressed. This means interrupting what you are doing.

3. **Try to work out why your child is upset**
    Try to work out what, if anything, is causing the distress or discomfort. While this can be very difficult at times, many parents become quite skilled at assessing the situation and taking prompt action that settles the child. Most parents get to know their child's cry very well. Is she hungry, wet, cold, hot or in pain due to nappy rash or wind? Is she grimacing? Does she appear to have a temperature or difficulty breathing? Has she vomited up milk or food? Does she need a change of environment, stimulation or attention

from you? Has she got into an awkward position in her cot? Does she have something to look at, touch, explore or listen to?

4. **Attend to the child's needs**

   Working out why an infant is crying is sometimes a process of elimination. Start by checking the basics relating to his physical comfort. While you do this – for example change a wet nappy or feed the infant – make sure you interact with your baby. Look into his eyes, talk, smile warmly, hold him or put something into his hands to hold. If the problem persists, try to distract him by rocking him, singing to him, putting him in a bouncinette, moving him into a different room or giving him a toy or object that makes a sound.

5. **Make sure you and your partner work as a team**

   Where crying is a persistent problem, particularly at night, it is an excellent idea for both parents to share the role of settling the distressed baby. Some couples successfully alternate the task of attending to the baby at night. If the child needs to be breastfed, the father can still get out of bed and bring the child to the mother, if she prefers to feed in bed.

6. **Avoid becoming impatient, irritable or angry**

   Crying is distressing for parents and children, particularly when it persists, and parents can feel very tired and vulnerable. However, it is crucial that you don't take your negative feelings out on your baby. If you get to the point where you feel you could harm your child in any way, have a plan for dealing with these times. Count to ten, take several deep breaths and remind yourself that your child is not trying to upset you; ring or visit a friend or someone else you trust; talk to your partner; take your child for a walk or a ride in the car. If you must let off steam, go into another room, give yourself time out in the bathroom or go and work in the garden.

Specific issues and problems of toddlers

At around eight to ten months, most children will start to crawl and will also begin to test the limits that their parents set to their behaviour. At the same time, parents must provide an emotional climate where their children feel secure and loved. Toddlers can be great company; they can also be demanding and exhausting. Many of the difficulties that emerge now are part of normal growing up, and parents experiencing them for the first time should not feel that their child has a problem. They must, however, be prepared to deal with the difficulties quickly to prevent more serious problems arising later. Toddlers need to get into good routines relating to sleeping, eating and play, and they need to learn the meaning of the word no.

Promoting independent feeding

During toddlerhood, most children start to have an increasingly varied diet and learn to eat what the rest of the family eats, a diet containing all the necessary nutrients: proteins, carbohydrates, fats, vitamins, minerals and water. They gradually become more independent in their feeding habits. Many parents experience difficulties in helping their child make the move from being a milk-fed infant to a youngster who can eat a mixed diet and feed themselves. One- and two-year-olds are not known for their wonderful eating habits, and mess in the kitchen is a normal part of helping toddlers learn gradually to feed themselves. Many a parent has felt mildly nauseous on discovering a toddler with an upturned bowl and food all over her hands, hair, high chair and the floor. Other parents become irritated when their toddler drops his spoon from the high chair for the fifth time and then screams until it is picked up. However, it is during this period that children become independent in the act of eating. As a child's coordination and physical control improves, she becomes more skilled at handling eating and drinking utensils. Parents require a lot of patience to prevent mealtimes turning into a battleground.

When toddlers are given many opportunities to feed themselves, there is a gradual but steady improvement in their feeding capabilities. By the age of twelve months, most toddlers can hold a cup with a lid and can drink liquids pretty well. However, spills are common, especially when drinking from cups without lids, as the toddler has trouble accurately coordinating the tilt of the cup to their mouth.

Between the ages of eighteen months and two years, children can be expected to control cups and small glasses quite well and to be less likely to drop or throw cups over the edge of the high chair.

Spoon control develops slowly, partly because toddlers like to use their fingers. In the six months following their first birthday, most toddlers have difficulty scooping food and getting it to their mouths. By eighteen months, scooping is improving but the load is still dropped frequently, sometimes just as it is about to go in the mouth. By the child's second birthday, wrist, elbow and shoulder movements are coordinated enough to get the spoon to the mouth with only a few spills.

Toddlers gradually become more adept at chewing, and with the arrival of a set of molars at around twelve months they start to grind some foods. By two-and-a-half a child has well-developed chewing motions and can handle most adult foods. From the age of two, the child is skilled enough to concentrate less on the task of getting food into her mouth, and it is then that many parents find the toddler is easily distracted during meals and has difficulty sitting still.

A healthy diet

Good nutrition is a basic requirement for healthy development. Children should learn to eat a variety of foods that provide all the necessary nutrients. Appendix 1 provides a list of sample menus that meet daily dietary requirements for children of different ages. During the child's second six months, most parents will introduce solid foods. This process often starts with the introduction of baby rice cereal, progressing to strained fruits and vegetables, dairy products, cereals and then other protein foods. At one year of age, most toddlers still prefer mashed, puréed, strained or moistened food because it is easier to chew. Cut harder food into small, bite-sized portions. Be particularly wary about food your child might choke on such as cherry tomatoes, nuts, hard sweets and popcorn.

Toddlers can enjoy and digest most foods eaten by other family members, but can be quite fussy and refuse to eat particular foods or eat at certain times. Your child may develop a particular fondness for a favourite sandwich and insist on it at every meal. This only becomes a problem if the child refuses to eat anything else and it continues for a long time. The primary goal during this time is to help your toddler learn to enjoy a wide variety of food and to become as independent as possible in feeding. Here are some steps to help with this process.

1. **Get everything ready**

    Prepare everything in advance to avoid having a hungry child fussing and protesting while waiting to be served. Use a high chair until the child is ready to sit at a table with the rest of the family, and provide unbreakable plates and cups.

2. **Have predictable mealtimes**

    Get your child into a set routine regarding mealtimes. Don't let him eat between meals throughout the day. Meals should be served at particular times that coincide as closely as possible to the times other family members eat. Five small meals or three larger meals each day is sufficient.

3. **Encourage self-feeding through finger foods**

    Begin by encouraging your child to finger feed. Infants signal when they are ready to do this by trying to grab your spoon or plate. Try putting finger foods such as sliced apple or peach, celery or carrot sticks, or cheese segments, on a plate or directly onto the high chair tray, then simply let your child at them. Many children accept meals more readily when they can participate. Toddlers will often gnaw on finger food and allow you to feed them at the same time.

4. **Offer your child a spoon**

    While you are feeding your child, offer her a spoon. Whenever she manages to get food on the spoon and into her mouth, praise and encourage her. As spoon control develops, you may need to gently guide your toddler through the motions of scooping and locating her mouth. Some spills are inevitable. As soon as your child loses interest in self feeding, continue to feed her yourself.

5. **Gradually phase out your help**

    As your child becomes more and more skilled at using a spoon, gradually phase out the help you provide. This means the child taking more and more control over the meal – as well as more mess to clean up initially.

6. **Introduce new foods one at a time**
   Take note of the time of day when your child seems to be most hungry. Introduce new foods one at a time at these meals. Introduce small portions of the new food along with familiar and accepted ones. Remember to praise your child and name the new food he has just eaten.

7. **Provide opportunities for your child to learn through watching**
   Toddlers learn a great deal about eating and mealtime behaviour through watching older siblings and parents, so, from twelve to eighteen months, occasionally let your child eat in her high chair at the family dinner table.

8. **Reward good mealtime behaviour**
   Encourage appropriate mealtime behaviour by providing plenty of praise and attention when your child is eating appropriately. Talk to, smile at and touch her when she tries a new food, uses a spoon for the first time without spills, sits without wriggling in her high chair or swallows a mouthful of food after having chewed it properly.

9. **Avoid rewarding poor mealtime behaviour**
   Do not provide positive attention for inappropriate mealtime behaviour. Avoid laughing at your child when he spits out or throws food, or throws or drops utensils, bowls or cups. The best initial strategy is to withdraw your attention. Turn your head away and simply wait a few seconds until the undesired behaviour has stopped. When it has stopped, look at your child to get eye contact, offer food again and then give positive attention as soon as he eats correctly.

10. **Don't expect toddlers to eat everything on their plate**
   It is better to serve small portions and allow the child to ask for more if she is still hungry rather than to have a battle over the last spoonful or two. Do not expect to provide the child's daily nutritional requirements in a single meal.

Crying

While most children cry less and less as their first year progresses, some cry a lot more than others. These temperamentally difficult children can wail after very minor upsets, bumps or falls. They may cry loudly when put to bed, when they don't get their own way and after mildly upsetting experiences such as a loud noise. Crying is often accompanied by attempts to get the parent's attention, which may involve being picked up and held, cuddled, reassured or offered a drink. This kind of reaction from a parent is quite appropriate if a child is genuinely hurt or unwell. However, children also learn that upset behaviour leads to positive attention. Some anxious parents feel that they are neglecting their children if they don't respond to all crying or distress. This kind of overprotectiveness is a mistake. Children have to learn to deal with a few minor knocks, discomforts or frustrations without always bursting into tears.

When children cry frequently for little or no apparent reason, it is better either to ignore the crying altogether or to respond very matter-of-factly to it. 'Up you get. Give it a rub,' not, 'Oh you poor dear. Did you hurt your little bottom? Come over here and have a cuddle. Mummy will fix it.'

If you think your toddler cries a lot, try the following suggestions but first ask yourself the following questions. Does the child receive sufficient time and attention from you when she has been good? Are there any signs of emotional disturbance or evidence that the child has had an emotionally traumatising or upsetting experience? For example, has he gone off his food, have there been any recent changes in his sleeping pattern, particularly more disturbed sleep, or does he seem fearful or fretful? If the child is generally in good health and the answer to these questions is no, then it is usually safe to proceed as follows.

1. **Quickly check on your child's state**

   When your child starts crying, quickly check to make sure no major disaster has occurred. Try to do this without your child seeing you. Sometimes simply listening to the nature of the cry will give you the best clue. Children who are genuinely injured and in pain will often have a deep, bellowing cry followed by a pause as they gasp for air. Other types of cries, particularly attention-seeking cries, are often less intense, are not interrupted by gasping for air and are not as loud.

2. **Ignore the crying**
    Withdraw all attention while the crying continues. Say nothing,
    turn your head away and continue with what you are doing.
3. **Listen for pauses in the crying**
    Wait for a pause of a few seconds in the crying and then attend
    to your child immediately. When the crying has stopped, try to
    distract your child with another activity.
4. **Do not pick up or cuddle the child while she is still
    fussing**
    If the child seeks your attention such as asking to be picked up
    while still crying or whimpering, use a neutral tone to prompt
    her to tell or show you what the matter is. Do not pick her up.
    Be neither overly sympathetic nor cold and harsh. A matter-
    of-fact expression is the best. For example, simply ask 'What's
    the matter?'
5. **Praise your child for being brave**
    If the child points to or tells you about the problem and at the
    same time stops crying, praise him. 'Aren't you a brave boy?'
6. **Set the child up in a new activity**
    Try to distract the child with another activity. If the crying con-
    tinues or turns into whining, use the strategy for dealing with
    whining that comes later in this chapter.

Promoting children's language

One of the most important changes that takes place during toddlerhood is in the area of language. Children move from understanding
an average of ten words at twelve months, to having a vocabulary of
800–900 words by the time they are three, when they understand
most of the adults' sentences they hear. This tremendous growth in
language use is closely related to intellectual development and the
child's general understanding of her world. How quickly children
learn to speak and the size of their vocabulary is influenced by their
interactions, between the ages of one and three, with their parents
and other family members. Children differ markedly in how quickly
they learn to speak. Some children are speaking complex sentences
by the age of three, while others are hardly speaking at all. If your

child's language appears to be considerably delayed compared with other children of the same age, then it is worth seeking professional assistance to have the problem assessed. Speech therapists are expert in assessing language problems and can provide concrete advice on dealing with the problem. Here are some ideas about how to promote language development.

1. **Be accessible**

   Being accessible does not simply mean spending time with your child. It means being available when he attempts to communicate through language and being prepared to listen to what he is saying.

2. **Talk to your child**

   A child's interest in speaking increases when her parents speak to her frequently. This does not mean that you must spend all day chatting to your one-year-old, but you should point out and name things your child looks at. Notice the objects she is interested in and tell her the names of those objects.

3. **Respond positively when children start a conversation**

   Learn to respond positively when your child attempts to use language. This involves listening to what he is saying, repeating it yourself and perhaps providing more information about the topic or thing that has captured his attention. This is the key to the incidental teaching we discussed in Chapter 4. If a child brings an object to you – such as a rattle – and makes a sound – 'tattle' – this is an excellent time to teach your child language. His interest is focused on an object and he has approached you to show you how it works. A good response here would be to stop what you're doing, look at the child, smile and say, 'What's that you've got?' Instead of simply saying, 'That's a rattle,' you have invited the child to tell you more about it. If this initial attempt does not produce any more language, simply say, 'That's a rattle. Can you say "rattle"?' If he can, praise him. If not, don't worry, there will be plenty of other opportunities. Toddlers benefit greatly from these kinds of interactions, particularly when they are brief and frequent.

4. **Provide a good language model**

   Try to avoid babytalking to toddlers. Provide a good language model by using complete sentences and correct pronunciation. Children learn more quickly to speak in grammatically correct sentences when adults use language that is somewhat more difficult than the child can yet produce. As children grow older, they will often ask the meaning of unfamiliar words and thereby extend their own vocabularies. Of course, you should not use overly complex sentences that have too many unfamiliar words.

5. **Describe what you are doing**

   Children often enjoy watching their parents carry out various tasks, for example cleaning the car or vacuuming. They enjoy it even more if they can participate in some way, or can hold a conversation while their parent works. Language can be encouraged if you take the time to describe what you are doing. These descriptions of simple everyday events such as weeding the garden, cooking, taking care of a baby, or building something, will often stimulate your child's curiosity and prompt her to ask further questions.

6. **Share your feelings, ideas and joys**

   Another aspect of describing what you are doing involves sharing your feelings and experiences: tell your child about your day, the things that amused you, what you saw on the way home from work, and the people you spoke to. Sharing information about oneself is a skill that some adults never master. Often, these skills have been modelled for them by their parents. Of course, in the meantime, it also helps to stimulate a child's interest in the world of words.

7. **Act as an information resource**

   Parents can and should be information resource centres for their young children. Encourage your child to ask questions by answering her in understandable language. This takes patience and a willingness to be frequently interrupted. The parent who tells her three-year-old not to ask so many stupid questions misunderstands the importance of this skill for a child's development. Children who stop asking their parents questions may have also stopped talking to them. This can be a sign of a poor parent–child relationship.

8. **Comment on your child's play**

   Some parents are able to participate in their child's play without dominating or directing it. The key to this is observation.
   Watch what your child is doing and then make a comment that
   extends his interest in the activity without interfering with it.
   One of the best ways to do this is to ask a question about the
   game or activity. 'Where does baby Sarah sleep?' 'Where do all
   the blue ones go?'

9. **Read to your child often**

   Toddlers love to have stories read to them and to look through
   picture books with an interested adult, particularly at bedtime.
   The world of words comes alive in books, and infants and
   toddlers should be read to from a very early age. Parents should
   obtain a good supply of books and read to their children regularly, at least once every day. Both parents should be involved.
   However, don't force children to listen to a story if they are
   interested in something else.

Whining

As children learn to communicate with their parents through
words, whining can become a problem. All children whine from
time to time as a way of gaining an adult's attention. Children
whine for a variety of reasons: they may be tired, hungry, bored,
unwell, have a wet nappy or want attention. Obviously, some children whine a lot more than others. Whining is a problem when
it occurs a lot and becomes the child's usual way of gaining
attention or making requests. If whining is successful because it
produces attention for the child, there is little incentive for the
child to learn to make requests appropriately. For instance, if a
child simply points and grunts or whimpers to get an object that
is out of reach, and then gets it, she does not need to learn the
name of the object or to say please. Children whine less when
they have the language to make their needs known. This involves
learning specific words and phrases related to making requests,
such as 'thank you', 'please', 'may I have', along with a pleasant
expression and tone of voice.

Your main aim is to teach your child an acceptable way to make requests. Parents should not allow themselves to be bullied by a demanding toddler, so do not give your child what he wants until his request is acceptable. The following strategy involves waiting until the form of the request is reasonable before considering the request itself. The idea is to model the correct way of asking and to reward your child when the desired behaviour occurs. Children under the age of two who have yet to learn to speak can point, smile or lead you by the hand to the desired object. As long as the child is not whining and makes a language response that you can understand, comply with the request but prompt him to label the object requested. Each time he wants help he has an opportunity to learn a new word. The following steps will help develop these skills in young children.

1. **Stop what you are doing**
    When your child approaches and makes a request in an unpleasant voice, stop what you are doing and gain his attention.
2. **Calmly describe the problem behaviour**
    'Sandy, you don't need to whine for a drink.'
3. **Describe the correct way of asking**
    Calmly ask your child to ask nicely. 'Say, "Mummy, drink please"' or, 'Say, "Truck please, Mummy".' Use simple words the child can say. Initially say all the words you want your child to use. Once he knows what to say, phase out your prompts. For example, you might say 'Pardon?', 'What's the magic word?', or even just look at the child expectantly with raised eyebrows.
4. **Praise your child for speaking nicely**
    Praise your child for speaking in a more pleasant manner. For example, 'That was a lovely way of asking.' The key is to make sure you offer praise any time the child asks properly without first having to be reminded, otherwise the child may learn to wait for the reminder.
5. **Decide whether the child's request is reasonable**
    If the child asks for food, you might decide that because dinner is being served shortly, you want the child to wait. The idea

here is not to say yes or no until the request is made in an appropriate form. If the request is expressed appropriately and it is reasonable, go along with it.

6. **If whining continues, give a further prompt**
   If the request is still unreasonable, prompt your child to speak properly once more. 'William, say, "Please Mummy, the truck".'

7. **If the child protests, provide a logical consequence for the behaviour**
   Describe the behaviour calmly but firmly. The most appropriate consequence is that the child does not get what he asked for. 'Okay. You can't ask nicely, so the biscuits go away for ten minutes. Try again then.'

8. **If the child becomes aggressive or throws a temper tantrum, immediately back up with quiet time for two minutes**
   Remember to describe again to the child what she has done wrong.

9. **If the problem continues or the child won't sit in quiet time, put him into time out for two minutes**
   Make sure the child is quiet before being allowed out of time out. Children, like adults, eventually have to learn that despite being tired or run-down it is not okay to be obnoxious to others. Be persistent and consistent, and your child will more easily learn what is required.

Avoid losing your temper and yelling, or telling the child to stop whining but giving her what she wants *before* she asks properly, or completely ignoring her. There are times when a bit more leniency is warranted, including when the child is physically unwell or has had an upsetting or frightening experience.

Whining often occurs in children who throw temper tantrums. Some parents worry that insisting on speaking reasonably might provoke a temper tantrum. However, don't let the threat of a temper outburst prevent you from dealing with whining as a specific problem. Tantrums can be dealt with as the need arises.

Minor fussing

Sometimes children whine for no apparent reason; they just seem in a grumpy mood. This sort of whining and whimpering can also occur when a parent refuses a request for something the child wants, such as food before mealtimes. It differs from the previous sort of whining because it is not immediately directed at the parent. Nor is it the result of the child having been hurt, or being wet or ill. Some children just seem to wander around aimlessly fussing and whimpering. They often receive attention at some point from their parent or a concerned grandparent, who says, 'What's the matter with you then?' The child may or may not settle when he receives such attention. The best strategy for dealing with such behaviour is to ignore it completely. Here are some guidelines to deal with minor fussing.

1. **Quickly check that your child is not hurt**
   When you observe your child whining, quickly check to make sure he has not fallen over, been hurt or has wet pants. If the child is okay, then proceed as follows.
2. **Completely ignore the behaviour**
   Remove all attention from the child for as long as the whimpering continues.
3. **Attend to the child when the behaviour has stopped**
   When the fussing stops, wait a few seconds and then attend to the child. That is, the child receives attention for having stopped. For example, you might say, 'Would you like to come and help me hang up the washing?' It is important to wait for a pause in the whining before trying to distract your child.
4. **Praise your child when they are busy**
   As soon as the child is engaged in play, look for an opportunity to praise her. Catch your child not whining.

Disobedience

During the toddler period, most parents first experience the problem of their child's disobedience. As toddlers become more mobile and independent they will touch things they are not supposed to. From the age of fourteen to twenty-four months, toddlers start to resist the will of their parents. They become more assertive. They may climb onto furniture that is fragile, run out on the road, try to put objects into power points, pull hair, strike their parents or other children, or pour drinks on the carpet. Toddlers must learn the meaning of the word no. Some children will deliberately repeat a forbidden behaviour to get a reaction from their parent. When the parent says no, it's like a dare. The child does exactly the same thing again, maybe even with a big smile or a grin. Toddlers are renowned for testing their parents.

Neil, a two-year-old, was told not to touch the television knobs; he then stood right next to the set, looked defiantly at his mother, and pretended to touch the knobs again. His mother rose to the bait every time this happened, saying , 'Neeeiil!' Occasionally she would be so amused by the child's antics that she would grin and say, 'You are a naughty boy.' Neil, of course, got a very confusing message, and it took a long time before he finally lost interest in the television knobs. Neil would have learned to leave the television alone much more quickly if his mother had dealt with the behaviour more firmly and decisively.

Discipline after disobedience should teach your toddler at least two things. First, no means stop what you're doing immediately. Second, the child should learn the appropriate behaviour. Deal with disobedience firmly and decisively when your child is a toddler rather than leaving the problem unchecked. Children need firm adult direction and guidance at this age. Parents who have taught their toddlers to respond to directions find raising preschoolers and school-aged children much easier.

Here are some guidelines for dealing with disobedience.

1. **Safety-proof your home so there are few 'no touch' areas**
   By reducing the number of times you have to say no, you will make each rule carry more weight.
2. **Get close**
   If a toddler does something that needs correction, move closer.
3. **Say no in a firm, controlled voice**
   Take hold of the child's hands and speak in a firm, controlled

voice. 'No, don't touch.' This will not hurt the child and is an alternative to smacking. When you say no, frown and shake your head from side to side.

4. **Suggest an alternative activity**
    If the child stops the inappropriate behaviour, suggest something else for her to do. For example, if the toddler pulls the cat's tail, say no, then show her how to stroke the cat gently instead. 'No, don't be rough with kitty. Stroke her like this.' Praise the child as soon as she complies or is engaged in an activity.

5. **Ignore whimpering or protesting**
    Sometimes children will whimper or cry after being corrected in this way. Simply ignore these protests.

6. **Use quiet time as a back-up**
    If the child repeats the behaviour within the next hour, use quiet time for one minute.

Hurting others

Toddlers can inflict nasty injuries on other children through biting. Apart from being painful, a bite that breaks the skin can easily become infected. It is unacceptable behaviour and should be dealt with firmly. Some children bite when they don't get their own way, others bite when they are frustrated or annoyed, and others do it just to see what will happen. Toddlers also occasionally pull hair and hit other children. Parents are sometimes the prime target for this type of behaviour.

Some parents try to deal with biting and hitting by hitting or biting back. The idea is that if the child knows how it feels he will be discouraged from trying it again. Unfortunately, this tactic involves modelling the very behaviour you want the child to control.

The key to overcoming biting is to provide close supervision in the early stages. You must watch your child closely for a few days while she is playing with other kids so that you can respond quickly.

1. **Give positive attention for not biting**
    When you notice your child playing well, give him attention or comment on the child's play. 'Aren't you playing nicely this

morning?' or 'What are you doing with that truck? It can tow that car easily, can't it?'

2. **Give a 'stop' instruction**

   When your child is about to bite or actually bites another child, act immediately. Give a firm 'stop' instruction, such as 'No, don't bite.'

3. **Put your child into quiet time or time out**

   Provide an immediate back-up consequence, such as quiet time or time out for two minutes. Follow this step and the previous one as often as you need to until the behaviour ceases.

4. **Allow the child to return to the activity**

   After the time-out period, return the child to the activity so he can practise playing without biting.

5. **Provide a back-up reward if no further disruption occurs**

   If the child manages to last out the activity without biting, provide a small back-up treat such as raisins, a favourite drink or a story. Explain why his behaviour has pleased you.

A variation of this strategy can be used when a child pulls hair, including your own. However, before you give quiet time or time out, get the child to spend a few seconds touching and stroking your (or the other child's) hair without pulling. If she struggles or resists, simply guide her through the motions and ignore her protests.

Sleeping and bedtime problems

'Mummy, I not tired', 'Stay wiff me', 'Your bed, Mummy', 'Daddy, more drink'. These are familiar cries at bedtime. The most common bedtime problems include the child refusing to sleep in his own bed, and getting out of bed after being put to bed.

Most parents need time to themselves at the end of a day. They are often tired and thus vulnerable to a child's night-time antics. It is important, therefore, for toddlers to get into a good night-time routine, so they have sufficient energy for the next day's activities and their parents will have some child-free time to spend with each other as partners and companions.

Children should have a definite and predictable bedtime, should be expected to sleep in their own bed and to remain there until morning unless something exceptional happens, such as the child being physically unwell.

Some sleeping problems are temporary and follow an illness or other disruption to the child's normal routine, such as having to sleep in a strange bed. These problems often correct themselves once the normal routine is re-established.

The most common difficulty parents experience when trying to settle their children in bed is the child's crying. The parent puts the child to bed, reads a story, says goodnight, and then it starts. As soon as the parent attempts to leave, the child starts to scream. This screaming can be quite distressing for many parents. However, if a child learns that screaming will bring his parents back into the room, or better still have them take him out of his bed and into theirs, there is little incentive for him to stay quiet. The crying pays off. What is more attractive than being able to snuggle in between Mum and Dad in a nice warm bed? Unfortunately, if this habit is established, you can expect the problem to continue, sometimes for many years.

Parents who give up trying to get their children to sleep in their own beds often have to put up with disturbed sleep themselves. Toddlers often wriggle, knee their parents in the back and disrupt parents' normal sex life. Here are some ideas for helping to get children into a good night-time routine.

1. **Establish a predictable, regular bedtime**
   Decide on a reasonable time (between 6.30 and 8.00 p.m.) and stick to it.
2. **Discuss the ground rules**
   Explain to your child that from now on you would like him to go to bed at a specific time, to stay in bed and not to call out.
3. **Make sure the child's room is well ventilated**
   The room should be neither too hot nor too cold. Purchase a night light if the child is afraid of the dark.
4. **Give a warning**
   Thirty minutes prior to bedtime, warn your child that he will

have to get into bed in half an hour. During this time, get him involved in a quiet activity. Make sure he does not run around or get too excited with boisterous play. Suitable activities include looking at a book, or listening to a story on a CD or cassette. Do not let your child watch television in his bedroom.

5. **Wind up pre-bedtime activities**
Five minutes before bedtime, ask the child to finish what she is doing and get ready for bed. Tell her that if she comes straightaway without a fuss you will read a story in bed.

6. **Help your child get ready for bed**
Help the child as necessary with teeth, toilet and getting ready for bed.

7. **Put your child to bed and review your list**
Put the child to bed and read the story, give him a kiss and a cuddle and then go through a list of all possible excuses the child may have for getting out of bed.
'Have you cleaned your teeth, David?'
'Yes.'
'Have you said goodnight to Daddy and Booma [the cat]?'
'Yes.'
'Have you been to the toilet?'
'Yes.'

8. **Remind your child of the rules before leaving**
Explain what will happen if he stays in bed or gets out of bed. 'If you stay in bed and don't call out, there will be a surprise treat under your pillow in the morning. If you call out, I won't answer you even if you yell. If you get out of bed, I will take you straight back to your bed. Okay? Goodnight.' If the child wants the door left open or a hall light left on, that's fine.

9. **Ignore calling out**
If the child calls out, completely ignore her. Say nothing at all and don't go back in. Be prepared for her to cry for quite some time on the first night, particularly if you have returned to her room when she has screamed in the past. If the child wriggles and squirms in bed, or lies there awake, ignore it.

10. **If your child gets out of bed, return him to it immediately**

    If the child gets out of bed, take him back to his room immediately. 'Steven, you are not to get out of bed. Now get back to bed.' Ignore protests and return the child to bed.

11. **Return your child to her bed if she wanders during the night**

    If your child wakes during the night and wanders into your bedroom, immediately return her to her bed. Give very little attention at this time. Spend no more than thirty seconds trying to settle the child – simply pat her back, say goodnight and leave. Ignore protests.

12. **Give a back-up reward in the morning**

    If the child remained in bed throughout the night, place a small gift or treat under the pillow and, if you are using a behaviour chart, put a smiley on his chart. Remember to praise your child for being a good sleeper if he has been successful. If he screamed or got out of bed, do not give a back-up reward.

If you follow this routine consistently, many problem sleepers will be sleeping in their own beds and going off to bed without protesting within a few days. However, many will cry for anywhere from a few minutes to several hours the first few nights. You must be prepared to let them cry themselves to sleep. If you go in after the child has screamed for a long time, you will probably make it worse. The child will simply learn to scream louder and longer. Remind yourself that in the long run it is for his own good.

Some parents become quite upset during this time and are very tempted to attend to the child. Don't. See it through. By the end of the first week, children will often have given up crying when they are put to bed or will whimper for only a few minutes. The first few days are the hardest.

It is very important that both parents follow this routine consistently. Remember that an adequate amount of sleep is a vital energy-restoring process. We cannot make a child go to sleep, but we can arrange things so sleep becomes more likely. If there is no progress after a two-week trial, double-check to ensure that you are following the routine consistently.

Temper tantrums

Almost every parent has heard about the 'terrible twos', when their previously placid, cooperative baby becomes very demanding, stubborn and uncooperative. Some toddlers will throw massive tantrums when they are not allowed to do something, or even for no obvious reason. The trigger can be quite minor, such as not being able to fit a block into a hole in a puzzle board, or being unable to open a packet of raisins. The first time a child throws a tantrum, her parents may be stunned into embarrassed silence, particularly if the supermarket floor is the venue.

Some temper tantrums are short-lived encounters, lasting only a few seconds, but other children can work themselves up into such a state that they can continue screaming for hours. They may throw themselves on the floor, throw objects, stamp their feet, even hold their breath until they are unconscious for a few seconds. It can be quite frightening to see your child change colour through lack of oxygen, but all breath-holders eventually take a gasp of air. Temper tantrums can also be a sign of more serious behavioural problems, particularly if they occur frequently and persist over a long time. It is best to deal with them promptly as they arise. Here are some guidelines.

1. **Gain the child's attention as best you can**
   Stop what you are doing and move close to your child, within arm's reach.
2. **Give the child an instruction to stop**
   Tell your child that the screaming must stop or he will have to go to time out until it does. 'Bevan, stop that screaming right now or you'll have to go to time out.'
3. **If the tantrum continues, describe the problem and the consequence**
   'You have not done as I asked. Now go to time out. Right now.'

4. **Take the child to time out**

   Explain what is wrong and the rules for time out. Give the explanation even though the child might be quite distraught.
5. **Follow the time-out rules consistently**

   Follow the guidelines for using time out in Chapter 4, and do not let the child out until the screaming has stopped and the toddler has been quiet for at least one minute.

When the child throws a tantrum, do not try to cuddle, reassure or in any other way give positive attention. Do not give in to the child's demands or he will learn to use temper outbursts to get his own way. Some parents try to ignore the tantrum as an alternative to using time out. This will only work if the child is completely ignored, and that may be difficult if other children are around or you have visitors. It is better to remove the child from the action. In doing so, he will learn an important message: 'When you have got yourself under control, you are welcome to rejoin us.'

Be prepared to put up with quite a storm in the time-out room. You may feel quite agitated to hear your child in such distress, and your natural instinct will be to try to calm and comfort him. This is a mistake and can actually make the tantrum worse. Children who throw tantrums, often five or six times a day, may need to be put into time out six to ten times on the first day. By the end of the first week, tantrums are usually occurring much less frequently and for a shorter time.

If there has been no progress after a few days of following this routine, check to make sure that you are following the guidelines for using time out correctly. If you are, and the problem continues, seek professional advice.

Wandering

Toddlers are notorious for getting lost. Parents are understandably concerned about their children wandering because they can run onto the road and get hit by passing cars or be picked up by strangers. These dangers are not apparent to two-year-olds who do disappearing acts. Wandering can occur on shopping trips, walking down the road or just playing in the backyard.

Some toddlers seem to take off whenever there is an opportunity. Parents have told me that it can take just a split second. The parent may turn away for a moment and the child disappears. Children like these may refuse to hold the parent's hand when walking.

It might sound very obvious, but the key behaviour to encourage in a wanderer is staying close to the parent. Remaining close has to become more rewarding to the child than the excitement of exploring on his own, at least initially. Here are some steps to help you teach your child to stay close to you.

1. **Set aside time to teach your child to stay close**
   This can involve taking your toddler on a series of planned short trips, about five to seven of them, around your neighbourhood. Don't take your child out less often because she is a wanderer, give her even more opportunities to learn to stay close. Start with a very short trip of, say, two minutes, perhaps down to the corner of the street. Each subsequent trip should be slightly longer, building up to about a ten-minute walk.

2. **Get yourself ready**
   Before setting out on each trip, get yourself ready, arming yourself with a packet of raisins or soft sweets that can be used to reward the toddler for staying within reach.

3. **Explain the ground rules**
   Explain where you are going and what the ground rules will be. 'We're going for a walk down to the shop for some bread. Would you like to come with Mummy?' Depending on the child's language, ask him to state the rules for going walking with you. Praise him for correctly stating the rules.

4. **Praise your child for staying close**
   Initially, praise the child every thirty seconds or so for staying close, before he has had a chance to wander. Each time you praise him, offer him part of a snack. As you walk, engage him in conversation. Point out flowers, birds, trees or any item of interest that catches your eye.

5. **Deal with wandering by prompting the correct behaviour**

   If your child starts to stray, immediately describe the incorrect behaviour. 'Paul, you are too far away.' If he returns, praise him for doing what he's told. 'Good boy for coming back to Mummy.'

6. **Provide a back-up consequence if wandering continues**

   If the child tries to take off again, grab him immediately and give a firm 'stop' instruction. 'No, you must stay close to Mummy.' Stop walking and give him quiet time for one minute. Quiet time can involve sitting him on the footpath. If necessary, wrap your arms around him and hold him firmly so he can't move.

7. **Continue the journey while remembering to praise your child for staying close**

   Once quiet time is over, continue the trip and look for an opportunity to catch him staying close.

8. **After the trip, give positive feedback**

   At the end of the trip, make a big fuss over the fact that your child remembered to stay close. Tell your partner and your child's grandparents or family friends, who can also give positive feedback.

9. **Let your child practise staying close with other adults**

   After your child has accomplished staying close on short trips, make sure he has a chance to practise staying close with both parents or even with grandparents.

10. **Phase out rewards and positive attention**

    Gradually phase out the rewards so that your child is required to last the whole trip before receiving the treat. If the improved behaviour continues, then phase out the back-up treats. Just give occasional praise for remembering to stay close.

The key to overcoming wandering is a quick, decisive response on your part. The child should be supervised very closely during outings where wandering occurs, and he should receive quiet time if he attempts to stray. Some parents use restraining harnesses with young children who wander. This can be a useful strategy but it does not actually teach the child the correct behaviour; it simply prevents him from running off. Parents often find that the problem resurfaces as soon as the restraint is not used. Take the time and make the effort to teach your child properly to stay close.

Toilet-training

Learning to use the toilet or potty is a complex task. The child must learn to recognise internal signals such as a full bladder, to hold on and not wet his pants, to tell his parents he needs to go to the toilet, or to walk to the bathroom and remove his pants, sit on the potty, urinate or defecate, wipe his bottom, pull up his pants, wash his hands, and return to play. It is a wonder that more children do not have problems.

It is best to begin a child's toilet-training when they are aged twenty to twenty-four months; the child has better control over the sphincter and abdominal muscles, and enough language to understand what is required of him. Toilet-training is accomplished quite quickly with some children; others take several months.

Here are some general ideas on how to toilet-train your toddler.

1. **Allow your child to watch**
    The best preparation for many toddlers is to watch what their parents do when they go to the toilet. Let your child follow you into the bathroom.
2. **Get everything you need ready**
    Buy a potty that is easy for the child to sit on without falling in, and a doll that will release water when squeezed.
3. **Choose a day to begin**
    Set aside half a day so you can concentrate on the task of toilet-training.
4. **Organise a practice session**
    Have a practice session with the doll to show the child what to do when she wants to go to the toilet. Set this session up as a game where the child can help Dolly learn to go to the toilet. 'Let's look at what Dolly does when she wants to go wee-wees.' Show the child how Dolly first comes and tells Mummy. Praise Dolly for letting Mummy know. Then quickly take Dolly to the

potty, take off her panties and sit her on the potty. Ask the child to tell Dolly how good she is for sitting on the potty. Then squeeze the doll so that water goes in the potty. Offer enthusiastic praise for going to the toilet. Next let your child play Mummy and you be Dolly. Approach the child with the doll and say, 'Mummy, I want to go wee-wees.' If the child spontaneously praises you (the doll) and takes you to the potty, praise the child for helping Dolly go wee-wees.

Next, let your child pretend to be Dolly. Start off by asking what you should do when you want to go to the toilet. If the child tells you, offer enthusiastic praise. Take the child over to the potty and say, 'What comes next?' If the child says, 'take off my pants,' or actually takes off his pants, offer praise and sit him on the potty for a few seconds. If the child goes, offer praise. Take the child to the bathroom to wash his hands and once again offer praise.

5. **Give plenty of fluids**
   After this practice session, give your child plenty of fluids to increase the chances he will need to go to the toilet. Put the child in loose-fitting pants with an elastic waist, and no nappy.

6. **State the correct behaviour**
   Remind your child what you want him to do if he needs to go to the toilet.

7. **Offer praise for each correct step**
   If your child lets you know she wants to go to the toilet, praise her enthusiastically for each step she accomplishes on her own.

8. **Ask your child if he would like to go**
   If your child does not approach you or the potty, then every few minutes ask him if he would like to go, particularly if you see him holding onto his penis through his pants or pulling a face that indicates he is about to go.

9. **Teach your child to wash her hands**
   After every successful use of the toilet, make sure your child washes her hands. Offer a back-up treat, such as a small packet of raisins or soft sweets.

10. **Deal with accidents by describing the incorrect then the correct behaviour**
    If the child has an accident, and almost all children will, describe

what he has done wrong. 'No. You don't do wees in your pants.' Tell him what he should do instead. 'You must do wees on the potty.' Make sure the child practises the correct behaviour. Take him by the hand into the bathroom, take down his pants and sit him on the potty. Use a firm, matter-of-fact voice. Ignore protests. Do not get angry or upset with the child.

11. **Phase out rewards and praise**

Once your child is telling you regularly when she wants to go, and is successfully completing the task, gradually phase out the amount of praise and back-up rewards. This can be done by waiting until the child has completed several of the steps, then all of the steps, before being praised.

It is often quicker to teach toddlers to urinate in the toilet than to teach them to pass a bowel movement in the toilet. Many children who are dry during the day will wait until their diaper is on during naps before they pass a motion. This is normal and should not cause any concern. However, if the child tries to pass a bowel motion while sitting on the potty, offer enthusiastic encouragement. If you notice your child straining to pass a motion, then quickly ask if she would like to go to the toilet and take her promptly to the bathroom. Many children will continue to wet themselves at night until the age of six or seven. Bedwetting is dealt with in Chapter 7.

Encouraging independent play

Toddlers are generally better able than infants to amuse themselves. Indeed, toddlerhood is a period of great discovery and excitement as children become capable of more complex play and games. However, they are not generally capable of truly cooperative play with other children. Their play tends to be parallel, where two children may be playing side by side but with no rules in common and each absorbed in their own activity. Children's play is extremely important. Through play they learn about their world. They discover that objects have different shapes, sizes, colours, textures, names, sounds and uses.

It is also through play that children meet and learn to relate to other children. Children's play can be tremendously rewarding for parents as well, and they can participate from time to time without dominating the play.

Problems can also arise with children's play. If a child simply won't play on his own without an adult joining in, parents end up feeling harassed and as though they never get a break when the toddler is awake. If every time the parent stops watching the child play the child cries or follows the parent around, it is probably time to teach the child to play more independently. Many of these problems are normal and all children go through phases of being clingy. They may seem to want to follow you around all day, becoming upset whenever you are out of sight. The problem usually sorts itself out with time.

Here are some suggestions for encouraging independent play.

1. **Make sure you have plenty of interesting activities available**
    Make sure the activities are easily accessible. Toys can be stored in low, open shelves within easy reach of the child. In general it is better for activities to be stored in areas where children spend most of their time, such as the family living room. Having a beautifully equipped playroom can be next to useless if the child wants to spend her time near you. Avoid storing toys in boxes that open from the top; this makes it harder for the child to select what she wants to play with. Set aside a low cupboard in the kitchen where there are things with which the child can play.

2. **Help the toddler get started**
    Ask the child what he would like to play with. If he does not select anything, take out a few toys and suggest something. Sometimes children will need to be shown how to play with particular toys.

3. **Use incidental teaching strategies to encourage the child to continue with the activity**
    Respond positively to children's questions.

4. **Once the child has started, use strategic exiting**
    Suggest something the child might do ('See how tall you can make that tower') and follow with an offer to return shortly to see how the child has got on. Always tell the child where you

are going. 'I'll just put on the kettle and then you can show me what you've done.' Initially, leave the child on his own for a very short period, say twenty seconds. If the child continues with the activity without stopping, come back and let him show you what he has accomplished. 'Isn't that a beautiful tower? You did it all by yourself.' The basic idea is to gradually increase the amount of time you are away before returning, so that the child gets used to you joining in then leaving his play. Your return should always be associated with positive comments or questions related to the child's activity, and the fact that he was playing all by himself.

5. **Ignore protests about leaving**
   If the child protests or stops as soon as you attempt to leave, simply tell her to choose something else if she has finished with that game and then leave anyway. Ignore further protests.

6. **Offer snacks while the child is busy**
   Don't wait until children have become bored and have interrupted their play before you offer snacks. By offering them while a child is still busy, you will increase your child's attention and concentration span. It also serves as a reward for sustained play activity.

The combination of making activities available, the use of incidental teaching when children are at play, and the strategic exit can be very effective in encouraging easily distracted youngsters to focus their attention on play activities. Don't be upset if the strategy doesn't work the first time; simply try again in a few days' time. Children who are very easily distracted can't concentrate on anything for more than a few seconds, and those whose play seems aimless may be hyperactive or have a developmental disability. If you see these symptoms in your child, seek professional assistance.

Dressing problems

Children begin toddlerhood needing a great deal of help with getting dressed. By the time they are three they should have acquired most of the skills involved in dressing themselves, but will need some help on occasions. During toddlerhood, parents should encourage more independence in dressing, but some children will resist these attempts and simply refuse to dress themselves unless the parent does everything. Teaching a child to dress is a long-term project and change will be gradual. Some dressing skills are much easier than others. For example, putting on a pair of shorts is easier than learning to tie shoelaces.

Dressing should be fun. It is not a time for pressuring or nagging children. A toddler has at least two or three opportunities each day to learn about dressing and undressing. Try the following procedure.

1. **Get everything ready**
   Organise your morning routine so that everything the child needs is ready before you start. Have it all in the one place so that the child does not have to wait. Avoid distractions such as having the television on, so the child can concentrate on what is happening.

2. **Praise independent dressing**
   Begin dressing your toddler, but any time he wants to do something let him do so. Praise him enthusiastically and frequently for any attempt to put on an item of clothing.

3. **Describe what is happening**
   Talk to him about what you are doing. 'First, we put on what?' 'Yes, that's right, your underpants.' Ask him questions about what he should do next. 'What goes in here?' as you point to the holes for his legs.

4. **Only give assistance when it is required**
   Only give your child as much assistance as she needs. For example, avoid pulling up her pants if she can do this. Over time, gradually reduce your assistance and withhold praising her until she has put on all but very difficult clothing items.

5. **Give your child time to learn the skills**
   Allow enough time for dressing so that you are not rushed and therefore tempted to simply dress the child yourself to avoid being late.

6. **Prompt the naming of items of clothing**
   Ask the child to identify each item of clothing. Praise the correct naming of items.

7. **Provide consequences for noncooperation**
    If the child struggles, resists, tries to run off or throws a tem-
    per tantrum during dressing, tell him to keep still. Back up this
    instruction with quiet time for one minute.

Sharing

Toddlers can become very possessive about their things. The word
'mine' surfaces early in the vocabulary of many children, and they
get quite upset if visiting children touch something of theirs.
Appealing to the child's sense of reason simply doesn't work. The
toddler may grab or push another child away from a favourite toy,
teddy, car or doll. This kind of behaviour is common and nothing
to be particularly concerned about. It often decreases once the child
attends a playgroup or moves on to kindergarten or preschool.

In the meantime it can be a source of frustration and embarrassment, especially if your child is allowed to play with other
children's things when you visit. Here are some ideas to help
toddlers get used to the idea of sharing.

1. **Tell your child who will be visiting and what to
    expect**
    When you know that other children around your child's age will
    be visiting, explain that you would like him to let the visitors play
    with some of his toys.
2. **Involve your child in selecting toys for sharing**
    Ask your child to select some toys she is prepared to let the visi-
    tors play with.
3. **Give the visitor permission to play with selected toys**
    When the visitors arrive, set out the toys and tell the visitors
    they are welcome to use them. Set the children up in an activity
    before you leave.
4. **Praise your child for sharing**
    Praise your own child every now and then for letting the others
    play with his things.
5. **Describe correct use of toys**
    If the visitor plays with your child's toys dangerously or roughly,

ask your child if she would like you to put the offending toy away. Tell the child concerned how the toy should be used and request that he do so.

6. **Deal with snatching and disruptions by describing the incorrect and correct behaviour**

   If your child tries to snatch, grab or push the other child away from his toys, describe what he has done wrong, 'Steven, you mustn't grab when Andrew is using it', and prompt the correct alternative behaviour, 'Give it back and let him have a turn.'

7. **Remove troublesome toys**

   If the child disobeys, simply take the toy from her hands and give it to the other child.

8. **Use quiet time as a back-up consequence**

   If your child continues to protest or throws a temper tantrum, put him in quiet time for two minutes. After quiet time is over, return the child to the activity and tell him when it will be his turn.

Sometimes difficulties can arise when older or bigger children take over and do not let your own child have a turn. In these instances, be prepared to intervene to ensure that the children share the activity. Your child cannot be expected to let other children use her things if they don't take proper care of them or refuse to share. Don't wait for other parents to come to your child's rescue. In your house, and with your child's activities, be prepared to insist on fair play.

Arrival of a new baby

The arrival of a new baby means some fairly major changes for both toddler and parents. The toddler may have been quite excited about the prospect of having a baby brother or sister, but the reality can be a different story. The toddler must get used to not having his parents' undivided attention and may resent all the interest shown in the new arrival, not only by parents but by others. If there have been problems with the delivery, the mother will be quite anxious about the new baby's every movement. The mother will often be exhausted and sore after the delivery, or may be depressed and need time to relax and recover when the baby is sleeping. This of course is the very time the toddler wants your attention, because he has you on his own.

Some toddlers can be very loving and caring towards a new baby, rushing to tell their mother any time the baby cries, and cheerfully watching and helping with nappy changes and feeds. Other children become quite jealous and aggressive towards the baby. They may hit the baby, pour things on her, or otherwise be too rough with her. Many of these problems can be minimised if the following steps are taken.

1. **Prepare your child in advance**

    Tell your child when the pregnancy is confirmed and the mother is physically 'showing': talk about the birth, let the toddler feel the baby kicking and let the toddler 'help' with the preparation of the nursery. Read your child stories about the arrival of new babies into the family.

2. **Involve the toddler in the care of the baby**

    After the mother returns from hospital with the baby, involve the toddler in the care of the baby. It is important for the toddler not to feel excluded.

3. **Make sure you spend some time with the toddler without the baby around**

    The toddler needs to come to terms gradually with not being the centre of attention all the time. This adjustment can be helped by making sure the toddler is not neglected.

4. **Praise your child for assisting with the care of the baby or attending to his needs**

    Let the toddler hold, cuddle and nurse the baby. Praise him for amusing, entertaining and being gentle with the baby.

5. **Provide consequences if the toddler tries to hurt the baby**

    If the toddler becomes aggressive by trying to pinch, hit or hurt the baby, describe the incorrect behaviour. 'Jamie, no, don't pull Amy's hair.' Describe the correct behaviour. 'Stroke her like this if you want to touch her.' Deal with this behaviour firmly and calmly. Don't overreact by being too emotional. It is quite normal for toddlers to feel some resentment towards the new arrival.

If the behaviour persists, put the toddler into quiet time for one minute with an explanation of what he has done wrong.

Despite your best efforts, your toddler may feel some resentment and jealousy towards the new baby. This resentment can become even worse once the infant starts to crawl and walk, and so become able to touch and interfere with the older child's possessions and games. Parents dealing with this situation should aim to teach the older child to distract the infant's attention to objects or toys of her own. The parent should praise the older child for doing so. It is also important to avoid always chastising the older child for becoming upset about the infant's 'disruptiveness'. Many of these early adjustment difficulties resolve themselves with time. However, sibling rivalry and jealousy can be a persistent problem and indeed can continue throughout adult life.

Conclusions

The parenting of infants and toddlers requires a great deal of patience. It is during this early period that children develop a basic sense of trust in their caregivers. A safe, secure and loving environment encourages children to form healthy attachments to their parents. As your baby becomes more mobile the need for a safe play space becomes essential to prevent injuries. During the second year of life children start to test parents and need to learn the meaning of the word no. Children learn many new skills as their physical coordination improves, and the growth in children's ability to understand and speak words is truly remarkable. Parents have to develop routines for feeding, sleeping and dressing, and strategies to deal with whining, fussing and occasional temper outbursts. The good news is that if these early behaviours are handled well, children will have fewer difficulties later.

CHAPTER 6

Preschoolers

During the preschool period, from age three until five or six, many important developmental changes take place. These include further development in language use and vocabulary, improvements in both fine and gross motor coordination, and the beginnings of complex play and games that involve simple rules, sharing and turn-taking. Preschoolers love word games, books, poems, tongue twisters and magnetic letters that can be rearranged on the fridge. During this time they enjoy active play, involving moving to music and dancing, which helps develop coordination. Their imagination develops and they become interested in dressing up, pretending, puzzles and sorting through things, colouring, cutting and pasting, painting and other artistic activities.

At this age, children often spend time at some kind of organised preschool and have to learn to handle these separations from their parents. Children become increasingly independent as many basic self-care skills are mastered, including being able to dress and undress themselves, learning to answer the telephone, developing table manners and learning to pick up, put away and take care of their possessions.

This is also the time when children need to be prepared for their entry into school. Preschoolers love books and should acquire many basic concepts about the printed word that are important for learning to read. Parents can help their children acquire these skills, including skills such as tracking words from left to right, locating the top and bottom of a page, and understanding the idea that words convey meaning. Some preschoolers learn to read before they start school.

During this time, children develop a stable notion of their own sex and begin to see themselves as either a boy or a girl. They also start to show behaviour patterns that are characteristic of their sex.

This chapter deals with the more common developmental and behavioural problems that can arise in preschoolers. Some of the problems covered, such as disobedience and temper tantrums, are extensions of problems that begin in toddlerhood. Others relate to a child's greater involvement with the world outside the family, such as shopping trips, travelling in the car, visiting friends or relatives, separation problems, dawdling while getting ready to go out and refusal to tidy away toys and other possessions.

Behaviour in the home

Disobedience

Disobedience is the single most common problem of children who are referred to mental health professionals for behavioural and emotional problems. Serious problems of this kind can be avoided if parents establish good routines to deal with disobedience when the child is a toddler. It is important that preschoolers learn to respect adult direction and authority if they are going to be ready for school. At school, children are expected to comply with many basic rules. Those who are very defiant or disruptive at the end of the preschool period often have difficulty in settling into the routines of normal school life.

One way to tell whether your child is becoming very defiant is to give her about ten instructions over a half-hour period. If she disobeys six or more of the instructions, you may need to do something to increase her cooperativeness. When non-compliance occurs more often than this, the parent is likely to experience difficulties with many basic family routines such as bathing, dressing and simple outings such as shopping. Very disobedient children often receive lots of negative attention from their parents, who struggle to gain any kind of control. These children are also quite demanding. Some are aggressive towards other children and their parents, and may throw temper tantrums if they don't get their own way.

It is important to remember that blind obedience to all adult directions is also very undesirable. Insistence on obedience at all times is over-controlling and unreasonable. Children's creativity, initiative and positive view of themselves can be threatened in such a highly authoritarian environment. However, if a parent has reasonable expectations and takes care to make fair and sensible rules, consistent enforcement of these rules will lead to more cooperative, better-behaved and happier children, as well as less-stressed parents. The guidelines below are for children who frequently ignore parents' reasonable requests. Read the guidelines outlined in Chapter 4 on pages 97–98 for giving instructions to children, which cover most of the basic principles. To increase your child's cooperation with your requests, follow the guidelines below.

1. **Set up a happy faces chart**

   Set up a chart (see page 93) with about thirty squares for each day and enough sheets for about fourteen days. Create charts for each child in the family who has a compliance problem.

2. **Choose a quiet day to begin**

   Organise your time so that you begin this programme when you will be at home for most or all of the day. Your child will find it easier to learn the basic routine if you avoid shopping trips or outings during the first few days.

3. **Give a clear, calm instruction**

   When you ask your child to do something, be careful to make sure that you get close to her and maintain eye contact, and that the instruction is both clear and timed not to interrupt an activity that is important to her, such as watching a favourite television show.

4. **Praise compliance with the request**

   If the child complies within five seconds of being given the instruction, praise him. 'Thank you for doing as I asked straight-away.' Put a smiley face on his chart.

5.   **Repeat your instruction and back up**
     If your child disobeys, repeat the instruction, wait a further five seconds. Back up this instruction immediately with quiet time if the child continues to disobey. Follow the quiet-time guidelines in Chapter 4 on pages 100–101.

6.   **Repeat the instruction**
     After quiet time is over, repeat the original instruction. Do not put a smiley face on the chart if a reminder was required.

7.   **Give back-up rewards as appropriate**
     Initially let the child have a back-up reward from a lucky dip after earning four smiley faces. If the child is put into quiet time, start the count again. For example, if the child has earned three smiley faces and then goes into quiet time, wait until four more instructions have been complied with before offering a reward. After the first two days, give the child a lucky dip treat after six, then eight and then ten instructions. Increase the number gradu-ally, and simply go back one step – for example from eight to six – if the compliance drops off as you increase the demands.

8.   **Make back-up rewards more unpredictable**
     After the first week, make the lucky dips more and more unpre-dictable. Sometimes after five, sometimes after fifteen, sometimes after eight. The idea here is that the child never knows when compliance is going to be rewarded. It becomes a surprise.

9.   **Phase out the happy faces chart**
     After the second week, phase out the happy faces chart. Don't put up a smiley face after every instruction your child complies with. Make the earning of smiley faces unpredictable but continue to praise your child occasionally for complying with requests. If you follow this routine consistently every time you give an instruc-tion, after three weeks your child should be complying with most requests. Often it only takes a day or two.

This programme requires parents to become very aware of when they give instructions. It works best when parents consistently follow the routine. Avoid giving your child a smiley face or lucky dip if she asks for one; simply tell her that she can't get a smiley just by asking. Make sure you don't forget to provide the lucky dip if you have promised one and the child has reached the goal.

Temper tantrums

Temper outbursts are not confined to the 'terrible twos', and displays of temper can occur throughout childhood and indeed adulthood. Anger is a normal emotion. However, in the process of growing up, children need to learn to express their annoyance and anger constructively. Failure to do so can produce young adults who resort to violence whenever something upsets them. Temper tantrums are common problems in preschoolers. The most common triggers include a child being asked to stop an activity they are involved in, such as being requested to turn off the television and get ready for bed; a parent's refusal to agree to the child's request or demand, for example to buy an iceblock; and fights while playing with other children. Some very difficult preschoolers can throw ten to fifteen tantrums a day. These children are often very disobedient as well. The tantrums and disobedience often need to be dealt with at the same time.

Some preschoolers only throw tantrums at home, never when they are at childcare, preschool or kindergarten. Preschool teachers can be quite surprised to learn how difficult a child is at home because the child is so well behaved at preschool. Others will throw tantrums anywhere.

Tantrums can be difficult to deal with, particularly when they occur in the middle of the night, in the supermarket or if the parent lives in temporary accommodation such as a shelter, a caravan park or with relatives. If neighbours hear a child screaming repeatedly, they may complain to the police or welfare agencies because they fear that the child is being abused.

Most of these guidelines for managing tantrums in toddlers apply equally well to preschoolers. However, tantrums with preschoolers can take a bit longer to bring under control, and some parents may have to endure several fairly long screaming episodes before the child finally learns that tantrums no longer work. Here are some guidelines to help you deal with your child's temper tantrums.

1. **Set up a behaviour chart**
   Set up a behaviour chart similar to the 'happy faces' chart on page 93, but this time make up a sheet with half-hour time blocks corresponding to the child's waking day. (See the example in Figure 3, page 161.)
2. **Discuss the time-out routine with your child**
   Rehearse the time-out procedure and prepare the child for what will happen the next time he loses his temper.
3. **Set the timer**
   Set your oven timer or stopwatch for thirty minutes. If the child lasts thirty minutes without throwing a tantrum, she earns a smiley face. Let her put the smiley on the chart if she wishes.
4. **Back up instructions with time out**
   If the child throws a tantrum, follow the procedure for managing tantrums in toddlers on pages 141–42: give an instruction to stop, back up with time out in the laundry, bathroom or hallway, let the child out of time out when he has been quiet for three minutes, and ignore the child completely while in time out. Follow the guidelines very carefully and remember to make sure that the room used for time out is safe.
5. **Phase out the chart and back-up rewards**
   After two weeks, if the tantrums have reduced to once or twice per week, phase the child off the happy faces chart and back-up rewards but continue to praise her for being cooperative.

Many preschoolers quickly learn not to throw tantrums at home but may still do so outside the home. If a tantrum occurs in the car, pull over and stop the car. Firmly tell the child to stop. If the tantrum continues, be prepared to put the child out of the car and onto the footpath for two minutes. (You should sit with the child to stop him from running away and/or out onto the road.) If necessary, hold him still. Ignore other people's reactions as best you can. When the tantrum has stopped, let him get back in the car and put on his seat belt, and then continue on your way. If it is simply not possible to put

FIGURE 3: A SAMPLE BEHAVIOUR CHART

Behaviour chart

Day   Date

times	faces	times	faces	times	faces
7.00 7.30		11.00 11.30		3.30 4.00	
7.30 8.00		11.30 12.00		4.00 4.30	
8.00 8.30		12.00 1.00		4.30 5.00	
8.30 9.00		1.00 1.30		5.00 5.30	
9.00 9.30		1.30 2.00		5.30 6.00	
9.30 10.00		2.00 2.30		6.00 6.30	
10.00 10.30		2.30 3.00		6.30 7.00	
10.30 11.00		3.00 3.30		7.00 7.30	

Today's
total

Place a smiley face in the faces columns for the appropriate time period to indicate the absence of a behaviour you wish to reduce, or the occurrence of a desired behaviour.

the child in time out – if, for example, you are in the supermarket – completely ignore the behaviour. Look away, turn away, and as soon as there is a pause in the screaming, thank the child for being quiet. Finish what you are doing as quickly as possible and put your child into time out in the laundry, bathroom or hallway as soon as you get home. Remind him of why he is going into time out.

If there has been no noticeable change in the tantrums after a week of the above steps, check to make sure you have been following the guidelines below.

1. Follow the routine every time. Grandparents and other child-minders should also be aware of the time-out routine and should follow the same guidelines.
2. Act, don't threaten. Don't say, 'If you don't stop, you will have to go to time out.' Say, 'You have not done as I asked, now go to time out.'
3. Do not let your child leave time out until she is properly quiet. Ignore whimpering or calling out.
4. Give the child sufficient positive attention when he is not in time out. Are there enough activities available for him? Time out works best when 'time in' is a positive and rewarding alternative.
5. Don't get trapped by the child's attempts to treat time out as a game. He may say things like, 'I like time out anyway' or 'Can I go into time out? It's fun.' Ignore such comments and follow through every time the problem behaviour occurs.
6. Make sure that the child cannot get out of time out before the time period is up. Some children may run out, open the door or climb out the window to avoid time out. If necessary, shut the door, put a lock on the door or window, or hold the handle so he can't get out.
7. Completely ignore the child while she is in time out. Sometimes children will call out things like, 'I'm quiet now, Mummy. Can I come out?', 'Mummy, I can't breathe.' These manoeuvres must be ignored; otherwise your child will use them to gain attention when she is in time out.
8. Keep calm. Some parents forget this and give time out only when they are really angry. They may shout and drag the child

into time out, giving her a whack for good measure. None of these things make time out more effective.

9. Make sure your child knows the rules. Sometimes parents will tell their child one thing but act as though different rules apply. For instance, the parent tells the child he will go to time out for hitting, then puts the child into time out for not coming to the dinner table quickly enough. If you change the rules, make sure the child knows what they are beforehand.

10. Don't let the noise get to you. Some parents abandon time out because the child's screaming upsets them. If you give in while the child is screaming in time out, it is likely you will make the problem worse. The child will simply learn to scream more loudly and for longer next time. Occupy yourself when your child is in time out, for example watch television, read a book, get a friend to hold your hand, get some ear muffs and remind yourself it's for his own good.

11. Make the time-out room an uninteresting place. Do not use the child's bedroom for time out unless there is no other suitable place.

12. If the child makes a mess during time out, for example by throwing clothes from a laundry basket around the room, make sure she cleans it up before she is allowed to come out. If necessary, physically guide the child through the motions of tidying the mess away.

If you are following these guidelines correctly and the child's behaviour is still not improving, you should seek professional assistance. However, if these guidelines are followed accurately, time out will be effective with the vast majority of preschoolers who throw tantrums.

Getting ready to go out

The early-morning rush of getting children ready for preschool or school can create chaos. It is a pressured time and one that often leads to behavioural problems. This is particularly likely if you were late waking up yourself and have to get yourself ready for work. Beds are left unmade, dishes are in the sink, the place is in a mess and children leave without having everything they need for the day's activities.

Some children add to these difficulties by being persistently slow or demanding. Just when you need them to be cooperative they run away, hide, refuse to get dressed or start to whine. When adults are under pressure they may yell and shout, and many a child has left for preschool after getting smacked at home. Other children just seem disorganised in the morning. They have to be reminded every step of the way, sometimes several times. Have you done your teeth? Been to the toilet? Got your kindy bag? And so on. The key to overcoming this kind of dawdling is organisation. Here are some guidelines to help you help your child to get ready to go out.

1. **Be organised**

    For activities that occur often, such as taking a child to day care or preschool, establish an organised morning routine. If you need to leave by 8.15 a.m. at the latest and you know it takes an hour to get ready, do not get out of bed at 7.30 a.m. Some parents are habitually late in bringing their children to organised activities such as preschool, parties or playing dates at other children's homes. This shortens the time a child has to enjoy these outings and creates unnecessary additional pressure on both parents and children.

2. **Avoid last-minute rushing**

    To avoid last-minute rushing, and perhaps arriving late, get ready the night before any items your child needs to take, then go to bed at a reasonable hour so you can get up early in the morning.

3. **Get yourself ready first**

    Explain to your child where you will be going, then get yourself ready first. If you get ready early it will give you the time you need to deal with any disruptions with the children.

4. **Discuss the day's activities with your child**

    Answer any questions your child may have about the day's activities.

5. **Use 'Ask, Say, Do' to help your child get ready**

    Assist your child to get ready on time by using 'Ask, Say, Do' as a way of teaching children to dress themselves as outlined in

Chapter 4 on pages 82–84. If you use this procedure your child will not only learn what she has to do when she goes out but will be able to help.

6. **Give positive attention for cooperative behaviour**
   Speak up and praise your child for getting ready without making a fuss. Initially, any time your child gets ready without having to be asked, praise this behaviour enthusiastically.

7. **Provide appropriate consequences for disruptions**
   If any disruptions occur, such as whining or temper outbursts, deal with them decisively, using the strategy suggested for the specific behaviour. Sometimes you will have to endure an outburst while the child is in quiet time or time out. Don't let this put you off. Be late if necessary. Next time it will be easier.

8. **Use the 'beat the clock' game as a way of dealing with dawdling**
   Beat the clock involves setting the child a goal of being ready before the clock alarm sounds off at a set time. If the child wins, he earns a small treat or reward for his efforts, such as a favourite snack in his lunch box.

9. **Explain what is involved**
   Explain to your child that you would like her to learn to get ready more quickly. Show her the timer on the stove or an egg timer and tell her that if she can get dressed and ready to leave before the alarm rings she will get a small treat. Set the timer for the amount of time that you consider reasonable. Avoid repeating instructions or nagging the child to hurry up.

10. **Reward your child for beating the clock**
    If the child is ready before the timer rings, offer praise and encouragement and give the back-up treat.

11. **Phase your child off the programme**
    Once the child is regularly beating the clock, phase out its use. This can be done simply. First stop the back-up treat, using only praise as the reward but keeping the clock going. Next, let the child set the clock and tell you when the time is up. Finally, leave it to the child to decide whether to have the timer set as a reminder. This can often be accomplished over a two-week period.

Some early-morning problems are difficult to solve because the child expects everything to be done for him. Watching television first thing in the morning can be very disruptive. It is often better to get children dressed before they have breakfast. If you feel you must have the television on in the morning, then make watching it dependent upon being ready and beating the clock. If the child beats the clock, put something special in her lunch box that day. Parents themselves should also try to model being organised and on time. A child who observes his parents being consistently late for appointments or outings may develop this behaviour himself. While you don't want to become too time-conscious, good organisation in the morning certainly helps. It also helps if children learn to help out with tidying up. Smooth organisation is much easier when all family members contribute.

Teaching children to tidy up after themselves

Preschool children should be encouraged to take care of their possessions. This includes learning to clear away toys and activities after they have finished with them. If children simply leave everything for someone else to clean up, they will quickly lose parts or pieces of their toys and games. Play equipment will be more likely to be damaged, the house will always look messy and there will be much more work for parents.

Have reasonable expectations. Having play things strewn all over the place is often part of children's play, and interrupting such play so that the house is neat and tidy can disrupt their interest and involvement in what they are doing. It is better to wait for natural breaks in children's activities before cleaning up. These breaks can occur when children move locations, from indoor to outdoor play, go from one activity to a new one (such as from dressing up to painting or colouring-in books), have a meal break, or when the family is getting ready to go out. Some parents decide that only one clean-up a day is sufficient, say before bedtime. The disadvantage of this tactic is that the task will be much bigger and therefore harder for the child, who may need a lot of help. Two or three quick tidy-away sessions are often sufficient to keep the house in order, and have the advantage of taking place immediately after the play activity.

Getting children to tidy away is another story. Some children refuse to cooperate and even insist that it's *your* job. It is better to focus initially on getting children to clean up shared family living areas rather than their own bedrooms. Here are some ideas for helping children learn to pick up and put away.

1. **Store children's toys so they are easy to find**
    Use low, open shelving where possible rather than boxes or containers which open from the top. Boxes make finding toys harder and often lead to everything being tipped out on the floor, which means more work later.

2. **Choose the right moment to ask the child to tidy away**
    Look for natural breaks in the play activity.

3. **Give your child a warning**
    Tell your child she will have to finish the activity and tidy away in a few minutes.

4. **Suggest a positive consequence for complying**
    'When you've put the Lego away, you can come and have a snack.'

5. **Calmly ask your child to begin**
    In a calm voice, tell your child you want him to begin putting away the game or toys. Be specific. Rather than 'Tidy up this mess, please,' say, 'John, put the train back in the box, please.'

6. **Pause, then prompt your child to begin**
    Wait for ten seconds to see if your child complies. If she does not or cannot, go over and tell her what to do. 'First of all put all your train carriages in this slot here. Show me how you can do this.' If the child completes this, give praise. 'Nicely done, Jane, those carriages are very neatly put away.' For each game or item that has been used during playtime, follow the previous two steps. You will notice that this strategy initially relies on you giving the child assistance in getting started by breaking down the task into smaller parts. This assistance can be reduced as the child learns what to do.

7. **Use a 'stop' instruction to deal with protests**
    If the child begins to whine or complain, or becomes aggressive,

give an instruction using a calm but firm voice. 'John, stop complaining right now. I want you to gather the crayons together and put them in your pencil case.'

8. **Use physical guidance to help the child get started**

   If the misbehaviour continues or increases, avoid becoming angry and distressed. Stay beside the child, ignore protests and physically guide the child's hands through the motions until the activity or game is completely cleared away.

9. **Provide a logical consequence**

   If the child has misbehaved during the clean-up time, tell her that the games were not put away in an acceptable way today and that there is a consequence: the games will be put away and out of reach for a period of time, maybe the rest of the day or until the next day.

10. **Speak up and praise cooperation**

    If the child cooperated during the clean-up time, praise him for being a good helper. 'Stephen, you picked up all your books and put them away beautifully today. Good job.'

11. **Gradually reduce the assistance you give**

    During subsequent clean-up times, gradually reduce the amount of assistance given to get the child started. This can be done by giving her more responsibility for deciding what to do first, for example asking, 'What do you want to pick up first?' followed by praise; you can also get the child to pick up several different items before praise is offered; and finally, you can get the child to pick up all items before receiving praise.

Some parents only experience problems when they try to get their child to clean up by herself. In other words, even though the child can do the task on her own, she refuses to unless the parent helps. This kind of behaviour can be very irritating and is often a form of attention-seeking. To overcome it you may need to be quite firm and deal with it as disobedience rather than a pick-up-and-put-away problem. Quiet time or time out can be used as a back-up consequence for refusal to cooperate.

There will be times, however, when the child needs help, or indeed when the parent decides to complete the task instead of making the child do it, for example, if the child is very tired or unwell, or if the mess is not of his making. Young children under-standably object to having to clean up other children's mess. They are learning to act and think independently and will resist tasks they think are unfair. It is important for parents to view the task of teaching their child to look after his possessions as a long-term process that takes time. There is an important balance between looking after possessions and being overly rigid, fussy and conscious of tidiness. Remember, a bit of a mess often makes a home appear lived in, relaxed and homely.

Difficulties during meal preparation

The period between 4.30 and 6.30 in the afternoon can be a dif-ficult time for parents of young children. Parents and children are often tired at the end of the day. Parents often have a lot to do at this time including preparing meals, helping older children with homework and getting children bathed, dressed and ready for bed. It is a time when parents often like their children to amuse themselves while household tasks are completed. The children may have other ideas. Common problems at this time include children whining and demanding attention or complaining about being hungry. These problems are often worse if the family is late arriving home from work, school or preschool – the child is more likely to be hungry and the parent disorganised. Children are often better behaved if there is something they can do to help during meal preparation. Not all parents like this idea and prefer the child to be out of the way so they can organise the meal without interruptions and distractions. These parents may often tell their child to get out of the kitchen and go and play. However, if children are eventually to learn how to run a home, they need to be given opportunities to learn what to do. This means occasionally putting up with a bit more kitchen mess than you might like. Both boys and girls should, under supervision, learn the same tasks, otherwise they may grow up seeing a particular parent as the kitchen slave.

The best way to overcome this problem is not to compel pre-schoolers to help, but to give them the opportunity to if they wish, always with close supervision to avoid accidents. Here are some guidelines.

1. **Involve your child in a weekly discussion involving the planning of the family's evening meals**
   Seek your child's opinions about the foods she and other family members like. Make a note of these suggestions. Thank the child for her help.

2. **Plan a weekly menu of balanced meals**
   Include some of the child's favourite meals and avoid serving meals that the child does not particularly like on consecutive nights.

3. **Prepare a shopping list**
   Write down all the things you intend to buy.

4. **Have a regular time for meals each day**
   Organise your time so that you have your family meal prepared at the same time each night.

5. **Plan meals for the following night**
   Decide on the meal for the following night. The idea here is to be one day ahead of yourself. Check that all necessary ingredients are on hand. Where necessary, make a note for the following day to take items from the freezer or to shop for specific ingredients.

6. **Before each mealtime, ask your child if he would like to help**
   Let your child know you are about to prepare dinner. Suggest something simple that the child can do safely while you watch, for example setting the table, helping prepare vegetables and getting items from the refrigerator. Sometimes children suggest things that are too hard or dangerous such as chopping vegetables. If they do, explain why they can't help in this way and suggest something else. If the child prefers to continue playing, then that is fine.

7. **Interrupt what you are doing every so often to praise your child for appropriate behaviour**
   This is particularly important for children who have been disruptive and demanding during meal preparation.

8. **If the child interrupts, demands or whines during meal preparation, describe the problem behaviour**
   Calmly but firmly tell your child that you don't want to be interrupted while you are preparing dinner. Offer a choice of either playing quietly or helping with the meal.

9. **If disobedience or whining continues, follow the steps suggested for dealing with these behaviours on pages 156–59**
   Try to pinpoint what might be contributing to the behaviour.

10. **Give your child a warning before serving the meal**
    Ten minutes prior to the meal being served, tell your child to clear away any game or activity and to go to the bathroom to wash his hands.

11. **Invite your child to assist you in serving the meal**
    Serve child-size portions and eat the meal.

If your child is frequently disruptive during meals, is a fussy eater or has specific feeding problems including vomiting and not being able to swallow, refer to the guidelines relating to severe feeding problems with preschoolers on pages 178–83 and the suggestions for handling mealtime disruptions below. Have a look at the diet you are offering your child.

These suggestions about meal preparation are designed to give children a chance to participate if they wish. There will be times, however, when this is not possible because you are running late and simply prefer to get the job done as quickly as possible without children underfoot. Or it may be a special dinner occasion. At these times let your child know why they cannot help and, if necessary, suggest an alternative activity.

Handling mealtime behaviour

When family mealtimes run smoothly, they can be an enjoyable part of the day. The family is all together in one place and can share the highlights of their day, plan family activities and enjoy each other's company. However, for some families the experience is quite different. The meal may be eaten while everyone is glued to the television, or children may complain about the food served, try to leave the table, refuse to eat or not use utensils properly. Some parents dread mealtimes because they seem to spend the whole time dealing with disruptions ('Don't be a pig.' 'Eat properly.' 'Leave your brother alone.' 'Come back here.' 'Sit down and be quiet.' 'Eat up your carrot, it's good for you.'). In other families, one partner arrives home late from work and there are effectively two mealtimes. Other parents have expectations that are hard to enforce, such as insisting that there is no talking at the dinner table.

If your family mealtimes are like this, you might find the suggestions below helpful. Before you decide to try any of these ideas it is important to make sure that your child is not underweight, does not show signs of malnourishment, has no physical disorder such as gastric reflux, and does not experience a specific problem with swallowing. These sorts of problems may need specialist assistance and you should consult your family doctor to get the problem thoroughly assessed.

If the child is physically healthy and active, most mealtime problems are behavioural problems, not medical problems, and respond well to a simple change in the mealtime routine.

1. **Eliminate between-meal snacking**
   Explain to your child that from now on she will not be allowed any food other than at mealtimes. This is to ensure that she is hungry when the meal is served. Tell her she must not go to the fridge or cupboards to help herself.
2. **Discuss the new ground rules**
   Involve your child in a discussion of the rules that will apply during mealtimes: remaining seated at the table until you are excused; using utensils appropriately; not speaking with your mouth full; swallowing one mouthful before attempting another; no whining or complaining.
3. **Reduce fluid intake immediately before meals**
   Do not give your child any milk or juice for one hour before the mealtime. If he is thirsty, give him water.

4. **Discuss the consequences of good mealtime behaviour**
   Explain to your child that if he follows the rules, he will be given a small treat, for example a story or family game of his choice.

5. **Get everything ready before calling the child to the table**
   This reduces the necessity for waiting at the table while food is still being prepared.

6. **Praise your child for eating nicely**
   Comment on specific good behaviour such as remaining seated, chewing properly before swallowing, using utensils correctly, and so on. 'That's a good-sized mouthful.' 'Well done for staying in your chair.'

7. **Allow conversation at the table**
   If the child is making good progress, ask her questions about her day and encourage pleasant conversation between mouthfuls. Be careful here, however. Some children will quite happily chat away and eat nothing, or will eat very slowly or hold food in their mouth.

8. **If the child refuses to eat, ask him once only to continue eating**
   Avoid threats such as 'If you don't stop playing with your food you'll get a smack.' Do not insist that the child eat everything on his plate but encourage him to try everything.

9. **If the child refuses to eat, have her remain at the table until everyone else has finished**
   If the child still refuses, calmly tell her that she must sit quietly and wait until the rest of the family has finished, and that there will be nothing else to eat after she leaves the table.

10. **Ignore complaints**
    If the child protests or complains, ignore him and continue your meal.

11. **Use quiet time or time out for disruptive behaviour**
    If the child leaves the table, won't sit still or throws a tantrum, put her into quiet time or time out until the crying stops for three minutes, then return the child to the table until the family finishes their meal.

12. **Give positive feedback for good mealtime behaviour**
    Speak up and praise any behaviour you liked during the meal.

'Kate, you had beautiful manners at the table tonight. Well done.'

13. Provide a back-up reward

Offer the child an extra back-up privilege such as some individual time with you, or additional playtime before bed.

14. Offer no other food

If the child did not behave well during the meal, do not make any reference to it. However, make sure that no snacks or other food are given either between meals or before bedtime.

Some parents are very reluctant to be firm over between-meal snacks because they are afraid that their child will starve or that it is unfair to send a child to bed without something to eat. However, if a child can eat whenever he likes, there is no incentive for him to learn to eat normally, and problems with food can continue over many years. It also makes it more difficult to take the child anywhere because he turns on such a performance. It is important to establish good eating habits and a nutritionally adequate diet as early as possible.

More serious feeding problems

A balanced diet is vital for a child's normal growth and development. However, some children are a handful to feed. It has been estimated that about 5 per cent of children have an eating problem severe enough to require specialist professional assistance. Children with feeding problems can exhibit a wide variety of behaviours. They may spit up their food, vomit during or after meals, only eat a narrow range of foods such as a bottle of milk or a sandwich, simply refuse to eat, try to get down from their high chair or table, play with the food, or refuse to feed themselves or use utensils. Other children have problems chewing and swallowing and may gag when they attempt to eat solids. You may know of children who only eat potato crisps and ice-cream, or who have biscuits and drinks as snacks but who never eat at the table. Every mealtime turns into a battle. Some children's feeding problems become so serious that they fail to gain weight, or begin to lose weight. However, the most common problem parents report is that the child simply won't eat. Most feeding difficulties with children are transient and decrease as the child moves through toddlerhood and the preschool years. However, other feeding problems are more persistent and require both medical and psychological evaluation before the problem is resolved.

Parents of children with feeding problems are often deeply concerned that all is not well, but they are assured by family and friends that 'it's just a stage', or 'they'll grow out of it'. The situation only seems to get worse.

During toddlerhood, a child makes the important transition from being a largely milk-fed infant to a child who independently consumes a mixed diet. Feeding problems can result from physical causes, specific food intolerances or behavioural problems relating to parents' feeding practices.

Physical causes of feeding problems

Physical causes that need to be investigated include central nervous system disorders such as cerebral palsy and epilepsy, or degenerative diseases that occasionally present as feeding problems. Swallowing problems can be due to a cleft palate, pharyngeal incoordination or gastroesophageal reflux. True food intolerances are a much less common cause of feeding problems than is often thought. However, occasionally children have a lactose (milk) intolerance. In many but not all instances these problems would have been diagnosed at an earlier stage of development.

Feeding practices

Some feeding problems result from the way parents organise family mealtimes. Unpredictable mealtimes can be a problem. If a child's evening meal is at five o'clock one day then eight o'clock the next, it is difficult to achieve a set routine. Between-meal snacking can reduce a child's appetite, particularly if it occurs within an hour of the scheduled mealtime. Some parents give up trying to get the child to eat at set times and simply let her eat whenever she wants. This usually makes the problem worse. While the parent may be relieved because the child is eating something, she may not be receiving a balanced diet of proteins, carbohydrates, fats, vitamins and minerals.

Juiceaholics and milkaholics are children who consume large amounts of fluids but rarely eat solid foods. Children can sit at the table like other children but spend most of their time sipping drinks and refusing to eat anything.

Parent–child interaction at mealtimes
Some mealtime problems are directly related to the parent–child interaction that occurs at the dinner table. Refusal to eat is sometimes a very effective way of gaining attention. By refusing, going slow or complaining about the meal, children usually get a reaction from their parents. Often this is in the form of an instruction. 'Tania, eat your dinner.' 'Don't play with your food.' At other times the parent may end up bargaining and negotiating with the child over the amount of food to be eaten. 'Why not try just a little spoonful of your carrots?' This is not necessarily a problem except when the child repeatedly manipulates the parent into allowing him to eat the most meagre of portions. Often these responses result in the child becoming the centre of attention at dinner times. This can be a hidden pay-off for refusing food.

The child's feeding problem may also result from the parent providing inconsistent consequences following food refusal. On some occasions the child is allowed to get away with eating next to nothing, at other times the same behaviour leads to the child being sent to bed, threats of no television, no dessert or other negative consequences. If these consequences are too unpredictable the child will not know whether refusal will be successful.

Avoiding a painful experience
Children who have suffered from gastric reflux problems as infants may associate the ingestion of food with pain and discomfort. Even though the child may have been treated quite successfully using drugs or surgery, she may still be a reluctant eater long after the original physical cause has been removed. An almost universal

response to pain is to try to avoid the thing that causes it. In this case, the result is that the child won't eat.

Fear and anxiety

Some older children develop an intensely fearful reaction to eating. Prior to meals they become tense and upset, and may cry or even shake. These children may be genuinely food phobic. A phobia is an intense irrational fear of a particular object, event or situation. For these children, eating is truly a major ordeal. The fear can occur in a child who is otherwise well adjusted. Young children cannot express why they are afraid. However, food phobia is sometimes related to a fear of choking or gagging.

Family chaos at mealtimes

All families with young children sometimes experience disorganisation at mealtimes. Parents can be rushed, exhausted, home late from work, or late in picking up their child from childcare. Unforeseen circumstances can lead to a temporary disruption to meal preparation and service. Such events don't cause major problems unless they occur frequently, but if they occur often, they can be a formula for producing feeding and other behavioural problems.

Unrealistic expectations

Sometimes parents can have unusual ideas and expectations relating to their child's meals. For example, parents who insist that every single morsel on the child's plate be eaten at every meal will often create unnecessary battles. Children, like adults, have food preferences. They like some dishes more than others. Parents who insist that children eat a specific vegetable when the child will quite happily eat something else just as nutritious make life unnecessarily difficult for themselves.

Consequences of feeding problems

Some quite serious problems, both physical and psychological, can result from persistent feeding difficulties. These include nutrient deficiencies leading to failure to gain weight. Common dietary problems include iron deficiency and protein deficiency caused by reliance on milk and fluids and late introduction of solids, lack of calories and vitamin B12 caused by a strictly vegan diet (i.e. exclusion of meat, dairy and other animal products). Other problems include dental decay due to bottle feeding for too long, and diarrhoea due to excessive juice or cordial intake. Severe malnourishment can also lead to behavioural and other emotional problems, bone malformations, intellectual deficiencies or even death.

Handling more persistent feeding problems

The goal of this programme is to help children with persistent feeding difficulties learn to eat independently and appropriately. It works best for children between the ages of three and seven.

1. **If necessary, consult your doctor first**
   If you are concerned about your child's weight or growth, consult your family doctor. They may suggest seeing a specialist before tackling the feeding problem on your own.
2. **Prepare a behaviour chart before the meal**
   If you have not used a good behaviour chart before, see Chapter 4.
3. **Set up separate areas for quiet time and time out**
   If your child behaves unacceptably at mealtimes, follow the guidelines for using quiet time and time out in Chapter 4 on pages 100–105.
4. **Seat your child at the table**
   It is important to warn your child that it will soon be time to eat so that he can finish what he is doing or stop his game at a convenient time. Most people eat sitting at a table; children with eating problems have often developed the habit of eating anywhere *but* at the table. By seating your child at the table, he will learn that this is a prompt to eat and also that he will be expected to eat.

5. **Give your child a balanced diet**

Prepare meals that provide a mixed, nutritious diet. The food you prepare will depend somewhat on the child's age. Appendix 1 gives some sample menus for children of different ages. If a child is eating solid foods but is very fussy about what she will try, then prepare the same meal as for other family members. Your child may initially eat only *some* of the same foods but by the end of the programme she will probably be eating *most* of the same foods.

6. **Set a goal for the amount of food to be eaten**

Tell your child how much he has to eat. 'James, I would like you to eat all of the vegetables and half of the stew.' Set a goal that the child has a reasonable chance of achieving. Don't try to make him eat everything on the plate. It is more important to sample the variety of foods presented. It is better, too, to serve small portions and let the child ask for more if he is hungry.

7. **Establish a clear time limit for the meal**

Sometimes it is necessary to set a time limit for eating. This should be clearly understood by the child. The time should be long enough to allow the child to eat the meal with time to spare, and short enough so that it doesn't interrupt normal family routines. Twenty to thirty minutes should be plenty.

8. **Expect appropriate table manners**

Some children with eating problems develop ways of eating that are different from those of other family members. They may gnaw at a sandwich, slurp juice or only eat with their fingers even though they are capable of using a fork or spoon. Sometimes parents are so pleased to see their children actually eating that they don't insist on the appropriate table manners, but this is a mistake. As soon as a toddler is old enough to hold a spoon or fork, she should be encouraged to do so. Before you start the meal, tell your child what manners you expect.

9. **Explain quiet time to your child**

Before you use quiet time, tell your child what behaviours will earn quiet time and calmly explain why you will be using it. Behaviours that should earn quiet time at mealtimes include throwing a plate across the room, screaming, shrieking, kicking and biting.

10. **Help your child get started**

    After serving the meal, wait for ten seconds to see if your child begins by himself. If not, help him get started by giving an instruction. 'Nicholas, eat your lunch, please.' If the child still does not start, give him a specific instruction relating to a food item. 'Steven, pick up your spoon and put some yoghurt on it.' Limit your prompts to one per mouthful.

11. **Praise and encourage your child for good eating**

    Eating becomes an unpleasant business for children with feeding problems. Mealtimes should be pleasurable occasions. This can be achieved by letting your child know you are pleased with what she is doing. 'You're chewing well, Carla.' 'Terrific. That's three mouthfuls you've eaten, Bea.' Be clear, specific and immediate when you praise good eating.

12. **Give smiley faces to start with**

    Initially, each time your child swallows a mouthful, offer praise and put a smiley face (or whatever shape your child prefers) on the chart. You might set a goal of five mouthfuls, perhaps two more than the child managed the night before, then draw up five squares on a piece of paper. The meal might go like this:

    'What would you like in the square tonight, Simon?'
    'Clown faces.'
    'Okay. Have your first mouthful, and when you've swallowed it we'll draw your first clown face.'
    Simon puts a spoonful of mashed potato in his mouth. While he chews he keeps his eyes on his father who is watching him, smiling.
    'That's good chewing, son.' Simon takes a big breath and swallows. This is a major achievement for Simon because the previous week he vomited up each mouthful when he attempted to swallow. He is pleased with himself.
    His father starts to draw the first clown face. As Simon swallows each mouthful, his father draws a clown face in each square and tells Simon how well he is doing. After the fifth mouthful he says, 'That's five, Simon, you've eaten well. That's all you have

to eat tonight.' Simon grins because he knows that he will get his back-up reward.

When your child reaches the set goal, increase it by one or two mouthfuls for the next meal. How quickly you progress will depend on your child.

13. **Use a drink as a reward**
Children with eating problems often drink a lot, particularly at mealtimes. You can use their preference for drinks to encourage them to eat. Let your child have a sip of her drink only after she has eaten a certain number of mouthfuls of food. In the beginning it might be only one or two mouthfuls, but after a while you should expect her to earn several smiley faces before she has a drink. This strategy will be even more effective if the child is not allowed fluids for about an hour before the meal.

14. **Use 'stop' instructions to deal with avoidance tactics**
Some children will try to avoid eating by playing with their food. If, for example, your child starts to stack slices of sausage on his plate, say, 'Stop playing with your food.' When he looks at you, say, 'You put a fork in your sausage to eat it.'

Some children will put a spoonful in their mouths then hold it there without chewing or swallowing it. Some will try to get out of their seat, move food around their plates without eating it or take tiny nibbles of food and chew it endlessly. These behaviours can be dealt with by describing what the child is doing wrong and then asking him to behave properly.

15. **Use quiet time for inappropriate behaviour**
Use quiet time for two minutes as a back-up for refusal to comply with the 'stop' instruction. 'Tracey, I have asked you to stop pushing your food with your fingers. Now go to quiet time.'

16. **Use time out for disruptive behaviour**
If the child refuses to go to quiet time, throws a tantrum or continues to protest in quiet time, put him into time out for two minutes. After time out, return him to his meal and continue as previously until he has reached his goal for that meal.

17. **Give a back-up reward**
When your child reaches her goal, have a back-up reward ready. This might be something like staying up ten minutes later or

having a dip in a lucky dip box. (A lucky dip box for a three-year-old girl might include cheap treats such as hair ribbons, little soaps, junk jewellery and fancy hair clips.)

18. **Phase out prompts**

During the first few meals, you may have to help your child get started by giving one prompt for each mouthful. Once your child is eating ten to twenty mouthfuls, you should start to reduce these prompts. Start near the end of the meal when there are only three or four more smiley faces remaining to reach the goal. Explain that to earn smiley faces the child will now have to eat a mouthful without being asked first. Get the child to tell you when the mouthful is swallowed. Give a time limit for each mouthful: one minute for mashed food and two minutes if they need to chew it. Check that your child is taking small-to-medium mouthfuls that can be chewed and swallowed easily in the set time. If your child does not swallow the food within the set time, put him into quiet time for two minutes.

When your child can eat several mouthfuls without prompting, withdraw prompts earlier and earlier until he is eating the whole meal without instructions.

Always make sure you stop prompting before you increase the number of mouthfuls needed to earn the back-up reward.

19. **Increase food variety**

Once your child is eating fifteen or so mouthfuls per meal, you can start to increase the variety of food she will eat. Add a very small amount of one new food to the meal – it might be a mandarin segment for lunch or a teaspoon of pumpkin for dinner. Reward your child with an extra smiley face and lots of praise for trying the new food. Only give one extra smiley face the first time she tries the new food. At the next meal try another new food, such as a 1-cm cube of cheese, or a teaspoon of broccoli. Once your child has tried these new foods, occasionally add them to the regular meals you serve. Gradually increase the amounts and keep adding new foods. If your child has a particularly negative reaction to one food, leave it out for a couple of weeks and try again. Don't worry about it. Everyone dislikes some food. The aim is to have your child eating a range of food from the different food groups in the same way as the rest of the family.

20. Phase out the smiley faces

When your child is able to eat fifteen to twenty mouthfuls, increase the number of mouthfuls required to earn each smiley face. Start by requiring two more mouthfuls for each smiley face for a couple of days, then increase to three, and so on. At the same time as you increase the number of mouthfuls for each smiley, decrease the number of smiley faces needed to earn the back-up reward. Take it slowly.

Some children will start to lose interest in the smiley faces fairly quickly once they have learned to eat independently. After all, the aim is for eating to be an enjoyable activity on its own.

Parents of children who persistently refuse to eat properly need to be consistent in how they handle mealtimes for the first few weeks. For some children, eating has become so unpleasant that going into quiet time or time out may not seem to work. After all, by refusing, the child can be sent to a place where no eating is required for a short time. The key to overcoming this problem is to make being at the dinner table as positive and rewarding as possible. This goal is best accomplished by setting reasonable, attainable goals and by providing positive attention for proper eating.

Having visitors

Have you ever had the experience of inviting friends or family over for a meal, perhaps a barbeque, a party, or just so the children can play, and then found that your own children were an absolute embarrassment? You are not alone. Many parents find this a try-ing time. Preschool children often get quite excited about having friends over, particularly children their own age. However, the real-ity of having someone else on the child's home patch can lead to problems such as silly, noisy and showing-off behaviour. Your child might be quite defiant, refuse to share, refuse to play with the visitor or constantly demand your attention.

Several aspects contribute to these problems. The first is having visitors stay too long. Children may be fine for a few hours but then become tired and grumpy if their normal nap time or mealtimes are disrupted. Second, children are sometimes left to their own devices and unsupervised for a bit too long. Problems can arise if children only get attention when there is a problem, and are ignored the rest of the time with no organised activity.

Having visitors in your home provides many opportunities for young children to practise social skills, such as learning how to greet visitors, how to be a good host, how to think of activities other children might be interested in, how to make polite conversation with other grown-ups and how to entertain friends. These are complex skills that many adults never learn properly. Here are some ideas to help your child learn to behave well when visitors arrive.

1. **Plan visits that do not disrupt the child's mealtimes and sleep routines**
   This is particularly important for children who are difficult at these times.

2. **Let your child know in advance about the visit**
   Explain who is coming and the reason for the visit. 'Sheila and Brad are coming over for lunch today.'

3. **Discuss the ground rules**
   Explain the rules for the visitors' arrival. 'What do you have to remember when visitors come?' If your child cannot tell you, let her know what you expect. 'When Sheila and Brad are here I want you to . . .' Ask your child to repeat the rules. 'Okay, so what do you have to remember?'

4. **Plan some appropriate activities**
   Invite your child to choose some things that she would like to play with during the visit. The idea is to encourage her to find something to do so she won't be bored. It may also be useful to think of activities yourself that might be suitable to entertain the children.

5. **Let your child practise greeting visitors**
   When the visitor arrives and greets your child, praise your

child for answering appropriately. If he doesn't answer, prompt him but don't force him to answer. A battle at the beginning of a visit starts the whole thing off on the wrong foot.

6. **Before starting your own adult conversation, set the children up in an activity**

   Before getting too involved in adult conversation, take a moment to suggest something that the children can do. If your child takes the initiative, you may not need to say anything. If necessary, help them get started.

7. **Interrupt your own conversation now and again to give attention to your child**

   Be prepared to interrupt your own conversation to speak to and praise the children for playing nicely; do this every so often *before* a problem arises. Ask a few questions about their activity, and before leaving say you will return shortly to see how they are getting on. When you have visitors, don't wait for problems to arise before you speak to your child.

8. **If possible, offer a snack or drink while the children are busy**

   This will help you avoid the trap of rewarding bored, disruptive children with food.

9. **Deal with rude interruptions by describing the correct behaviour**

   If your child whines for attention or rudely interrupts while you are talking, ask her to say 'Excuse me' and to wait until the adults have finished speaking. Do not expect your child to wait for long if she has interrupted politely.

10. **If the interruption or demanding behaviour occurs again, give a 'stop' instruction and back it up with quiet time if necessary**

    It is important for your child to realise that you mean what you say. There is no point in having rules unless you are prepared to enforce them.

11. **Give your child positive feedback**

    Praise your child enthusiastically if he behaved appropriately during the visit. Spend some time with him after the visitors have left.

Complex skills take time to master. You should not expect your child to be well behaved when you have visitors unless you have put in the time to teach her how to behave appropriately. Many parents ignore misbehaviour when they have guests so as to avoid a scene. This is a mistake because children quickly learn that having visitors is a time when their parents are vulnerable. Many problems can be avoided with a little planning about how to keep your children amused. Once a child has learned that you are not constantly on call when you are entertaining, things often go much more smoothly.

Interrupting

Preschoolers have to learn to occupy themselves when their parents are busy, for example when they are speaking on the telephone, engaged in conversation with visitors, speaking to the doctor or speaking to their partner. Some preschoolers seem to resent it when their parents direct their attention to anyone else.

There are three important things to remember about teaching children to wait and not to interrupt. First, we have to be realistic. It is quite reasonable to expect a four-year-old not to interrupt while you have a five-minute telephone conversation. It is quite unreasonable to expect the child not to interrupt if the conversation lasts an hour, or if it's the tenth conversation that morning. Second, while children need to learn how to wait, they should be given something to do while they are waiting. Third, children need to learn how to enter adult conversations appropriately. It is polite to say, 'Excuse me, Mummy' and wait for her to finish what she is saying. It is rude to barge into a conversation by demanding instant adult attention.

Several problems get in the way of teaching these kinds of social skills. Sometimes parents of preschoolers are desperate for adult contact. After spending perhaps days on end without speaking to anyone over the age of five, parents need social outlets where adult conversation can take place. Unfortunately, some parents in this situation can expect too much. For example, they might visit a friend and simply stay too long. The children may have been able to amuse themselves for a couple of hours but not four or five. Other parents completely ignore their children when visiting, happily chatting until there is a crisis. Children learn to amuse themselves best when they receive some attention from adults while they are busy. Don't wait until your child interrupts before giving attention.

If your child frequently interrupts or is naughty while you are on the telephone, follow these guidelines to overcome this problem.

1. **Explain that you would like your child not to interrupt when you are on the phone**

    Explain the ground rules to be followed when the phone rings. These could include answering the phone unless Mummy wants to answer it (see guidelines for teaching the child to answer the phone, pages 189–90), finding something to do quietly while Mummy is on the phone and not interrupting while Mummy is on the phone.

2. **Ask your child to state the rules**

    'What do you have to remember when the phone rings?' Praise the child for correctly stating the rules.

3. **Set aside a morning to help your child learn the correct thing to do**

    You need to decide here whether to teach your child the necessary behaviour in a single session or to spread it out over several weeks. The former is quicker but requires you to be organised and to set aside the time.

4. **Get out some quiet toys or activities that the child can play with while you are on the phone**

    Examples of quiet activities include colouring books, picture books, soft toys, puzzles and blocks. It is also a good idea to purchase a toy phone the child can use while you are on the phone.

5. **Remind your child of the rules**

    On the day you start, restate the ground rules.

6. **Dial a number**

    Dial your own telephone number. Speak briefly on the phone as you normally would. If the child continues to play with the toys, speak for a few seconds more and praise the child enthusiastically for letting you speak on the phone without interrupting. 'I liked how you waited while I was on the phone, Danielle. Well done.'

7. **If your child interrupts, prompt the correct behaviour**
   If the child stops what he is doing and tries to interrupt, prompt him to find something to do. 'Remember the rules. When Mummy's on the phone, find something to do.'

8. **Praise compliance with the rules**
   If the child complies, praise her for finding something to do.

9. **Use quiet time as a back-up consequence**
   If the child does not comply, say 'excuse me' to your pretend caller and immediately put the child into quiet time.

10. **Increase the length of the pretend calls**
    Practise this basic routine with pretend callers about ten times, gradually increasing the length of the conversation up to about two minutes until the child is performing the correct behaviour. Spread these calls out over an entire morning.

11. **Arrange for a spouse, friend or neighbour to call you at a specific time**
    Keep the conversation brief, between two and three minutes. If the child copes with this real call, praise her enthusiastically and offer a snack or treat as a back-up reward. Over the next few days give the child several further practice runs.

12. **Phase out reminders**
    Gradually phase out reminders of the rules before beginning to speak on the phone. Every time the child complies without having to be reminded, offer praise enthusiastically.

13. **Keep calls brief**
    When your child is around, try to keep calls brief. If you wish to have a long conversation, wait until your child is having a nap, is in bed at night or is at preschool. Any time your child interrupts, be prepared to back up your instructions with quiet time as soon as the problem arises. Don't wait until the child is screaming before you act.

Teaching children to answer the telephone

It is also important for children to learn how to answer the phone politely and, eventually, to make their own calls under supervision. They need to know what to do if the phone rings when the parent is outside, on the toilet, in the shower or otherwise temporarily unavailable. Some children never learn these skills properly. Many problems can be avoided if parents teach their preschoolers correct telephone etiquette. It is interesting that even some adults find making telephone calls a difficult experience, and become anxious whenever they have to ring someone other than close friends or family. Some simply avoid using the phone unless they absolutely have to.

When preschoolers answer the phone they can make several blunders. They may pick up the phone and then not speak; they may use a silly, rude, cheeky or impolite voice when answering; or they may answer but not tell the person for whom the call was intended, and so on. One way to teach a preschooler to answer the telephone is to buy a toy phone to practise on. Using the telephone correctly is quite a complex skill and preschoolers should always be supervised when they answer the phone. Here are some steps to help you help your child.

1. **Choose a time when you have about thirty minutes to spare**
   Ask your child to get her toy phone.
2. **Explain the rules of the telephone game**
   The rules for answering could be: when you hear the phone ringing, first ask Mum or Dad whether you can answer it. If the answer is yes, then lift the receiver and say hello and your name. 'Hello, Julian Palmer speaking.' Speak in a nice voice. If the caller wants to speak to Mum or Dad, say, 'Just a minute, please', then put the phone down and quickly get Mum or Dad.
3. **Ask the child to state the rules**
   'What do you do when the phone goes ring, ring?' If the child can state the correct sequence, praise her. If only some parts are correct then praise the correct parts and tell her what she missed out. If after three attempts the child is still confused, move to the next step.

4. **Model the first step in the sequence**
    This might involve an interaction such as the following:
    'Watch what I do. Let's pretend the phone rings. "Ring, ring." What should I do first?'
    'Mummy, can I answer it?'
    'Good girl. Yes, you ask Mummy or Daddy first.'
    'Mummy, the phone's ringing. Can I get it?'

5. **Let the child practise the first step**
    'Okay. You try it. "Ring, ring."' If the child correctly performs the first step, offer praise and encouragement and move on to teaching the next step in the same way.
    'Now let's do the first two steps. Watch what I do.' Let the child pretend he is you. Pretend the phone rings, ask the child for permission to answer, then pick up the receiver, say hello and give your name. Now let your child practise the first two steps.
    'Okay. It's your turn now. "Ring, ring."'
    'Mummy, can I get it?'
    'Yes.'
    'Hello, Rebecca Smith speaking.'
    'That was excellent. You remembered to ask and then said your name very nicely.'

6. **Practise all other steps**
    Continue in the above manner until the child masters all steps in the sequence.

7. **Arrange for a friend to call you**
    If the child remembers the first step, praise her immediately. If she needs help, offer it. It may take several weeks before she can answer the phone confidently. Offer praise each time the correct sequence is remembered.

8. **Deal with silly behaviour on the phone by immediately taking the phone from the child**
    Tell the child what he did wrong.

9. **Back up your action with quiet time**
    If the child becomes disruptive, back up with quiet time or time out as necessary.

Behaviour in the community

Shopping trips

Shopping with children can be an exhausting experience, particularly when they are tired or hungry, or when they misbehave. In one study we conducted, 99 per cent of the parents who were interviewed as they were leaving a major supermarket said that shopping with children was difficult for most parents, and 66 per cent had actually experienced problems with their children on that trip. Common problems include children demanding that parents buy them things, touching merchandise without permission, running up and down aisles, getting lost, whining and occasional temper tantrums.

Most preschoolers tire quickly and become bored easily. This is especially so if the parent has a lot of shopping to do or becomes so preoccupied that the children are ignored until they become disruptive. Many parents prefer to shop without their children but others simply have no choice. If parents work full time they may have to shop at times when the stores are very busy.

The main reason children become difficult on shopping trips is that there is nothing for them to do. Bored kids often become disruptive. This is particularly likely if the parent does not involve the child in the shopping trip and simply ignores him unless he is naughty. This is a formula for bad behaviour.

The following suggestions form a step-by-step guide that teaches children to become good shoppers and to behave appropriately when they are on shopping trips with parents. Rather than seeing shopping as a headache, try to view each shopping trip as an opportunity for your child to learn something about becoming a skilled shopper. Focus on what the child should be doing rather than on how to stop bad behaviour.

Plan a series of brief shopping trips over a period of a week. Your first trips should be quite short, about five minutes, gradually increasing up to a thirty-minute excursion to the supermarket.

1. **Discuss with your child what you expect from good shoppers**
   Gain the child's attention through either a simple request for a chat or a direct instruction. 'Tim, come here, will you? I'd like to talk to you about what we're doing this morning.'

2. **Prepare the child for the outing by describing what is going to happen**
   'We're going to the supermarket this morning.' Tell the child how long the trip will take.

3. **State briefly, simply and calmly what the problem was the last time you went shopping**
   'Jeremy, the last time we went shopping you forgot to stay close to Mummy.'

4. **Describe the four rules for being a good shopper**
   i. Good shoppers stay within arm's reach of their mother or father.
   ii. Good shoppers only touch things on the shelves or displays when their parents say they can.
   iii. Good shoppers always speak in a clear, pleasant voice.
   iv. Good shoppers do not ask for things during the shopping trip.

   Tell the child why you would like him to obey these rules. 'I don't like it when you demand things when we go shopping. Shopping together will be a happier time for us both if you remember our shopping rules.'

5. **Ask your child to state the rules for being a good shopper**
   Praise your child for stating the rules correctly. Help out if she can't remember them all.

6. **Discuss rewards for being a good shopper**
   Explain to your child that good shoppers can earn special privileges for keeping to the rules. Every two minutes that the child obeys the rules he will be able to earn coloured buttons or a sticker, which can be exchanged for money at the end of the trip. Ask the child if he has any questions. Praise him for being involved in this planning ahead of time.

7. **Get everything you need ready**

   Check to make sure you have everything you need: a watch, a child's purse or wallet and about twenty coloured buttons.

8. **Plan the trip to avoid disrupting your child's normal routine**

   Plan the shopping trip so that it does not disrupt your child's usual mealtimes and avoid shopping trips just before lunch. Plan your day so that the shopping trip occurs after rather than before a nap. This reduces the chance that your child will be tired. Just before leaving, remind the child of the rules for being a good shopper.

9. **Praise your child for being a good shopper**

   If at any time during the trip the child does something you like or tries hard to keep to the four rules, look directly at her and say what she has done. 'Good girl, Peta. You are staying nice and close to Mummy today.'

   Break the trip up into two-minute time periods. At the end of each two minutes, if the child has kept to the rules, take out a coloured button and place it in her purse or pocket. Tell her that she has kept to the rules and how much you like it and how helpful it is. 'Jeannie, that's lovely, you have remembered the shopping rules. Here's your next button for being so helpful.'

10. **Keep your child busy**

    Find something for your child to do during the trip, such as asking him where certain items are; asking him to pass things to you; asking him the price of an item; asking him what he would like to eat; giving him information about certain products; having him help you place items in the trolley; letting him help unload items from the trolley at the checkout; and having him help you plan a shopping list.

11. **Deal with disruptions by making your child wait**

    If your child misbehaves by breaking any of the four rules, stop what you are doing, gain your child's attention, and say that she can't earn any more buttons for two minutes. 'Sarah, you touched something without asking. Now you will have to wait another two minutes before you get a button.'

12. **Allow your child to do some shopping**

    Once you have completed your shopping, count the number of

buttons the child has earned, exchange them for money and let the child shop by himself for some small item. Each button could be worth between five and twenty cents; therefore, a twenty-minute trip could be worth one to two dollars. One way of working out how much each button should be worth is to simply calculate the amount you usually spend on your child on shopping trips and then divide that mount by the number of two-minute blocks on the planned trip.

13. **Review the trip**

Praise your child's accomplishments. Briefly and calmly describe any rules the child forgot to follow. This programme tries to overcome the problem of this behaviour on shopping trips by preparing the child in advance, setting clear rules, giving the child something to do to help, catching her being good and giving her a chance to practise being a good shopper. The money children earn becomes their budget. They need to find something they can afford. They have to learn to handle money by paying the correct amount and by receiving change if there is any. If we expect children to learn to make wise choices in their purchasing when they have pocket money or work for wages, we must start preparing them as early as possible.

The above programme works best for children who are reasonable at following directions. If your child is also difficult at home, use the plan for increasing compliance with requests before you tackle this programme. When children practise a new skill such as becoming a good shopper it is better for parents to give their child more opportunities to master the skill. This is why several short trips over a period of a few days is better than taking your child shopping only once a week.

Leave difficult shopping trips, such as shopping for clothing or a long supermarket trip, until your child can cope with shorter ones without difficulty. In the first few weeks, avoid situations that require the child to wait for long periods.

Travelling in the car

'Jaasson! Daddy, Jason's on my side!' Family outings can become disasters when children play up in the car. Kids often seem to choose the car to try out some of their most irritating behaviour, whether it be whining, complaining, screaming, refusing to stay in their seat belts, fighting, teasing or generally being a pest. These behaviours can be quite dangerous; they can distract the parent from concentrating on driving and thus cause accidents and even fatalities.

All passengers, including children, should wear safety restraints at all times while travelling in the car. Children must also be taught to behave themselves in the car so that the driver can concentrate. Parents are often vulnerable while they are driving. Kids in the back are not within easy reach and the adult has to try to concentrate on two things at once: the road and the children's behaviour. It is a time when many parents are quite inconsistent and don't enforce ground rules.

From the child's point of view, car travel can be boring. It can seem to them that the ride takes forever, particularly if they have nothing to do. Some children are fine on short trips around town but become quite difficult on longer journeys. Others are difficult every time they get into the car. Here are some ideas to help your child learn more acceptable behaviour in the car.

1. **Avoid disrupting your child's normal routines**
    If possible, plan your trip for shortly but not immediately after a meal so children don't get hungry or tired too soon.
2. **Discuss your travel plans**
    Tell your child the destination and how long the trip will take. Answer any questions about the trip.
3. **Have some special activities available**
    Select some special activities or games (such as hand-held computer games) for the children to amuse themselves with on the journey.
4. **Discuss the ground rules**
    Explain what you expect in the car by describing the desired behaviour. 'Elizabeth, when we travel in the car, I want you to remember to stay in your car seat and sit quietly. Don't squeal

or ask me to buy you anything. Can you remember that? I will be trying to drive us all safely to the shops and home again.'

5. **Ask your child to repeat the rules**
'So, what do you have to remember?'

6. **Speak up and praise your child for cooperative behaviour**
'That's right. You remembered what you have to do when we're in the car. Well done.'

7. **Explain consequences for good and bad behaviour**
Let your child know what will happen if she behaves well on the trip, for example there might be a small treat when she arrives. Let her know, too, what will happen if the car rules are broken. You should decide ahead of time exactly how to deal with disruptiveness.

8. **Keep your child busy**
Engage your child in an activity shortly after setting off. Speak to him, ask questions and offer praise every so often during the trip. If the trip is a longish one (over an hour), offer a snack when he is behaving appropriately. On long trips, schedule breaks every few hours so that he can get out, run around, go to the toilet and so on.

9. **Deal with disruptions by describing the problem behaviour and then the correct behaviour**
If a disruption occurs, gain the child's attention. Calmly but firmly describe what the child has done wrong. 'Tanya, don't push your brother.' Then describe what she should do instead. 'Keep on your side of the car and get out your scratch-and-sniff book if you want something to do.'

10. **Back it up with a 'stop' instruction and a warning**
If the problem continues, give an instruction and a warning that further disruption will lead to you stopping the car. 'Peter, sit up properly and leave Daniel alone. If it happens again I'll stop the car.'

11. **If the problem occurs again, stop the car**
Tell the child that her behaviour is unacceptable and must stop immediately. Stop the car and put the child out on the side of the road for one minute of quiet time. Stay close and ignore protests.

12. **Review the trip**

    If your child has behaved well on the trip, praise him, describing the correct behaviour.

13. **Provide a back-up reward**

    If the child kept to the ground rules, offer any back-up rewards that you agreed to before the trip.

Business trips

Sometimes it is necessary to take children to places that involve standing in a queue or sitting in a waiting room, for example banks and doctors' surgeries. These kinds of situations can result in misbehaviour, particularly if children need to remain in one place for a long time. They get bored, squirm, wriggle and make a fuss. For important business trips that you know will take considerable time it is better to leave your child with someone. Sometimes, however, this is simply not possible. Here are some suggestions for dealing with children during such outings.

1. **Tell your child where you will be going and what you expect**

    Prior to leaving, explain where you will be going. Tell the child she will have to stand or sit quietly next to you and wait until it is your turn to be seen by the doctor or served at the bank.

2. **Find something the child can do**

    Ask your child what he could do while he waits. Suggestions could include sitting quietly, playing with toys, looking at a book or drawing on a piece of paper. If the appropriate materials are unlikely to be available, suggest what might be taken along. Ask the child to get these items ready.

3. **Select a suitable back-up reward for good behaviour**

    Ask the child what kind of small reward, activity or treat she would like to earn for behaving appropriately on the business trip.

4. **Praise your child for good behaviour in the car**

    If the child behaved appropriately in the car, praise him.

5. **Remind your child of the rules**

    Once you have arrived, remind the child of the ground rules that apply when you both go inside.

6. **Set your child up in an activity**

   Set up the child in a chair or on the floor away from the main thoroughfare and provide an activity, for example a pencil and paper. Before turning away from the child to seek services, ask her if she remembers what to do.

7. **Attend to your child periodically while you wait for service**

   If you have to stand in a queue, tell the child where you will be moving to and invite him to bring what he is doing to show you every so often. Use these instances as opportunities to praise his good behaviour and to make comments that will extend play. 'That's a great horse you've drawn there, John. Can you draw a fence around the horse?' If you have to sit in a waiting room, follow the same procedure.

8. **Give a 'stop' instruction to deal with misbehaviour, and provide back-up consequences**

   If the child misbehaves, go to her and give an instruction to stop. Calmly but firmly describe what you want her to do. If the misbehaviour continues or increases, go to her, tell her you don't like it when she ... (describe the behaviour that bothers you). Ignore further protests and attempt to restrain the child either by picking her up or holding her firmly at your side until she has calmed down. Avoid cuddling the child or nagging about the misbehaviour. As soon as she is quiet, attempt to set her up in an activity while you wait.

9. **Provide positive attention for good behaviour**

   If the child has behaved well on the trip, praise him then offer the small treat or reward previously selected.

10. **Describe any problem behaviours that arose**

    If any misbehaviour occurred, calmly explain what it was and describe what you want the child to remember next time. Do not provide the back-up treat. Tell the child she can try again next time you go on a trip to the bank or doctors' office.

Leaving children with friends, relatives or in childcare

All children have to learn to cope with temporary separations from their parents. Parents need time to themselves occasionally. They get sick, need a break from constant childcare, start work, meet appointments and so on. Children often benefit from the opportunity to spend time with someone else. However, some will not tolerate separation from their parents. They may appear terrified by the prospect of separation and cling, scream and protest quite furiously if the parent tries to leave.

Giving in and deciding to never go out on your own because of your child's reaction to temporary separations is a mistake. It will encourage more clinging behaviour and, rather than relieve the child's anxiety, it can make it worse. You should also investigate as best you can that your child-minder, whether friend, relative or paid help, looks after your child properly. Some children are neglected and can even be abused while in the care of others.

If you have persistent problems when you attempt to leave your child with sitters, check to make sure that the problem has not been made worse because of the way the separation takes place. Prepare your child in advance and follow these guidelines.

1. **Get everything ready**
   Make sure you have all the materials that the child-minder needs to take proper care of your child, for example medicine, favourite toys, games and equipment.
2. **Explain what is going to happen**
   Prepare the child for the separation by explaining where she will be going, where you are going and when you will return to pick her up.
3. **Ask your child what he should do**
   Tell your child what he can expect and ask him to tell you how he is expected to behave while you are out. If he can't tell you, describe the expected behaviour yourself. Answer any questions he has.
4. **Take something special**
   Make sure your child takes a special toy or other item.
5. **Introduce your child to the child-minder and any other children present**
   Many preschoolers need their parents to pave the way in new situations.

6. **Set your child up in an activity**
   Suggest something the child might like to do.
7. **Prepare the child-minder**
   Explain any special needs to the child-minder, and always give a contact number in case of emergencies.
8. **Say farewell to your child**
   Remind your child of where you are going and when you will return. Say farewell to the child without fussing. Ignore protests or complaints and leave.
9. **Greet the child warmly as soon as you return**
   Ask questions about what he did and about his day. Spend some time alone with him. Be prepared for him to be a bit clingy; this is quite common after brief separations.
10. **Praise your child for any accomplishments**
    If the child-minder tells you about something interesting the child has done or accomplished, show an interest and praise your child for not fussing when you left.

Conclusions

During the preschool years children can differ a lot in their social, emotional and language skills. At this time, differences in children's language abilities show up partly as a result of the way parents speak to their children. Some children enjoy extended conversations with their parents and can be great company, while others talk very little. Preschoolers like and need routine, and are often keen on doing things for themselves. It is during this time that many of the skills they will need for school are being established – the ability to follow simple instructions, find and go to the toilet when they need to, and recite their name, address and telephone number. Children are also learning to mix and play with other children.

CHAPTER 7

School-age children

The start of formal schooling brings with it some important changes in the lives of both children and parents. When a child starts school, their parents' influence on the child's development begins to change. Parents, while remaining the most important figures in a child's life, start to realise that their child is increasingly affected by experiences outside the home. Children's experiences at school have a major impact on their development. Their academic success and relationships with teachers influence how they view themselves and their opportunities in life. Their friendships with other children and peer relationships affect their self-esteem and how they handle social situations. By the time children reach seven or eight they become capable of more complex thinking and problem-solving. They also become more independent and are able to undertake many more tasks for themselves.

School-age children can contribute to the running of the household. They should be encouraged to help with making beds, washing dishes, helping with house cleaning and other chores. Many parents start giving children pocket money during this time. Children begin to develop their own interests and need less help to get started with activities. Children often want to be involved in music, sport, drama, art and other recreational activities outside the home. Some will be enrolled in organised lessons or after-school activities.

The period from the age of six or seven until eleven or twelve, when many girls and some boys start to mature physically, can also be a testing time for family relationships. If parents have not established basic cooperation with family rules by the time the child reaches ten or eleven, they can have a very difficult time indeed. Children at this age are bigger, stronger and more difficult to handle. Parents can experience a variety of new challenges relating to their children's development and behaviour. Several issues can arise relating to school, including difficulties in getting a child to attend school, problems with reading, maths and other academic areas, problems with disruptive behaviour at school and problems with completing homework. At home, many of the behavioural problems seen during the preschool period, such as disobedience, aggression, sibling rivalry, excessive demands and complaints, can continue. Other children develop more internalising problems during this period, such as fear, worry and anxiety, depression, shyness and low self-esteem.

As children move through their primary schooling, parents' strategies for dealing with behaviour also need to change gradually. Though most of the principles and strategies used with younger children can still be used with school-age children, older children are better able to think of solutions to their own problems, particularly after the age of nine or ten. Parents need to look for ways of encouraging children to solve more of their own problems. Children start to have opinions about how they are treated, and they will express them. They will also express opinions about fairness and justice, and about how they or their friends are treated. They can also become more secretive and skilled at breaking adult rules.

Some parents whose children have been generally cooperative up to the age of eight or nine may be unprepared for challenges to their authority as their children approach adolescence. Parents need to be able to compromise and seek out children's opinions. They also need to help children learn to be respectful and to express their opinions and disagreements in acceptable ways.

Specific issues relating to school

Starting school

In most countries, children start school at the age of five or six. Most children will have had some kind of preschool experience involving separation from the parent for periods of time, but starting regular primary school somehow seems different for both parents and children. For some parents, this may mean that for the first time they have time to pursue their own career or other interests. It is also a reminder to many parents that their child is growing up. This is something many parents have mixed feelings about.

Some children cannot wait to start school, and eagerly look forward to their first day. For other children the reality of starting school creates anxiety and worry. It is a time of transition for most children and several important adjustments have to be made. The excitement of getting new uniforms, clothes, books and other school materials is often counteracted by fears of leaving the familiar routines of home and preschool. Children cope better with these transitions when they are prepared for them, and parents have an important role in helping their children settle into school and, indeed, throughout the whole of a child's education. Here are some ideas for preparing children for school entry.

1. Choose a school that will meet your child's needs

For some parents there will be little choice available. The child may be required by local education authorities to attend the closest school unless parents are prepared for the expense of sending the child to a private school. The advantage of attending a local school is that the child will get to know other children in the neighbourhood, there will be less travelling to and from school, and it will be easier for the parents to become involved in the child's school activities. It is often extremely difficult for parents to gauge the quality of education a child is likely to receive at a particular school, whether public or private; it very much depends on the particular teacher and classroom your child is placed in each year. A school is only as good as its current complement of teachers. Schools develop reputations both good and indifferent for reasons other than the quality of education they provide. There are many excellent teachers in schools in less affluent areas, and there can be incompetent teachers in more advantaged schools. A parent may not know who their child's teacher is going to be until just before the beginning of term. There is an element of luck involved, and in any case parents need to accept that teachers have to cater for the needs of all the children in the class.

As a parent, you can do much to find out about schools. Speak to other parents whose children have recently attended local schools. Find out who will be taking your child's class and seek opinions from parents who have had children in that teacher's class. Don't speak to just one parent, talk to several. Speak to the teacher personally and to older children at the school who know the teacher. When you enrol your child at the school, ask specific questions about its general philosophy and approach. Find out whether the school provides special programmes for slow learners, remedial help, extension programmes for children with special abilities in maths, languages and reading, and so on. Find out about school rules and policy on discipline problems. Find out what the child needs to bring on the first day. All schools provide some information to parents on many of these issues. However, be prepared to seek clarification if you are unsure about particular points. Take note of how the school principal and office staff deal with your questions and concerns. Do they answer your questions openly and honestly? Do they suggest ways in which you might help the school or become involved in school activities?

2. **Talk to your child about starting school**

Long before your child actually begins school, you can raise the topic. This is best done in the six months or so prior to the child starting school. Answer your child's questions about school, but try not to overload the child with information all at once. It will be confusing and possibly upsetting as they gradually get used to the idea of starting school.

3. **Read to your child about starting school**

There are a number of children's books concerned with starting school. Check out a local bookstore or library that specialises in children's literature. These books can be read to children as a way of preparing them for what lies ahead.

4. **Tell your child when they will be starting**

Tell your child the starting date about two months beforehand.

5. **Take your child to visit the school**

Ask the principal if there is an open day at the local school. Otherwise, one weekend, take your child down to the school to have a look around. It is helpful if you can take an older brother or sister who can explain where the junior classes are, where the toilets are and what happens on the first day.

6. **Let your child know that you will be there on the first day**

On the first day, most schools permit parents of new entrants to stay with their children until they are settled into the new environment. This is often reassuring to a youngster who may be feeling anxious. If you say you are going to stay, make sure you do.

7. **Involve your child in buying things she needs for starting school**
This will include stationery, a schoolbag and lunch box, clothes or uniform, and other items required by the school.

On the first day at school stay with your child as long as you are required. Make yourself as unobtrusive as possible but gently prompt the child to become involved in the classroom's activities rather than clinging to you. Some children who have had separation problems at preschool will experience similar problems now. If your child usually gets upset when you leave but settles quickly once you are gone, be prepared to explain that you are going, say goodbye and leave. It might take a few days for the child to get used to being in the new situation. Most children quickly adapt to the excitement and challenge of starting school. Occasionally, children can develop a fear of going to school (school phobia). Usually such children are not frightened of school per se (although some can be) but are afraid of separating from their parents. If your child is extremely difficult to get to school, complains of aches and pains on school mornings, or screams and in other ways protests about going to school, be prepared to seek professional advice about how best to handle the situation. Generally speaking, it is very important that such a child miss as little school as possible. Speak to your child's teacher or principal, or your family doctor, who can tell you where you can obtain appropriate professional assistance.

Getting children into a good morning routine

School mornings go much more smoothly for everyone when children get themselves into a good morning routine. This means learning to do what is required in the morning and doing most things for themselves without their parents having to give constant reminders. At this age children can be expected to become more independent in getting themselves out of bed, getting dressed, eating breakfast, brushing their teeth, packing their schoolbag with everything they need for their day's activities, and being ready to leave at a particular time.

Parents can get into difficulties in the morning when they try to do everything for their child, or are disorganised or late in getting up. In some homes the morning routine is unpleasant, with parents having to yell at their children to get them out of bed and moving. Some children, particularly those who have trouble concentrating on a task, are easily distracted and disorganised and can find the morning a very difficult time. Here are some ideas for making your morning routine more pleasant and less stressful for everyone.

1. **Make sure your child goes to bed at a reasonable time**
   This is important because children with insufficient sleep find it hard to wake up, and are often grumpy and irritable in the morning.

2. **Be organised**
   Each night, prepare everything you and your child need for the following day. Place your child's school clothes conveniently in the child's bedroom so that they are easy to locate and put on. Get up early, because if you are running late, you will not have time to let your child do the things they need to do without your help (such as getting themselves dressed).

3. **Start an activity chart for the morning routine**
   An activity chart can help a child learn the steps they must follow in the morning. The first step is to make the chart and cut Velcro into strips. On each strip, place words, a picture or a drawing that illustrates a step or activity the child must complete. The chart can be attached to the wall in a convenient location such as in the kitchen or child's bedroom. When the child completes each step, the corresponding Velcro strip can be added to the space next to the activity. For the first few days, the child can be given one prompt or reminder to complete the step. Praise your child enthusiastically for doing each step on their own.

4. **Keep reminders to a minimum**
   Children will not learn to do things for themselves if they become reliant on reminders. Once a child can complete each step with only one prompt or reminder, phase out reminders. Pay particular attention to your child when they perform a step on their own without first being reminded.

5. **Avoid getting angry or irritated**
   Speak pleasantly to your child in the morning. Seeing you get angry and irritated makes it harder for children to learn what is expected of them.

6. Provide a back-up reward

If the child completes all the steps without having to be reminded, give her a back-up reward, such as a special snack treat in her lunch or a special game or activity after school (if there is not time in the morning).

FIGURE 4: GETTING READY FOR SCHOOL

Place the activity star next to the corresponding task once completed.

Getting children into a good homework routine

As children progress through school they will be expected to spend at least some time doing homework and independent study. Schools and individual teachers vary in the amount of such work expected. Children from Grades 4 to 7 can expect anywhere from ten to sixty minutes of homework each night. In order for children to make satisfactory progress in their studies, it is important for them to get into good study habits. Most homework is revision, and children will normally have done similar examples or exercises at school.

Many parents experience difficulty from time to time over their child's unwillingness to do their homework, and children sometimes make it hard for parents by asking for help the night before a project is due, help that may require a trip to the library to obtain resource material. Some children refuse to do homework at all, or their attempts are poorly done with little care. Parents often blame the child's attitude for such problems and can accuse her of being lazy and irresponsible. This often makes the problem worse. One father I know used to require his ten-year-old to do at least one hour of maths study each day. He would sit next to the boy with a ruler and quiz him on his times-tables. Every time the boy got a sum wrong, the father would yell at him and whack him with the ruler. The child did not learn his tables correctly and became so worried about school work that his grades became worse and worse.

Nevertheless, parents do have an important role in helping their children get into proper study habits and routines. This includes organising a well-lit space where children can work with few distractions, taking an interest in their work, assisting them to find resources and other materials, and establishing consistent rules relating to completion of homework.

Remember that you are not your child's teacher. Children are expected to tackle problems in the way they have been shown at school. Children differ widely in their abilities and the time they need to grasp concepts and new ideas. Doing homework should not be a time of stress or pressure. It should be a pleasant time where parents can offer encouragement and help if the child needs it. Here are some guidelines for dealing with homework problems.

1. **Let your child relax after school**

   Children need time to wind down after school, just as adults do after work. Let your child tell you about her day at school. Have a snack prepared so that she associates coming home with a pleasant interaction before commencing homework. Do not let your child turn on the television or computer as soon as she walks in from school.

2. **Arrange a proper place for your child to study**

   Primary school children often want to do their homework in the family living area rather than in their bedroom. A space should be cleared at the kitchen table and all distractions eliminated. Children do not need absolute quiet to work; after all, the classroom is rarely peaceful. Nevertheless, it is a good idea to get your child a desk with a desk lamp to do some project work. Once in high school, children can be expected to work completely independently in their bedroom or study.

3. **Select a specific time for doing homework**

   Homework is probably best done immediately after children have had time to wind down after school but before they are allowed to go out and play or watch television. If other children come around to play, tell them to come back at a specific time when your child has finished his homework.

4. **Ask your child about homework**

   Most children will tell their parents honestly what they are required to do. It might involve learning spelling words, writing a sentence or two, working on a project, summarising a paragraph or doing a few maths problems. Find out when the work has to be completed.

5. **Help your child get started**

   Many children who have difficulties with homework, either because they don't understand the work or because they would rather be doing something else, need some help in getting into a good routine. Helping your child get started does not mean doing the work for her. Be prepared to sit down at the table with the child. Ask them what needs to be done. Remind your child of the ground rules. Playing or watching television comes *after* completing her homework.

6. **Offer praise and encouragement while your child is working**

   Comments such as 'You're working well on your homework tonight' or 'Great. That's five questions you've done already' are particularly useful in the early stages to encourage your child to remain on task and to persist with homework.

7. **Wait until your child asks for help before giving it**

   Children should be given the chance to tackle the task on their own before parents come to their rescue.

8. **Deal with requests for help by using incidental teaching**

   Requests for help are a good time for parents to use the incidental teaching strategies discussed in Chapter 4. The basic idea is not simply to give the answer to a question but to prompt the child to solve the problem himself. Be careful not to overdo it. For example, if a child asks you how to spell the word 'factory' without having attempted to spell it first, you could say, 'How do you think you spell it? Get out a piece of paper and try to spell it yourself first and I'll come and have a look.' Offer praise when the child attempts the word. If he gets the word right, offer further praise. If the word is wrong, rather than saying, 'No, that's wrong,' point out the letters that are correct first. 'That's nearly right. The first four letters are right. Have a look at the ending. Is it "ery" or "ory"? Yes, "ory", that's right. Well done.' If after one prompt he still cannot get the correct answer, tell him what it is. Children will sometimes get frustrated if every question they ask is met with responses such as 'Look it up in the dictionary first'. Parents will find that their children are more cooperative if help is given relatively freely initially, with perhaps one or two attempts at incidental teaching.

9. **Avoid criticising the child's work**

   When children are doing their homework, they need encouragement for correct work and for attempting the task, rather than criticism for mistakes. You may be very tempted to criticise work that is messy or incorrect. Such criticism often backfires and only discourages the child, particularly if it occurs often. It is a good idea to encourage children to do rough copies of work first; a final, neater copy can be done for handing in at school.

10. Check your child's work before finishing

Children often want to show their parents the work they have completed. Some will ask whether it is correct or ask you to give your opinion on how good the work is. Do not feel you have to make sure your child's work is perfect before allowing her to hand it in. It can be upsetting for a child who has worked hard for fifteen minutes writing a paragraph only to have the parent point out twenty spelling or punctuation mistakes. The ideas the child has expressed in the story may be very good. When checking work like this, correct, if you must, only two or three mistakes. Try to find something positive to say about the child's effort.

11. Offer a reward following the completion of homework

This could involve praising the child for finishing his homework or allowing him to watch television, play on the computer or go and play before dinner. Some parents may feel that a more powerful incentive is needed if the child has been very difficult at homework time in the past. For example, Jonathan and Andrea, Peter's parents, set up a special homework chart on the refrigerator like the one in Figure 5 (page 212).

Each day that Peter completed his homework without a fuss he could earn points, which were exchanged at the end of the week for a back-up reward. His parents wrote down three things he had to do each night: bring home his homework book (one point), start his homework by 4.15 p.m. without complaining (two points) and work on his homework without interruption for a minimum of fifteen minutes (five points). If he earned thirty-six points by the end of the week, he received his back-up reward, which was $5 towards a new skateboard he wanted.

If after following the above programme your child continues to have problems with schoolwork, be prepared to discuss the problem with her teacher. Your child may need remedial assistance or help in one or more subject areas. Remember that children's learning and academic performance is strongly influenced by motivation as well as ability. One of the best ways to encourage better motivation is to focus on the child's successes rather than the things they do incorrectly. Giving a

FIGURE 5: A SAMPLE HOMEWORK CHART

Homework chart

Week beginning _____

Tasks	Points	Mon	Tues	Wed	Thurs	Fri	Total
Brought homework book home today	1				1	1	2
Started homework by 4.15 p.m. today without complaining	2	2		2		2	6
Worked for fifteen minutes without interruption	5	5	5	5	5		20
Total points earned	8	7	5	7	6	3	28

Fill in the points earned for each task and add them up at the end of the week.

child lectures and pep talks, or scolding, nagging or threatening because of their 'attitude' to schoolwork often achieves very little other than making the child feel less capable than they really are.

Parents need to accept that their child is not brilliant, and that no amount of pressure to succeed will alter this. Parents can, however, encourage their children to perform to the best of their abilities by helping them get into good work habits and routines and by providing encouragement, support and help as needed.

Behavioural problems at school

One of the most worrying problems for parents relates to their child's conduct at school. Common problems include inattentiveness, not following the teacher's directions, distracting other children through silly behaviour such as swinging on chairs, pulling faces or making loud noises, getting into fights in the playground, failing to complete set work, calling out and wandering around the classroom when they should be seated. Teachers generally expect a certain standard of conduct from students. Children who persistently break basic classroom rules will find themselves getting into trouble, and it can be very difficult for parents to know what to do in this circumstance.

Children can be disruptive for a variety of reasons. Sometimes, disruptiveness at school can be an extension of disruptive behaviour at home. These children are generally uncooperative and defy adult authority. Other children can be disruptive because the work is too hard, or not challenging enough in the case of very bright children. Disruptiveness can also be due to a teacher trying to enforce excessively rigid rules. Many factors that cause behavioural problems at home can be at work in the classroom, for example the teacher ignores good behaviour and only attends to the child when she is disruptive. A child may have a lower intellectual ability than the majority of his classmates, or a specific learning difficulty in one or more subject areas such as reading or maths, which influences his behaviour at school.

There are several things a parent can do to try to resolve a school-related behavioural problem. Most of these strategies require the active cooperation of the child's teacher. A home–school behaviour contract is one such strategy.

1. **Clarify the problem**
    Be clear about what the child is doing that is causing a problem. Make an appointment to speak to your child's teacher at a convenient time – after school is often the best time because the teacher will have fewer distractions.
2. **Share information with the teacher**
    Tell the teacher about the relevant difficulties you experience with your child and let her teacher know what steps, if any, you have taken in trying to resolve the problem, such as taking the child to see a psychologist. Teachers can often gain a better appreciation of your child and her circumstances if you tell them

about the steps you are taking or intend taking in dealing with home problems.

3. **Ask the teacher what you can do to help solve the problem**

Before suggesting a solution, find out how the teacher thinks the problem might be solved. This will convey your interest in trying to help solve the problem and will also encourage the teacher to share his own ideas on handling the difficulty. If the teacher is considering referring the child to a school psychologist, for example, or requesting that the child be suspended, you need to know about this. Some teachers will make quite specific suggestions about things you can do to help, such as supervising homework and making sure the child brings to school everything required for the day's activities.

4. **Find out what specific rules the child needs to follow in the classroom**

This involves encouraging the teacher to be as specific as possible about what the child is expected to do. For example, a Grade 4 pupil might be expected to begin set work promptly, put up their hand if they want to speak rather than calling out, work quietly on set work without disrupting other children, and write down their homework for that day.

5. **Suggest a home–school daily report card as a way of dealing with the problem**

Take along a sample booklet of cards for the teacher to look at, similar to the one in Figure 6. The main idea is that a system of communication be established between home and school regarding the child's behaviour in the classroom. The agreed set of rules the child is to observe in class is written down in the column marked 'classroom goals'. The child carries the home–school card booklet to and from school each day. If she observes the rules during different lessons in the day, the teacher signs the report and allocates an agreed number of points. These points are then exchanged at home for an appropriate back-up reward. If, however, the child fails to earn the agreed number of points, the parent can provide back-up consequences.

FIGURE 6: HOME–SCHOOL DAILY REPORT CARD

Home–school daily report card

Week beginning 26 November

Home goals before school	Possible points	Points	Signature	Comments
Take homeowrk to school	2	2	S. Jones	
Be ready to leave for school by 8.20 a.m.	3			

Classroom goals	Possible points	9.00–10.30	10.45–12.30	1.15–3.00
Begin set work straightaway	2	2		
Obey teacher's instructions	4	4		

Comments   Worked well in the

first session today.

Teacher's signature   *J. Smythe*

Points earned in class (6) + home (2) = 8

Fill in the points earned for each task and add them up at the end of the week.

The main advantage of having the teacher record the child's behaviour is that you as a parent are more likely to receive accurate information about what is happening at school. If the teacher is willing to try the programme, offer to work out the details and discuss the plan with your child. Some teachers may prefer to do this themselves. Suggest that the programme be tested for one week initially and arrange another time to review progress.

6. **Explain the programme to your child**
    Tell your child that you are concerned about his conduct in class and have spoken to his teacher. Let him know he will have to take the signed card booklet to school each day and give it to the teacher. The teacher will fill in the card three times each day and then sign the card at the end of the day. The card must be brought home each day, and you and your child should add up the points together.

7. **Select appropriate rewards for satisfactory performance**
    If the child earns 80 per cent or more of the possible points on that day, provide an appropriate reward on the same day. If the child earns 80 per cent or more of the possible points over the whole week, then another back-up reward should be provided. Andrew and his parents worked out that for the daily reward he would be allowed to either choose his favourite dessert, watch an extra thirty minutes of television or have a game of cards with his father. As a reward at the end of the week he chose being able to have a friend to sleep over on Saturday night and to watch a video.

8. **Select a suitable consequence for poor performance**
    If the child earns below 80 per cent of the possible points on any day, provide an appropriate consequence. Andrew's parents decided that he would not be allowed to watch any television and would be banned from using the family computer on that night.

9. **Trial the programme for one week**
    Tell your child that the programme will stop at the end of one week and his progress will be reviewed at that time. During the first week, make sure you praise your child for good behaviour at school, check the daily points, sign the cards and ensure the cards go to school each day. Provide rewards and consequences as agreed.

10. **Review progress with the teacher**

    Arrange to meet with the teacher to discuss progress. Make any necessary adjustments to the programme, such as providing clearer definitions of the goals. Make sure you thank the teacher for her efforts in helping your child overcome the problem, and arrange for the programme to continue for a further two weeks.

11. **Phase your child off the programme**

    This can be done over a two-week period as follows. In the first week, only give rewards every second day. To earn a back-up reward, the child must earn 80 per cent or better on two consecutive days. When this goal is achieved, increase to three days, then require a whole week before the child receives any back-up rewards. As you phase out the rewards, make sure you keep praising the child for his good performance. Then phase out the use of the monitoring card. Do this by alternating the days on which the child has to take the card. As you phase out the monitoring, arrange to ring the teacher at least once in the week to ensure that the child's behaviour has continued to be satisfactory. The following week the child need not take the card at all. If the child's behaviour deteriorates during the process of phasing him off the programme, simply go back one step and try again.

Discussing problems with teachers

It is important that parents have open channels of communication with their child's school, particularly if the child is experiencing difficulties. To accomplish this, here are a few tips that can help.

1. **Avoid speaking negatively about your child to the teacher**

    Most teachers react negatively to parents being overly critical of their children, even if the child has been quite difficult to deal with at school.

2. **Avoid criticising the school or the teacher's handling of your child**

    This will lead to defensiveness and will often make the school less receptive to your ideas and suggestions about how to solve the problem. If you have a major concern or complaint about a school matter that you feel you cannot discuss with the child's teacher, it is a good idea to discuss the matter with the school principal.

3. **Avoid becoming defensive and making excuses for your child's conduct**
    If there is clear evidence that your child has done something wrong, accept this reality. Don't go on and on and try to justify or explain away your child's behaviour.

4. **Avoid becoming upset and angry**
    Some parents become very upset when their children are in trouble. This strategy often backfires and can make others irritated and defensive. It is never appropriate to threaten or intimidate your child's teacher.

5. **Avoid claiming that your child has special gifts or abilities, unless you know this for certain**
    Some teachers become annoyed by parents who insist that their child is very bright despite the fact that the child has never done very well at school. Parents can easily over-estimate their child's ability. Your child's teacher sees your child's performance in relation to hundreds of other children of the same age.

6. **Avoid telling teachers how they should teach**
    Teachers understandably react negatively to advice from parents about how they should run their classroom.

Parents have an important role in supporting teachers and school in general. Having a positive relationship with your child's teacher is about learning to communicate your child's needs (where appropriate) in a way that is respectful and understanding of the school's responsibilities for all children, as well as your own.

Remedial reading with your child

Reading is perhaps the most important academic skill children are expected to learn at school. Despite the generally recognised value of reading, a significant number of children experience difficulties in learning to read. The reasons are complex, but it is becoming increasingly clear that parents can play an important role in helping children work through reading problems.

'Pause, prompt, praise' is a way of training parents to become remedial tutors for their children at home. The procedures were devised to help children who had fallen several years behind in their reading. The basic idea behind the programme is that parents create a positive atmosphere in which to regularly listen to their child read material of an appropriate level of difficulty. Parents also learn how to positively attend to correct reading performance, and how to correct their child's mistakes. Children's ability to read is strongly influenced by motivation. Children feel discouraged and don't enjoy reading when their efforts are unsuccessful or meet with disapproval. Children with reading difficulties are often afraid of being wrong, and it takes patience and persistence to help them to regain their confidence and sit down and tackle the task again. Here are some guidelines for helping your child improve their reading skills.

1. **Arrange a suitable time and place for hearing your child's reading**

    Set aside ten minutes, three or four times per week. Choose a time that does not clash with your child's favourite television programme or other important activity. Sometimes a few minutes just before bedtime is a good time. To avoid interruptions, ask someone else to answer the phone and make sure other children have something to do. It is important that distractions are minimised, so make sure the television is turned off. Sit beside your child, either on the couch or at the kitchen table. Make sure the session lasts no longer than ten minutes.

2. **Select suitable books for your child**

    This is one of the most important steps in helping your child with a reading problem. Most schools use a series of learning-to-read books that are graded from simple to difficult. Different schools use different series. Often, teachers can send home books for the child to read that are at the same level or below the level the child is using in the classroom. Ask your child's teacher to send home a book that is at an appropriate level of difficulty for your child.

3. **Check the difficulty level of the book**

   Count off fifty words of text and note this point in the book. On a piece of paper write the date and the name of the book. When your child begins reading, put a mark on the paper for each mistake made. Mistakes can be of several different kinds including leaving words out, adding words or reading different words from those in the text. Count only one mistake for each text word incorrectly read. Don't count mistakes that your child self-corrects. Count the number of mistakes made. Take this number away from fifty to give you the number of words read correctly. The book is too difficult if there are more than ten mistakes, and too easy if there are fewer than four mistakes. If your child makes a number of mistakes between these two numbers, the book is at the right level of difficulty. Speak to the child's teacher if your child needs a book of a different level.

4. **Use 'pause, prompt, praise' to help your child become an independent reader**

   This involves helping your child learn to solve problems for himself. The problems referred to are the words that he gets wrong. Figure 7 shows the basic technique. The procedure is divided into two main parts: the steps to follow when your child reads correctly and those to follow when he reads incorrectly. When a child reads correctly, he should be praised. When a child makes a mistake, you should wait for a few seconds (the pause component) to give him a chance to correct the mistake. If he does not accurately self-correct, then prompt with a clue to solve the problem. When he gets the correct word or words, offer praise and encouragement. This basic strategy eliminates any need for the critical comments that are so discouraging to reluctant readers.

5. **Check on your child's progress**

   It is important to continue to assess whether the material your child is reading is at an appropriate level. To do this, simply repeat the procedure you used in assessing the difficulty level to select an appropriate book. Make sure during this check that you don't

FIGURE 7: 'PAUSE, PROMPT, PRAISE' HOME-TUTORING PROCEDURES

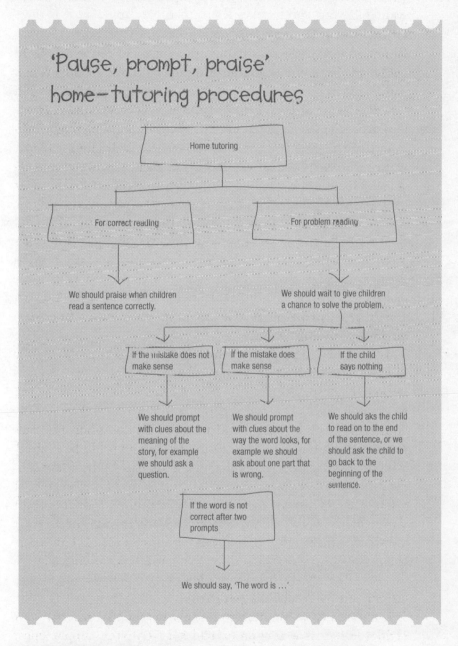

From McNaughton, S.S., Glynn, T., & Robinson, V. 1987, *Pause, prompt, praise: Effective tutoring for remedial reading*, Positive Products, Birmingham, England. Reproduced with permission.

give your child any help if a mistake is made, or praise for correct reading. If your child makes fewer than four mistakes it is time to move on to a more challenging book. Speak to the child's teacher to get one a little harder, or search out the appropriate level at the local public library using the expertise of the professional librarian.

If you are to become an effective remedial tutor for your child, it is important that the time you set aside to listen to your child read is a positive experience. If you are feeling irritable or impatient, it is not a good time to listen to reading. Your feelings will come through and make the activity seem a chore. Success in helping your child improve his reading also involves getting into a consistent routine for regular practice, as this is what your child needs more than anything else.

Bullying

Being bullied can be very traumatic for children and can seriously affect a child's academic progress and attitude to school. Bullying can range from minor teasing to threats of violence and actual assault, such as pinching, pushing, tripping or fighting. Children terrorised by a bully may complain about feeling sick and suffer stomach aches before school; their sleep can be disturbed with nightmares, and bedwetting may be a problem. Bullying can take many different forms, such as older children demanding younger children give them money, the stealing of a child's school lunch, being tripped up, pushed, made to stand at the back of a line, or being ridiculed or called names. Some bullies will exclude other children from their games, spread rumours about them or harass them through phone calls, texts or email messages. Children with perfectly normal features, such as ginger hair, freckles, awkward gaits, big noses, ears that stick out, or who are members of a minority group, can be prime targets. Children who are small for their age, shy and not very assertive or very athletic, or who are effeminate in mannerisms, can be teased and tormented.

Some of the worst bullying occurs when several children decide to pick on a child, making that child's life a nightmare. Parents of children on the receiving end of bullying are often extremely worried. They are frequently at a loss to know how to advise their child to deal with the problem, particularly when the child pleads with the parent not to contact the school. Children often fear reprisals if they are seen to have told tales or dobbed in the culprits. This is a particular problem with teenagers who are immature for their age. They may put up with months of bullying without telling anyone.

What should parents do if they discover that their child has been bullied at school? Parents can sometimes help children handle minor teasing and bullying by helping them change the way they deal with the problem. Many children who are bullied make the problem worse by acting in ways that reward the culprit. For example, many bullies continue victimising particular children because the harassment pays off. The child reacts, becomes upset, cries, gives in, pays the money, gives the bully his lunch, and so on. These reactions may reward the bully who is used to being able to hurt or threaten others to make them give in to his demands. Often the behaviour at school is an extension of how the child behaves at home. Parents can help their child by using a two-pronged approach: coaching the child in better ways of reacting, and working with the school to address the problem. Here are some guidelines for helping children reduce bullying.

1. **Encourage your child to tell you what has happened**

   Listen carefully as your child describes what has happened; ask whether it has happened before, and if so how often. Ask what the child did to deal with the problem. 'When he called you a sissy, what did you do?' Children will sometimes give vague answers, such as 'Nothing' or 'I tried to ignore him', and if this happens, prompt your child to elaborate and be more specific. 'When you say you did nothing, tell me exactly what you said or did.' Role playing can be useful here. 'Okay, I'm Bill, I come up and call you a sissy and push you out of line. What do you do?'

2. **Stay calm**

   Some parents immediately overreact and threaten to call the offending child's parents or the school. This often backfires and may make your child clam up or plead with you not to say anything. Sometimes parents assume that it's all the other child's fault, when their own child may be far from blameless. Children who are teased or bullied need to feel they can talk to you about the problem.

3. **Ask your child how they have tried to deal with the problem**

Sometimes a child who is being bullied has tried their own ways of dealing with the problem, and these methods could work if consistently employed. Typically, however, the child will try a tactic once or twice and then give up because the bullying persists. Ask your child to describe exactly what happened when she tried each strategy. In other words, determine how successful the tactic was.

4. **Summarise the problem as you understand it**

A summary draws together and highlights the key facts and issues involved, and it also serves to focus the discussion. 'Okay. So, since the beginning of term, Bill and Andrew have been teasing and bullying you at school by doing three things: calling you names, pushing in front of you when you line up waiting to go into class and threatening to belt you up after school. This has made you scared about going to school and you've been feeling sick in class. So far you've tried ignoring them but this seemed to make it worse, and once you told the teacher. Is that right?'

5. **Acknowledge that a problem exists**

Let your child know that you think the bullying is definitely a problem and that you need to work out a solution together. 'This is just not on. We need to figure out a way of getting them to stop.'

6. **Explain some possible reasons for the bullying**

Children are more likely to try a new way of handling the problem if they understand what is going on and are offered a plausible explanation as to why the problem continues. Many children will give very concrete reasons for bullying. 'Oh. He's just a bully.' 'He's always like that. Everyone hates him.' 'He's always getting into trouble.' Most children explain the problem in terms of the bully's negative personal characteristics. This rarely provides a basis for thinking of a way to deal with the problem. Sometimes it is helpful to give children some alternative ways of thinking about the problem. 'Let's try to think about why this happens. It sounds like Bill doesn't have many friends. When he teases you, do any of the other kids laugh and join in?' . . . 'Yes, I thought so. Maybe he does this to show the other kids how smart and tough he is. So, one possibility is that he does it to get attention. Another one is that he picks on you because it works; he gets what he wants. Remember that you said that last time when he pushed in front of you he got away with it? Maybe he's like a fisherman. You know, when you go fishing you put some bait on a hook and dangle it in the water to tempt the fish to bite. When a fish comes along, it takes the bait and is hooked. If the fish keep biting, the fisherman thinks he's pretty cool and keeps coming back to the same spot. But what happens when the fish stop biting?' . . . 'Yes, that's right, the fisherman gives up. Maybe Bill is so used to getting a bite when he teases you that he keeps doing it. What do you think?'

7. **Ask your child for their opinion on how to deal with the problem**

The next step involves engaging your child in a problem-solving process. Many children are initially at a loss to know how to solve the problem and may need help generating ideas. Start by asking your child a fairly general question. 'So, how do you want to handle this problem?' 'What else could you try if Bill teases you again?'

8. **Suggest brainstorming as a way of tackling the problem**

If the child appears stuck, get out a piece of paper and ask her to think of as many solutions to the problem as she can, no matter how crazy the ideas might sound. If your child suggests something, write it down and repeat it. Do not pass judgement on whether the idea is a good one or not. Just say, 'Okay, that's one option. Let's think of a few more before you decide what to do.' If you think of other options, write them down after your child has finished. There are a number of things that a parent might suggest. These include teaching the child to ignore the teasing by yawning and walking away as soon as it occurs; encouraging the child to make friends with other children so she is not on her own during recess; teaching her to make assertive statements, and so on. It is also a good idea for children who are victims of bullying to be friendly and pleasant to other children, and to avoid making smart comments, bragging, teasing or in other ways annoying other children.

9. **Review your list of possible solutions**

Once you have generated about eight to ten options, ask your child's opinion about each one. Put a tick beside those options that seem reasonable and cross out those that seem impractical or unlikely to work.

10. **Practise the selected solution**

This involves role playing with your child exactly what he should do the next time the problem arises. You should play the role of the problem child and your child should play himself. It can be introduced like this: 'Let's pretend I'm Bill and I come up to you and say, "Why don't you get lost, sissy?" What should you say? You show me what you will do.' Provide feedback on the things you liked about what he did and then suggest things he might do differently. Keep practising and giving feedback until the child is able to carry out his plan reasonably well.

11. **Consider other options**

If the bullying is serious and involves violence or threats, you should also consider contacting the child's teacher about the problem. Some bullying stops as soon as the school becomes aware of the problem and the culprit is spoken to and monitored more closely for a while. However, many children want to deal with the problem themselves. Respect these wishes unless the problem continues. Some children cannot carry out their plans because they lack the skills and confidence to confront their assailant. If this is the case, you could also consider getting your child into a social skills training group run by a professional therapist. Some parents immediately consider countering aggression with aggression, and send their child to karate, judo or other self-defence classes. This strategy can backfire if the child has no real interest in these activities.

12. **Keep track of how your child makes out**

For the first few weeks, ask your child each day about school and about how her plan is going. Praise your child for employing her strategy, and take notice of any signs that she is worrying less about the problem.

13. **If the problem persists, arrange a conference with the child's teacher**

    Discuss your concerns with the child's teacher, find out whether the school is aware of the problem, and talk about what can be done to overcome it. Follow up this discussion (if necessary) with a formal letter of complaint to the school about the incident. Be as clear and specific as possible and include details such as the alleged dates and times and the names of the children involved. A conference with the offending child and his parents may be arranged by the school.

Issues relating to children's behaviour at home

Stealing

Many families go through a phase when money goes missing at home or a child brings something home that does not belong to them. Most children will stop stealing when they are caught and the problem is dealt with, and will not go on to develop serious problems. However, some do develop major problems with stealing. One twelve-year-old I worked with found out his mother's personal identification number (PIN), took her credit card and, over a period of three days, withdrew $650 from an automatic teller machine. This child was also caught stealing money from a teacher's purse at school and taking things from other children's bags. Stealing is a potentially serious problem, particularly when it occurs outside the home, and it needs to be handled carefully. Children need to learn that it is wrong to take something that does not belong to them.

Children are more likely to steal when parents are not careful with their money, for example if they leave notes and coins around the house in easily accessible places. Some children start to steal because of peer influences. They may be involved with older children who have stolen from their parents. Others continue to steal because they get away with it. Because stealing is sometimes hard to detect, there are likely to be many times when the child has stolen and was not caught. Stealing is often a problem in children who spend a lot of time unsupervised. Parents should always know where their child is, what they are doing and who they are with.

Persistent stealing can be a sign of serious family problems. Some children come from homes where one or both parents have a drinking or drug problem, have been in trouble with the law or perpetrate violence within the home. Negative home environments can contribute to a child stealing.

Children who steal a lot are at risk of becoming delinquents later on. The majority of criminals started their life of crime well before their teenage years. Children who repeatedly steal often have other problems as well, such as difficulties at school, aggressive behaviour, disobedience, poor peer relationships and low self-esteem.

The best time to deal with stealing is when it first begins. When children start stealing they are not very skilled and are often fairly easy to catch. For example, the child might arrive home from school with items that you know you have not paid for, claiming they were gifts from another child. But, if a child has been a successful thief for several years, he is likely to have become quite good at it.

The key to overcoming stealing is to reduce the opportunity for stealing to take place, to supervise the child's activities more closely and to use a no-stealing behaviour contract to prevent any further theft. Here are some guidelines for introducing a behaviour contract for stealing.

1. **Keep track of your money**
   Make sure you know exactly how much money is in the house. Count notes and change before your child goes to bed each evening. Do this laborious task every day for at least a month.
2. **Keep your money in a safe place**
   Do not leave it in the kitchen or family living areas where it may be a temptation.
3. **Check your child's room**
   Check your child's room twice a week while he's out, and be on the lookout for any unexplained money or items that you have

not paid for and know your child has not been given the money to buy.

4. **Make sure you know where your child is at all times**

Minimise the amount of time your child spends unsupervised either at home or out of the home. This is particularly important if your child has been stealing from local shops.

5. **Start an allowance system**

Give your child a regular allowance that he has to earn by doing chores and odd jobs. This will ensure that some of the things he wants can be bought with money he has earned rather than stolen.

6. **Establish an 'honesty and trust' contract with your child**

This should be a written contract signed by the parents and the child. (An example of such a contract appears in Figure 8 on page 230.) The contract is an agreement between parent and child which states in very specific terms what the child is expected to do, and lists the incentives and penalties that will follow if the child breaks the agreement.

The contract in Figure 8 was worked out between Phillip, aged ten, and his parents after a policeman brought Phillip home when he was caught shoplifting at a local newsagent. Phillip had also been taking small amounts of money from his mother's purse for about six months. The contract was used for four weeks. There was one episode of stealing in week two, then not a single episode that the parents knew of for the next two years.

7. **Involve your child in other activities and help foster positive interests and hobbies**

The turning point for some children who steal comes when they develop an interest or hobby that captures their imagination. Many kids who steal have very little to do in their spare time other than watch television. Give preference to activities that have adequate adult supervision. This might involve learning a new sport, learning to play an instrument or joining a sports team.

8. **Monitor who your child spends time with**

Be prepared to ban your child from playing with children who seem to be a bad influence. If your child is mixed up

FIGURE 8: A SAMPLE BEHAVIOUR CONTRACT

Behaviour contract

I _Phillip_

hereby agree to the following conditions for a period of 4 weeks commencing 3 June.

1. I will return home each day from school by 4.15 p.m.

2. I will come directly home from school and not go near the shopping centre on school nights.

3. I will not take anything that does not belong to me (steal) from my parents or anyone else. This includes money and any other items.

We _Jayne and Mark_

hereby agree to the following:

1. That one of us will be at home each school day by 4 p.m. to greet Phillip.

2. We will be available each school day to help Phillip with his homework should he want help.

3. We will provide Phillip with the agreed incentives should he keep to the terms of this contract.

Incentives

For each day Phillip keeps to these conditions, he will be able to earn $1.00 towards a new skateboard.

Penalties

Each each time Phillip breaks condition 1 or 2, he will be fined 50 cents. If he breaks condition 3, he will be fined the entire amount saved up to that point plus be grounded for a period of four days.

Signatures

Child's name _Phillip Hanson_ Date _10 October_

Parent's name _Jayne Hanson_ . Date _10 October_
Mother's name

Mark Hanson
Father's name

Commencement date _11/10_   Termination date _24/10_

with children who are unsupervised for much of the time, or are involved in stealing, smoking, drinking, drug taking or other antisocial behaviour, severely limit the contact your child has with them. This may be more easily said than done, particularly if they attend the same school. One way of tackling this problem is to help your child get involved in organised activities that none of these children attend. If this is not possible, encourage your child to bring children home to play so you can keep an eye on what happens and can provide supervision.

9. **Establish firm rules relating to the time your child must arrive home from school and the amount of time your child is allowed to spend away from home**
This is particularly important for children who have been getting into trouble outside school hours. Wherever possible, make sure there is someone at home to greet the child after school. Primary school children should not be left unsupervised after school. If necessary, arrange after-school care. Don't leave the responsibility to older siblings, particularly if the older child does not get on well with the younger child.

10. **If you find your child stealing again, act on your informed suspicions**
If you discover money or other items missing and you strongly suspect that your child is involved, be prepared to act on your suspicions rather than waiting for absolute evidence.

11. **Confront the child with the facts**
'Two hours ago I had two fifty-dollar notes in my purse and now there is only one. We are the only ones at home and I haven't been near my purse.'

12. **Ask the child to return the money**
Many children will at this point hand over what was taken if it is still in their possession.

13. **Do not force your child to admit they stole**
Many children who steal also lie about it. Asking for a confession often simply gives the child an opportunity to lie to cover his tracks.

14. **Impose an appropriate penalty**

    If the child admits taking the money and returns it, firmly and matter-of-factly impose the penalty in the contract. Do not lecture, nag or shout. Simply state the problem and the consequence. 'Brad, that is stealing. You are grounded for three days, have lost forty points from your contract and are banned from going to the movies with Henry this weekend.'

15. **Ignore protests**

    If the child protests and claims her innocence, ignore it and carry out the penalty. While this may seem a bit harsh, it is even more of a problem if the child is lying and gets away with it. 'I am not saying you did it. I don't know this for a certainty. However, I strongly suspect that it was you and so you'll have to suffer the consequences. If I'm wrong I'm sorry, but what I've said goes.'

16. **Create opportunities for your child to show you they can be trusted**

    Your child must learn to resist temptation. Once your child has stopped stealing, let her show her honesty. This can be done quite simply by starting to leave money where you know your child will discover it. Do not tell your child that you plan to do this. If she resists the temptation or returns the money to you, give enthusiastic praise. If the money goes missing, deal with the problem immediately and decisively, and impose the penalty on the contract. Let her go down to the shops to purchase groceries on a shopping list. Give her more money than the goods will cost. If the child returns the correct change without having spent anything, thank her for being responsible with money.

17. **Start a savings plan**

    Help your child open a savings account and encourage him to deposit a portion of his pocket money each week. The idea here is to encourage the child to learn to save money he has earned rather than always spending impulsively when money is received. Make sure there is a portion available to spend or save as he sees fit.

Sometimes you discover long after the event that something has been stolen. For example, on routinely cleaning your child's room, you may uncover some unexplained item. You don't know where it came from, how long it has been there or how it was paid for. It is better to establish a basic rule that your child doesn't bring anything into the house that is not his, including borrowing or looking after things for friends. The only things the child is allowed to bring into the house are articles of his own that have been paid for by you or that the child has bought from his allowance. You can then assume that a strange item has either been stolen or brought home without permission. The rule should not be relaxed until there have been no incidents for at least three months.

Lying

Lying involves deliberately deceiving another person. Children lie for many reasons, such as to avoid getting caught when they have done something wrong. When children are under threat of punishment, many will do things that enable them to avoid or escape the punishment, and one of those things is to lie. Lying is more likely to continue if it is successful and allows the child to avoid punishment.

Children also lie as a way of gaining attention and approval from peers. Children can tell lies about some strange things: they may tell other children or teachers lies about what they have done, seen or own. These kinds of boastful lies are often short-lived once a child starts school and has been caught out once or twice.

Lying becomes a problem when children start to be deceitful in an attempt to cover up activities such as getting into trouble at school, stealing, cheating and behaving inappropriately in the community. These children are often engaged in activities they know their parents disapprove of, and lying and deception allow them to continue these activities without getting caught. When lying has become a well-established pattern of behaviour, it can be difficult for parents to deal with. Parents may feel unable to trust their children and become sceptical about many truthful things their children tell them. When children persistently lie, parents may need to make a number of important changes in their approach. These changes may include the amount of time and positive attention the child receives for good behaviour, the severity of discipline the parents typically use, a child's acquaintances, and the amount of supervision the child receives. Here are some guidelines to help you deal with this problem.

1. **Discuss the problem with your child**
   Explain to your child that lying is unacceptable behaviour and that it must cease immediately. 'Daniel, I would like to talk to you about what happened last night. You lied to me about where you had been after school, and as this is the fourth time this has happened in the last two weeks, I think we have a problem. It is important that I can trust what you say, and I would like this lying to stop.'

2. **Describe the problem from your perspective**
   Briefly and matter-of-factly point out how lying affects you and why you consider it a problem. 'I feel angry and disappointed when this happens, and it makes me want to question other things you tell me. You'll find that if the problem continues, other people simply won't trust you.'

3. **Ask your child about the problem**
   When they are caught lying, many children don't have much to say about why they lied, but occasionally they will make excuses or even try to blame someone else for the problem. Avoid getting into a 'yes, but' argument with your child if this happens. Simply restate the problem as you see it and close the discussion with a statement of what you would like to happen from this point on.

4. **Create opportunities for your child to tell the truth**
   This involves identifying when your child is telling the truth about her activities and then responding positively to these reports. To do this, you need to know that your child is telling the whole truth. The best way to do this initially is to ask your child questions about events and happenings around the home on which you are fully informed. 'Have you tidied your bedroom?' 'Done your homework?' 'Finished raking up the leaves in the yard?' 'Cleaned your teeth?' These are examples where you can quickly check on the facts before asking the child. The reason for doing this is that the child

can practise telling the truth and you can detect deception immediately if it occurs.

5. **If the child tells the truth, give praise and positive attention**

If the child accurately describes the event in question, give positive attention and feedback, regardless of whether the child has or has not done whatever she was supposed to do. 'Thank you, Rachel, for telling me the truth.' The idea here is that the child is always praised for owning up and telling the truth, regardless of whatever else has happened. Try not to create the impression that you are continuously suspicious.

6. **If the child lies about what has happened, give corrective feedback**

Simply describe the problem. 'Kevin, you are not telling me the truth about that. You have not finished raking the yard.'

7. **Back up with an appropriate consequence**

The consequence will depend on the circumstances. However, for failing to report accurately on chores, you might require the child to do extra work. Alternatively, time out could be used as an immediate consequence for a child up to age nine. The important point here is that the consequence is provided for lying, not for failure to complete the task or chore.

8. **If your child lies to cover up some other inappropriate behaviour, deal with each problem separately**

Deal with the lying first, then the problem that prompted the lie. Provide appropriate consequences for both. If money is found in the child's room and he lies about where it came from, provide a consequence for the lying, such as withdrawing privileges. Then provide an additional consequence for the stealing itself, for example loss of points on a contract as described earlier.

9. **Consider establishing a 'telling the truth' behaviour contract**

If the problem is persistent, establish a behaviour contract similar to the one on page 230 for managing stealing. An alternative is to incorporate lying (as a behaviour) into an existing contract for another problem.

Lying can be a difficult problem to solve when parents aren't sure if the child is lying. Younger primary school children, however, usually give the secret away by smirking or smiling while telling you a lie. Sometimes the child's story simply doesn't add up. For example, when asked to explain how they happened to have $10 in their room, they might tell an unlikely tale about finding it on the way home. Questions about when, where, who was with them or the sequence of events, lead to a confession. Most children eventually confess when confronted directly, but others will maintain a lie in the face of the strongest interrogation. These children have become skilled liars and are often involved in other antisocial behaviours as well.

The best time to deal with lying is when it first begins. Children need to get the consistent message that, regardless of what they have done, they need to be honest with you. After all, parents cannot assist children who get into trouble, whether at school or in the community, unless they know what has happened. Many of the strategies discussed earlier in relation to fostering good communication with children can also help in overcoming lying.

Swearing

Children often learn to swear from their peer group, between the ages of seven and eleven, although swearing can occur in preschoolers if they have older siblings or indeed parents who swear a great deal. Swearing in children is considered by most adults to be unacceptable, particularly at school. Swearing in the peer group may meet with the opposite reception. Some children swear as part of projecting a tough, aggressive image. It can be used to intimidate or threaten other children into submission, as an alternative to direct violence. Swearing in both adults and children is much more common in some groups than others. For many street kids and runaways, swearing is a part of life and a way of defying adult authority.

Swearing in the home can occur as part of an outburst of anger or rage. It can be a form of abuse directed at siblings or, less frequently, at parents. There are hundreds of choice expressions that children can discover. Parents may find some expletives offensive while others not a problem, and indeed may themselves use them.

You really need to decide for yourself which potentially offensive words, phrases or expressions are acceptable and permissible in your home and which ones are not. The guidelines below are designed to help children learn more socially acceptable expressions.

1. **Decide which words, phrases or expressions are acceptable**

    It is generally best to have a small number of completely banned words that are commonly used but you find personally offensive, than to have a large list of unacceptable words that will be difficult to enforce. Remember, you might be able to control the language your child uses at home but you can't control what happens in the playground at school, or on the street.

2. **Make sure you do not model swearing**

    You cannot expect your child not to swear if you use offensive words.

3. **Only use words, whether in general conversation or as expletives, that are on your list of acceptable words**

    Every parent gets frustrated at times. We break things accidentally, hit our fingers with hammers and bang our shins or elbows. These are the times that many parents will let out a swear word. It is very hard to control what we say when we are in pain, but if you must swear, try to choose a non-offensive word.

4. **Explain the ground rules to your child**

    Hold a discussion with your child relating to swearing at home. Describe the problem from your point of view: 'James, I don't like it when you use that word in this house. Don't use it again.' Describe acceptable alternatives. 'If you must use that sort of language, you may say [list the acceptable words].'

5. **Provide an incentive for complying with the ground rules**

    Start a behaviour chart for monitoring swearing at home as shown in Figure 9 (page 238). You will notice that it has one column for each day of the week. At the end of each day, your child can earn a merit award if she has gone through the whole day without swearing. At this time, you should thank and praise

FIGURE 9: A CHART FOR MONITORING SWEARING

A chart for monitoring swearing

Date	20/6						
Day	Sat						
Merit award	1						
Daily total	1						
						Weekly total	

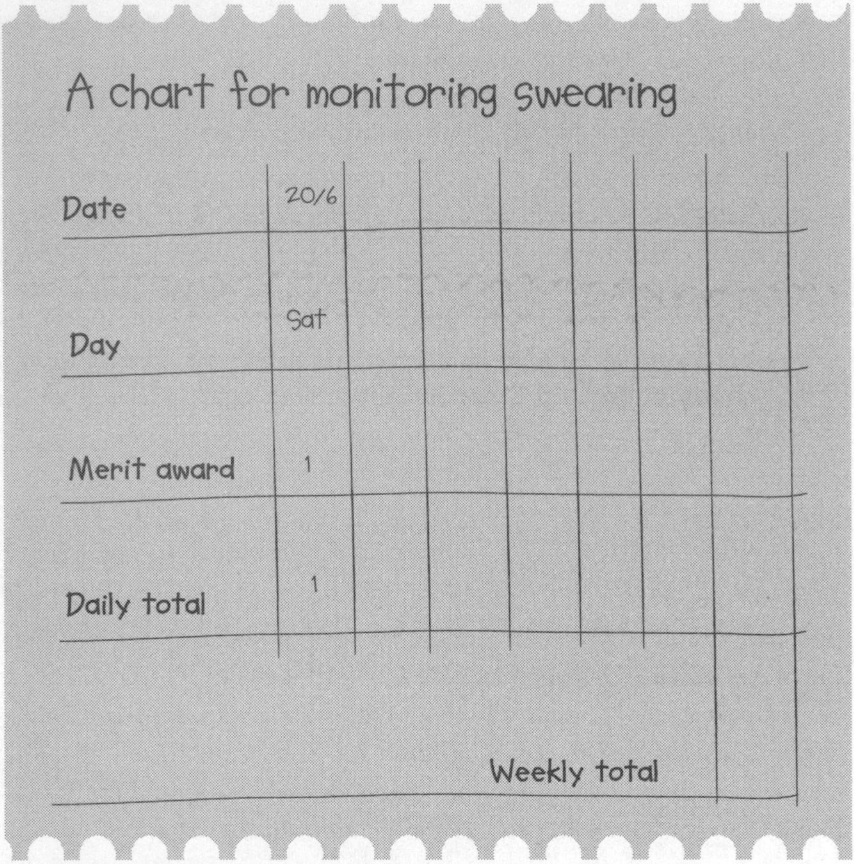

Fill in a merit award for each day that swearing does not occur, and calculate the total at the end of the week.

her for speaking properly at home during the day. When the child has earned seven awards in a row, give her a back-up reward. Keep this chart posted in the kitchen and have enough copies for three to five weeks.

6. **Deal with swearing by using a 'stop' instruction**
   If you hear your child swearing at home, give her a firm instruction. 'Jane, stop using that language immediately. That word is banned in this house.'

7. **Describe the correct behaviour**

Tell your child what would have been a more acceptable way of dealing with the problem. 'If you want to borrow some paper from your sister, ask her pleasantly.'

8. **Describe the back-up consequence**

Tell your child that he will not get his reward today. Decide on an additional back-up consequence such as the withdrawal of a privilege, for example watching his favourite television show or time out for three minutes.

9. **Ignore protests and follow through with back-up consequences as necessary**

After stating the consequences, simply remove yourself from the room, ignoring protests. Make sure you follow through if it happens again.

One problem that can arise with this strategy is that other siblings may begin telling tales to get the offending child into trouble. Telling tales can be as much of a problem as swearing, so you need to be prepared to deal with this as well. One way of doing so is to act only on things you have heard first-hand. It might mean that you have to keep a closer eye on your child's activities for a few days so that you detect swearing before other children feel they have to tell. If telling tales occurs frequently over other things as well, then read the guidelines on pages 85–89 for establishing clear ground rules.

Chores

How old should children be before they are required to regularly help out around the house with chores such as doing dishes, tidying their bedroom, clearing away the dinner table, cleaning the house and working in the yard? The answer to this question will depend on at least three things: first, whether you view running the household as a shared responsibility or something that is the sole province of the parents (usually mother); second, whether you believe children should have regularly assigned tasks as opposed to 'helping' now and again; and third, whether the child has the physical and mental capacity to carry out the necessary task.

Children need to learn the value of work from an early age. By having regular chores that are their own responsibility, children can learn to apply themselves to a task, as well as learning the skills involved in running a family household and practising self-discipline. However, the key to helping children learn to undertake these responsibilities cheerfully and competently is to move slowly. The process starts right back during the preschool years when young children are taught how to take care of their belongings and to tidy up after themselves. By the time children reach the age of eight or nine, they should be encouraged to have regular household chores. If you do this, you will find that your own work is more manageable and that you have more time to spend with your children on other activities, as well as more time for yourself and your spouse.

It is often better to introduce all children in the family to chores at the same time, even though they may differ in age and therefore have different capabilities. Children often accept new responsibilities if they don't feel they are being singled out. Here are some ideas for establishing a family roster for household duties. However, remember that an introduction to unsuitable tasks too early will often turn the child away from such tasks in the future. Here is a programme that will help you introduce your children to household chores.

1. **Call a family meeting**

   Arrange a meeting with all family members at a convenient time. Eliminate distractions by making sure the television is off. It is important that both parents have discussed the plan in advance and agree that there should be greater role-sharing within the family. This can be a problem for couples where one or both partners assume that it is the mother's responsibility to do the majority of the work around the home. Reluctant fathers might more readily accept that children should do more, than that they themselves might need to change.

2. **State the issue from your perspective**

   Explain to the children that from now on they will be expected to help out with chores around the house. Tell them that every family member will have certain assigned responsibilities each day. There will also be occasional jobs that need to be done less often.

3. **Explain why children must be prepared to help out around the home**

Try to keep the explanation simple. 'Living in a family involves a lot of work. Our family will run more smoothly and there will be more time for things we can do together as a family if everyone pitches in and helps. It is not Mum or Dad's job to do everything to keep the place clean and tidy. You are now old enough to share in some of these jobs. One day you will have to know how to run your own house. Now is the time to start learning about these things.' Ignore protests or claims that none of their friends have to do any work. Simply restate the fact that from now on they will all have set jobs to do.

4. **Generate a list of the daily, weekly and monthly chores that need to be done**

Use a piece of paper or a blackboard to make a list of jobs that need to be done around the house. Involve your children in this process by asking for their opinions. Write each item down. Try to select items that children can do with minimal adult supervision and that are not too time-consuming, such as placing their dirty clothes in a clothes basket in the bathroom and taking their plates from the table after dinner and placing them in the sink or dishwasher. The list should show the chores in order, from the beginning of the day until bedtime. At this stage do not assign jobs to children, simply write down what needs to be done.

5. **Put your name beside any chores on the list that you feel you should do**

You might decide for a variety of reasons that there are specific things, such as loading the washing machine and preparing meals, that you should continue to do, either because the children are too young or because you feel these should be adult responsibilities.

6. **Ask the children for their opinion on any chores they would like to do**

Children should be given an opportunity to express their opinion on jobs they would like to take on. Be cautious here because some children will suggest things they are not capable of doing competently, such as cooking the evening meal, and other children will say they don't want to do anything. Don't be put off by this. Be prepared to insist that certain jobs are their responsibility, or suggest alternative things they can do. Keep in mind each child's age and capabilities.

7. **Finalise a job list for each child**
   This involves writing down a final job list that will be included on the jobs chart. The child's responsibilities should be broken down into daily, weekly and monthly jobs. Try to have the same number of items for each child. However, older children should be expected to take on more complex tasks than younger ones.

8. **Prepare a large jobs chart**
   A jobs chart similar to the one in Figure 10 can be used for keeping track of whether children complete their assigned jobs on time. A large whiteboard is useful for this purpose. The columns and headings can be written in permanent felt pens and the individual items for each child in pens that can be erased. An alternative is to use a large sheet of cardboard or a sheet generated from a computer. This chart is also used as a reminder to children of what their responsibilities are and as feedback on whether or not they have completed the tasks.

9. **Involve your child in preparing the chart**
   Many school-aged children love being involved in preparing charts. They can help with ruling columns, reading items from the draft list while you write them on the board or writing them down themselves if they have neat handwriting.

10. **Allocate a list of duties to each child**
    Fill in the chart with jobs assigned to each family member. Some families prefer to have only the children's names on the chart. Others want the adults' names as well.

11. **Select incentives for improved performance**
    Children are more likely to cooperate if their efforts are acknowledged and rewarded. There are several things that parents can do to motivate their children. These include providing praise and positive attention during or immediately following the completion of assigned tasks, and giving positive feedback at the end of the day (before bedtime) while you fill in the

FIGURE 10: FAMILY JOBS CHART

Family jobs chart

Job	1	2	3	4	5	6	7	8	9	10	11	12	13	14	15	16	17	18	19	20	21	22	23	24	25	26	27	28	29	30	31
Carlie																															
1. Set the dinner table																															
2. Load the dishwasher																															
Stephen																															
1. Clean dinner table																															
2. Dry dishes																															
David																															
1. Feed the dog																															
2. Put away clean dishes																															

Month _____

List the jobs assigned to each family member and tick off the jobs completed each day.

chart for that day. It is also possible to link the family roster to a pocket money system by assigning a monetary value to each item. Guidelines for establishing pocket money are detailed on pages 246–50.

12. **Select consequences for failure to complete chores**

    If the programme is linked to a pocket money system, those children who fail to do their assigned jobs simply do not get the amount specified for that job. Logical consequences can also be used, such as insisting that chores be completed before children are allowed to watch television or go out and play. Don't get trapped into allowing the child to do something if she promises to do her chores when she has finished. Children often manipulate parents into agreeing to this and then fail to keep to the bargain.

13. **Explain the incentives and consequences**

    Let your children know what will happen if they complete their chores or fail to complete them. Then test the system for a week.

14. **Remind your children of the rules before you start**

    In particular, ask your child to describe what has to be done today.

15. **Select times for doing daily chores that give the child some choice**

    Generally homework should be done before chores are tackled. Give the child a specific time by which the chores must be completed but let the child decide when and how the tasks will be done.

16. **Avoid hassling your child about starting the chores**

    Give one reminder that chores need to be done by the specific time and then leave your child alone. Don't get trapped into giving repeated reminders or instructions to begin.

17. **Attend to your child while he is busy**

    Try to catch your child being good, and praise him during or immediately after completing individual tasks.

18. **Help your child get started**

    Children may initially need help getting started, particularly if the job is a new one. Use 'Ask, Say, Do' (see pages 82–84).

19. Provide back-up consequences at the agreed check time

At the agreed time, check which tasks have been completed and fill in the chart for each child. It is important that children learn to complete each task satisfactorily. You should not reward sloppy or half-completed jobs. At the same time, don't expect a perfect performance. You will need to make a judgement here about whether the job is done well enough.

20. Hold another family meeting to review progress

At the end of the first week, hold another family meeting to review progress. This should involve giving children feedback on tasks they have completed regularly and asking for their opinions about how the first week has gone and any changes that might need to be made. You should also offer your own views on changes. For example, there may be certain jobs that can be rotated, such as raking up leaves, vacuuming a swimming pool or drying dishes. It is often easier to rotate on a weekly basis rather than on alternate days to avoid the problem of children saying, 'I washed the dishes last night, it's Rosemary's turn tonight.'

21. Use reminder cards

Write down each child's daily and weekly chores on a large card and stick it on the child's bedroom wall. These cards can be useful in the early stages as a reminder.

22. Decide whether to phase out reminders, monitoring and incentives

Once children are in a good routine and are completing chores with a minimum of fuss, you will need to decide whether to phase out the jobs chart. Some large families find it very convenient to continue to use the chart and often do so for years. However, in smaller families, the chart can be phased out once the children know what to do. If you decide to phase out the chart, use the following strategy. Start off by reducing the amount of positive attention you give to the child while she is completing the chores, but continue to praise your child at the end of each day. Next, wait until two then three days pass before checking off the chart. Once this has been done, take down the chart altogether.

23. Increase the number of chores

As children progress through primary school, they become capable of learning more complex and responsible tasks. New tasks can be introduced and added to the new chart. When this occurs, simple daily chores that have become habits can be left off the chart.

It is only recently that children have not been expected to work. In the nineteenth century children as young as five worked in British coal mines for up to twelve hours a day and were considered a vital part of the workforce. Child labour laws were necessary to protect children from this kind of abuse. By contrast, many children in modern families contribute very little to the running of the family. The pendulum perhaps has swung too far. Common sense and balance should prevail. One eight-year-old girl I worked with was required to prepare breakfast for a family of five, and to wake her mother at 8.30 a.m. with breakfast in bed. The child also made school lunches and did all the dishes on her own. In my opinion, this child was being abused.

Always remember that chores should not be so time-consuming that children's needs in other areas are neglected. They still need time for play, fun, hobbies, exercise and homework.

Pocket money

At what age should children be given an allowance? Many parents start giving children a small regular allowance during primary school years. The allowance given obviously depends on the family's financial circumstances. Some children earn as little as twenty cents, others are given $10 or more. From the age of seven or eight an allowance is generally a good idea. It gives children an opportunity to learn to save and manage small amounts of money. They can also learn the value of money and the cost of items they would like to buy, as well as make the connection between work and financial reward. Many problems over the money children receive from parents can be avoided with a properly planned allowance system. Some children expect parents to have an unlimited supply, a myth supported by parents who give their children whatever they ask for. Many families start a pocket money system but don't operate it consistently. One week the child gets it, the next week they don't. Sometimes the allowance is in return for chores, at other times it's not. As they approach adolescence, many children complain about the amount they receive compared with their friends, and so on. Sometimes parents refuse to give their child pocket money because they believe they will spend it all on junk food.

Here are some ideas for setting up a pocket money system that is within your family's budget. It is often a good idea to start off a pocket money system with a savings plan for your child.

1. **Decide on the amount you can afford**

   Before speaking to your child about pocket money, chat to neighbours and friends about the going rate and the way other parents handle the issue. Work out approximately how much you already spend on each child on extras such as sweets, toys, gifts, outings, movies and so on. Some of this money may be able to be used as pocket money. Look at your family budget realistically to decide what you can afford. It is not a good idea for young children to have access to large amounts of money. As a rough guide, a seven- or eight-year-old could earn between $1.50 and $3; an eight- to nine-year-old from $3 to $5; a ten- to eleven-year-old from $5 to $7, and twelve-year-olds up to $10. There are no hard and fast rules. The amount will depend on your means.

2. **Decide how much should be spent by the child and how much banked**

   A 50/50 split often works well. As your child is likely to be banking small amounts, it might be a good idea to establish a bonus system. For example, you might match every $5 your child saves if she is saving up for a new pair of skates.

3. **Decide how much should be received automatically and how much earned**

   It is a good idea to give the child one-third to one-half of the allowance automatically, with the rest to be earned through doing chores and odd jobs. In essence, the child gets a bonus for helping out around the home.

4. **Discuss the plan with your child**
   Hold a discussion with your child to introduce the plan. Explain what you propose and what she is required to do to get money. Let your child know she may spend one-half or one-third of the money on whatever she likes and must bank the rest.

5. **Decide on a regular pay day**
   It is important that you stick to this. Make sure you always have enough small change or notes to pay the required amount. Every Friday night or Saturday morning is a good time.

6. **Open a bank account with your child**
   Many schools have a school banking facility. Get your child to fill out the relevant application forms under your guidance and open the account with a starting deposit.

7. **Encourage your child to set savings goals**
   Some children will immediately want to set themselves a savings goal, for example for a new bike, skateboard or CD, and this should be encouraged. Suggest but don't insist on a savings target. Some children just like the money to accumulate.

8. **Keep track of chores completed towards pocket money**
   Use a chart similar to the one in Figure 11 for keeping track of whether your child has completed the chores linked to earning pocket money. Not all chores should attract pocket money. Routine daily jobs should be left out. Weekend and other odd jobs are good for earning pocket money.

9. **Let your child spend the money he has earned without too much interference**
   If your child asks for your opinion on what to buy, give it. But let him make the decision. Let him spend some of his money on sweets if he wishes. (There may, of course, be some things you need to ban for children on special diets.) Children should be encouraged to compare the prices of similar items in different shops to get value for money. Wise shopping comes with opportunities to make choices and with practice. Children's banking and shopping can be linked to your own. Be prepared to allow children some time to do their shopping after or during the time you do your own.

FIGURE 11: POCKET MONEY CHART

Pocket money chart

Month:

Chores to be done	Value	Week 1	Week 2	Week 3	Week 4
1. hang out washing	50c	50c			
2. clean up leaves	$1				
3. sweep out garage	50c	50c			
4.					
5.					
Amount earned	$2	$1			

List the chores to be done and the value assigned to each task, then calculate the total pocket money earned each week.

10. **Give children positive feedback for good purchasing**

    Take an interest in what your child wants to buy. Offer praise and attention any time your child shows evidence of having shopped wisely. For example, if your child compares two similarly priced items and chooses the one that is sturdier and likely to last longer, let her know why you think it was a good choice.

11. **Avoid criticising your child's choices**

    Don't get too upset if your child wants to buy something you consider a waste of money. He will become more skilled with practice.

Try to avoid letting large amounts of money accumulate in your child's moneybox. Let him bank even small amounts on a regular basis so that he can see the balance grow. An efficiently run pocket-money system is an excellent way of giving children opportunities to become more independent and more skilled at making decisions to do with money. You should be prepared to adjust the allowance periodically because of inflation and the fact that the child is getting older. Sometimes younger siblings will object to older siblings earning more money. Don't get trapped into feeling you have to treat each child the same way. However, be absolutely consistent so that when the younger child reaches the older child's age, he receives the equivalent amount.

Television

There has been much written about the effects of television on children. It has been blamed for the increase in violence and juvenile crime, family break-ups and children's poor school performance. Many parents are concerned about the amount of violence children see on television.

There is little doubt that television has a major impact on children. However, the connection is a complex one. The average seven- to eleven-year-old watches twenty-one hours of television each week. This is an enormous slice of their time. In some families, watching television is the only hobby the family shares. The television set is on from the time a child wakes in the morning until she retires at night.

Television has both positive and negative aspects. The good aspects include the fact that suitable programmes are both enjoyable and informative for children. Television can encourage fantasy and enable children to see people, animals, places, things and events they may never actually experience. Shows such as *Sesame Street* have gained such a good reputation because young children both enjoy them and learn from them. Television can also be used as a way of helping children relax and unwind after school or boisterous activity.

The negative aspects of television for children include the fact that there are very few high-quality productions designed especially for children. Many stations rely on filling children's television time with violent cartoons or repeats of old comedies or soaps. Apart from the quality of programming, if children spend huge amounts of time watching television, other important activities can be neglected, including homework, outdoor play, exercise, reading and communicating with parents. Television watching is a passive activity. Activities that are interactive tend to be remembered more easily and therefore help learning. In other words, children often get more out of doing rather than simply watching.

The effects of television on children depend on a host of factors. These include how much they watch, whether their viewing habits are monitored by parents and whether they have an opportunity to talk to their parents about confusing or upsetting programmes.

Television is neither good nor bad for children. It can be both under certain circumstances. It is important for parents to establish good television routines in the family. Here are some ideas about how to avoid problems, especially arguments, over television watching.

1. **Decide how many hours per week you will allow your child to watch television**

    This is probably one of the most important decisions you can make. In making this judgement, estimate how much your child watches at the moment; you may be staggered by the result. I would recommend a maximum of one hour per day during the school week and a little longer on the weekend.

2. **Tell your child about the plan**

    Tell your child that from now on he can only watch programmes he has selected in advance from the television guide.

3. **Ask your child to select the programmes she wants to watch**

    Go through the television guide with your child and write down the shows she wants to watch. Some children may want to watch several programmes on a particular day. That is fine so long as the total weekly hours are not exceeded.

4. **Explain the new ground rules for television time**

    These should include the following: only watch selected programmes; the television will be turned off for the rest of the day if there are any arguments over channels or if the child turns on the television at any other time; no television before homework is completed; no boisterous play or fighting while watching television.

5. **Reach a compromise if children want to watch different programmes at the same time**
    You may have to make the decision, if children can't work it out for themselves.

6. **Keep a lookout for interesting and suitable programmes**
    Be prepared to let children watch extra television if a particularly suitable programme is scheduled. These can be bonus extras you give to your child at your discretion.

7. **If children break the rules, follow through with the planned consequences**
    It is important that you break the habit children have of turning on the television 'just to see what's on'. Any time this, or any other, rule is broken, cancel the child's viewing for that night. Ignore protests. If it happens again, unplug the television and if necessary remove it from the lounge room.

8. **Reward children for keeping to the rules**
    If your child sticks to the rules, hire a video or allow him to watch extra television on the weekend as a treat.

9. **Praise your child for participating in other activities**
    Children will be less interested in television if they receive praise and attention for selecting activities at times that were previously used for watching television.

10. **Control your child's access to other television sets**
    If you have more than one set, you'll need to be especially watchful. It is much more difficult to enforce consistent rules if children have sets in their bedrooms. Consider selling such sets.

Sometimes parents contribute to problems over television because they themselves have become addicts. Some people use television as company, or to provide background noise in much the same way that the radio used to be used. The early-evening viewing time can be a particular problem if one of the parents likes to watch the news on arrival home from work. The programme will be easier to enforce if you watch most of your television after your children are in bed.

Many families who have made the decision to cut down on television watching report some important changes in their family: parents start to talk to each other more, children get interested in hobbies and outdoor activities, parents and children have more time for each other, and children start to show an interest in reading again. Children may also learn to amuse themselves without having to be entertained all the time.

Computers

Many families invest in a home computer to help children with their schoolwork. Indeed, computer skills are being introduced to children at school at an earlier and earlier age. Many of the same issues that are relevant to children watching television apply to the use of computers. Computers have become a major source of entertainment for children. The major issues relating to computers are the amount of time children are allowed to spend on the computer, the type of Internet content they can access and conflict between siblings over use of the computer. Here are some ideas for preventing problems with home computers.

1. **Put the computer in a family living area rather than in a bedroom**
    Having the computer located in a family area enables you to monitor and supervise your child's use of the computer and reduces the chances that children will access unsuitable content such as violent or pornographic material.
2. **Decide on how much computer time is allowed per week**
    Similar rules to watching television should apply here. I recommend sixty minutes maximum per day during the school week.
3. **Introduce ground rules for use of the computer**
    Children need very clear, firm and consistently enforced guidelines. The main ground rules could include keeping to the agreed

time allowance, using the equipment properly, leaving siblings alone to play when it is their turn and turning off the computer when requested without arguing.

4. **Decide what kind of content and games your child is allowed to access**
   There are many excellent software programs for children. Always check that any program the child obtains from someone else is suitable and is a legal copy.

5. **Restrict access to unsuitable Internet content**
   Although this can be difficult to monitor at times and sometimes children can accidentally discover unsuitable sites, children should be encouraged to come and tell you if they hit a pornographic site by mistake. Some of these sites can be quite upsetting to children. Do not store anything on a home computer that is unsuitable for children.

6. **Monitor your child's use of the computer**
   If children know that their parents have certain values and expectations about what is acceptable, it is easier for them to follow the rules. However, do not leave children unsupervised for long periods when they are using computers.

7. **Provide suitable consequences if the rules are broken**
   If the rules are broken introduce an appropriate back-up consequence. For misuse of the computer, the child can be refused permission to use it for a suitable time (such as the rest of the day), or for a longer period for repeated misuse and breaking of rules. If the computer is causing continuing friction in the family, consider putting it away for a few months.

Issues relating to children's activities

Sportsmanship

Primary school children are often expected to participate in activities that involve being a member of a team. Team games occur in physical education programmes and as part of organised school sports teams. Children may also join a club out of school hours, where they receive coaching in a variety of competitive sports such as soccer, rugby, hockey, netball, basketball, tennis and cricket. Many children find being a member of a team a very enjoyable experience. It is not only an opportunity to develop their physical coordination and receive regular exercise, but is also an opportunity to meet other children, make new friends and learn about teamwork and competition. Children's sporting activities are also a source of pleasure and pride for many parents, particularly if a child has talent.

Such activities can also be a source of great frustration. As a coach of junior rugby I often witnessed the pressures that parents can place on young children. It is not uncommon for children to experience tears and stomach aches on Saturday mornings before matches. Parents have been known to berate and abuse their children from the sidelines for dropped catches, missed tackles, not running hard enough or appearing uninterested in the game. Winning often becomes the all-important goal for both parents and coaches, and too much pressure from either source can create anxiety and other emotional problems in children. Parents may be unable to accept that their child dislikes, is not interested in or has limited ability in a particular sport, especially if the parent was good at the sport as a child.

Other children are bad sports. They might gloat when they win, be ungracious in defeat or refuse to try a new activity if they think they can't do it. Some children will reluctantly join in with a lot of prodding from their parents but then refuse to join in, or complain bitterly about playing the game. Coaches of children's sports have a big responsibility to ensure that children receive encouragement and proper instruction but still have fun while playing sport. This is not an easy task, particularly when coaches may be volunteers with little or no training in coaching techniques and have to deal with large numbers of children. They have to ensure that the activities are closely supervised and that children receive proper skill development to make sure the game is played safely. This is particularly important in contact sports where injuries can and do occur. Some children can also be quite disruptive and disobedient when participating in sporting activities, and are capable of ruining the enjoyment of other children because of their behaviour.

What can parents do to encourage children to participate in

sporting and other recreational activities and to develop sportsman-like behaviour?

1. **Spend time with your child to help her develop her coordination**

    During toddler and preschool years, be prepared to spend time with your child playing games that involve developing coordination and physical activity. There is a wide variety of activities that promote children's muscle development and coordination, including hopping, skipping, jumping, playing catch, rolling a ball to each other, throwing a ball, balancing games, walking, jogging, bushwalking, backpacking, climbing and kicking a ball. Children often love to play active games with their parents, particularly if the parent is encouraging and avoids criticising their child for not being able to master a skill. Parents who are active through regular exercise are more likely to raise active children. They learn a lot through observation as well as practice. Remember to give lots of praise and attention for small improvements in skill in these activities.

2. **Take note of those activities your child is interested in or seems to enjoy**

    Children differ a great deal in their coordination, and a child who appears poorly coordinated as a six-year-old may catch up and be particularly good at a sport at fifteen. If children express an interest in playing a particular sport or joining a team that their friends belong to then be prepared to let them join, even if it is not a sport you are particularly interested in. Children often develop interests in sports they play at school, have friends involved in or that their parents show an interest in. There is little doubt that children's interests in particular sports can be influenced by parents, but it is important for parents to avoid narrowing their child's choices too soon. This can be done unintentionally when parents are critical of specific sports or fail to show an interest in the child when he talks about or tries to play a sport. Unless you feel the sport is particularly dangerous or too expensive, have an open mind and encourage experimentation so children can decide for themselves which sport they would like to play.

3. **Let children experience many different sports**

Parents should allow children to change their minds at the end of a season about the sports they wish to play. If a child wants to play netball one year then change to tennis the next, let her do so. It is not a good idea to allow children to withdraw from a sport once they have started a season unless you are concerned about how they are treated by the coach or the child is obviously distressed by the experience. The main reasons for encouraging children to continue until the end of the season are the expense involved in changing and the fact that some children learn quickly that if they kick up a fuss they will be allowed to avoid activities about which they initially lack confidence. The problem here is that the child might try the same tactic again. Children need to learn that confidence comes with practice and persistence, not by avoiding problems or uncomfortable situations.

4. **Attend training sessions and games as often as possible**

It is a good idea for parents to attend training sessions as often as possible, particularly the first few times. Children often approach new activities with some hesitation, and this can be eased by knowing that their parent is there taking an interest. It also gives you an opportunity to see the coaching methods and approach employed; if the team's coach spends the whole time yelling at the kids, you might be better off finding another club. During training sessions and matches, watch your child closely and take particular note of what he does well. Remember that because your child is learning a sport, his performance should be compared with his previous efforts rather than with the efforts of other children. Specific comments after the game or practice session will assist the child's motivation to improve further.

5. **Offer to help**

Junior sport often suffers from a lack of parental support and involvement. Some parents act as taxi drivers for their children and leave all the rest of the work to other parents. If your schedule permits, take an active interest. Offer your help. Don't wait to be asked, and don't feel you have to be an expert in the sport to be of assistance. (Don't be disappointed if your offer is declined, because at least you've made the effort.) Your involvement can heighten your child's interests in the activity.

6. **Encourage regular attendance and make sure your child is on time**

There is nothing more frustrating for coaches than to have children who simply don't turn up. If your child is ill or there is an emergency that prevents regular attendance, make sure you ring the coach or manager of your child's team. Don't give your child a bad name by always being late.

7. **Avoid harassing your child during a game**

Comments from the sidelines during children's sport have to be heard to be believed. Grown men have been known to come to blows over refereeing decisions or the outcome of games. They abuse referees or opposition players, question decisions and swear at their own child for not playing well. This type of behaviour provides a bad model for children and is usually motivated by an excessive emphasis on winning rather than on participation and enjoyment. There is absolutely no place for violent or abusive behaviour from parents during children's sport. This does not mean that parents should not enjoy the game, become excited and cheer to offer support and encouragement. Many children, particularly when they first start organised sport, have no idea of the score or indeed who won, and usually it doesn't matter to them. This situation changes rapidly when children reach the age of nine or ten.

8. **Provide encouraging feedback at the end of the game**

Find something positive to say about the team's and your child's performance; leave negative feedback to the coach. If your child asks you for ideas about how the team's performance could be improved, offer your suggestions. Children respond better to one or two quite specific suggestions that you can demonstrate for them rather than a whole list of faults.

9. Dealing with poor sportsmanship

Poor sportsmanship can come in many different forms, ranging from cheating to abusing opponents or referees, or displays of temper. Children who are bad sorts are quite competitive, and their parents may have observed similar behaviour at home during children's games. Children need to understand that sportsmanlike conduct involves keeping to the rules of the game and acting in an appropriate manner whether you win, lose or draw. If you notice poor behaviour during a game, wait until the activity is over and then describe what the child did wrong. 'Throwing your racquet into the net is being a bad sport.' Describe what the child should have done instead. 'If you feel frustrated during the game, take a deep breath and count to ten.' Then provide an appropriate back-up consequence.

The consequence you select should be appropriate to the problem, as the following example illustrates. During a holiday at the beach, the Smith family was playing a game of cricket with two other families. There was an equal number of adults and children on each side. Robert, aged seven, was batting at one end and his mother was at the other. Robert swung and missed the first ball he received. The second ball bowled him middle stump. At that point he burst into tears and stormed off the pitch, throwing his cricket bat as he left. He refused to join the fielding team. It was a very embarrassing episode for the mother but she took the following decisive action. She immediately ran over to the child, reprimanded him for being a bad sport, took him back to the batting crease despite the struggle, and twice made him practise placing the bat down in the proper way. She then made him sit in quiet time, off the pitch, for two minutes. As soon as the two minutes were over, she took him by the hand to take up his fielding position. The action was powerful and decisive. Robert quickly learned that temper outbursts during cricket matches would not work.

Many parents have mixed feelings about competitive sport, particularly if their child shows talent. While a child's achievements are a source of pride and pleasure, parents often feel uncomfortable about the competitive aspects of sport. High achievers in many sports have to make tremendous sacrifices in normal family life. These include long hours of training and reduced opportunities to experience activities undertaken by other children of the same age. Children's sport can come to dominate a family's existence if parents let this happen, to the extent that every weekend is committed, families don't go on outings and schoolwork and normal recreation activities are neglected. It is important to maintain a balance so children can still experience a full range of opportunities and experiences. No single activity should be allowed to take over completely, whether it is sport, music, schoolwork, watching television or anything else.

Other parents become concerned about the competitive nature of sport itself. They feel that too much emphasis on winning, training and competing, rather than on participation, can be harmful, particularly for young children. These are reasonable concerns, and parents and coaches of young children need to make sure children are protected from unnecessary emphasis on winning at all costs. Excellence does not necessarily mean beating the opposition.

Many of the issues raised in relation to children's sport also apply to other activities, such as learning a musical instrument or becoming involved in performing arts. Because sport is so highly prized in our society, it may lead parents to neglect children's interests and abilities in artistic, musical and literary fields. Parents should allow children to pursue and develop these interests as they emerge, and provide as much encouragement and support as they would for sporting involvement. Too many parents label certain activities as 'sissy' or 'unladylike' and try to discourage their children's interest in them.

Encouraging creativity

Children can gain great pleasure from participating in performance arts such as music, dance and drama, and visual arts such as drawing, painting, photography and sculpture. The arts provide many opportunities for children to explore their identity and to express thoughts, opinions and feelings. Listening to music or watching a painting can generate a range of emotions. The arts help promote children's language, social and intellectual development. Here are some guidelines to help support your child's creative endeavours.

1. **Take notice of activities your child likes**
   Help your child get involved when they show an interest by finding out where lessons are held and where equipment can be obtained.
2. **Offer to help**
   By getting involved you will show your child that you really are interested in their activities. There are lots of ways of helping – you can offer to make costumes for a performance, or supply art equipment such as darkroom equipment or a pottery wheel.
3. **Create family activities that support your child's interest**
   Singing and dancing help children develop a sense of rhythm, melody, harmony and timing. Encourage dramatic play by providing clothes that your child can dress up in. Notice, share and talk about everyday things of natural beauty such as a pattern of bark on a tree, the shape of a seed pod or veins on a leaf, and help your children notice details such as patterns, colours, shapes, lines and textures. Where possible take your child to concerts, pantomimes and plays, and stop to watch street performers.
4. **Encourage your child's attempts**
   Show an interest when your child is practising an instrument. If she brings home a piece of art from school, put it up on the wall. Praise her efforts and avoid critical comments such as, 'Leaves aren't really pink are they?'
5. **Encourage regular attendance**
   If you want your child to value the lessons they receive, be on time. Try not to cancel lessons unless your child is sick or there is some other unavoidable circumstance.
6. **Teach your child to look after equipment**
   Art and music equipment can be expensive, so teach your child to take care of it. Encourage your child to clean brushes, cover clay and put lids back on paints and pens so they do not dry out.

7. **Continue to encourage your child**

Parents need to be prepared for children to lose interest from time to time. This loss of interest is quite common. At these times it can be useful to show a bit of extra attention to their efforts to renew their interest – spend a little time with them while they practise, or offer to frame artwork. If the child's loss of interest continues, let them stop.

Issues relating to stress and emotional problems

Handling children's fears and worries

All human beings are afraid of something. Fear is a normal emotional reaction to threatening or dangerous events and the possibility of bad things happening. Fear creates feelings of anxiety, physiological changes that include increased heart rate, blood pressure and quickened breath, sweating, shaking and avoiding or trying to escape from the feared object. When children are frightened of something, they may also shriek, scream or run to their parents for comfort. Children's fears are much more common than was once thought. More than one-third of children between the ages of two and fourteen experience fear that is intense enough to interfere with their daily lives.

There is a wide range of things that children can be afraid of. The exact fear depends somewhat on the child's age. Table 3 includes a list of common fears experienced by children at different ages. You will notice that the specific fears experienced by children change with age.

Table 3: Common fears across age groups

AGE GROUPS

8–10 years		11–13 years		14–16 years	
Item description	% reporting this fear	Item description	% reporting this fear	Item description	% reporting this fear
Nuclear war	68	Nuclear war	80	Nuclear war	69
Being hit by a car	72	Not being able to breathe	62	Not being able to breathe	55
Not being able to breathe	68	Being hit by a car or truck	62	Bombing attacks – being invaded	53
Bombing attacks – being invaded	65	Bombing attacks – being invaded	62	Being hit by a car or truck	50
Earthquakes	62	Earthquakes	51	Fire – getting burned	48
Falling from high places	58	Fire – getting burned	51	Falling from high places	42
A burglar breaking into our house	56	A burglar breaking into our house	47	A burglar breaking into our house	39
Fire – getting burned	52	Falling from high places	46	Snakes	39
Being sent to the principal	47	Snakes	40	Spiders	36
Getting lost in a strange place	46	Death or dead people	39	Earthquakes	35

Adapted from King, N.J. et al., 1989, 'Fears of children and adolescents: A cross-section Australian study using the Revised Fear Survey Schedule for Children', *Journal of Child Psychology and Psychiatry*, vol. 30, pp. 775–84. Reproduced by permission.

When fear is intense and out of proportion to the objective danger and interferes with a child's normal activities, it is called a phobia. Why do children develop fears and why do some fears persist? Some fears are learned through direct experience with the feared object. Children may associate a particular event, such as the sight of a dog, with another event, such as a dog barking or growling, which produces fear. For example, a child walking home from school might be confronted by a dog that approaches and barks loudly. This loud, unexpected noise may produce an automatic fear reaction. The child may also learn to fear other things associated with the original frightening experience or event – seeing a large dog or walking past a particular house. The child's fear of a specific dog might be transferred to other dogs, even if they are some distance away. Whenever they see a dog the child may cling, shake, hide or in some other way try to avoid the feared object. This process of avoiding a feared object prevents the child from confronting his fear and thereby overcoming it.

Fears can also be developed through observation. For example, if a child observes a parent or older sibling scream and shriek at the sight of a spider or cockroach, the child may also learn to fear these objects. Many children learn to be afraid of precisely the same things their parents fear.

Fear can result from being directly rewarded for a fear response. For example, if a child displays fear in a particular situation, such as when her bedroom light is turned out at night, and the parent gives the child a lot of attention and reassurance, or spends time soothing, stroking or calming the child while leaving the light on, the child may be directly rewarded for her fear reaction or, more accurately, for not confronting the basis of her fear.

It is believed that the capacity to develop fear is partly inherited. Children appear to differ from birth in how easily fears can be conditioned or learned. Children who from very early in life react with distress to sudden changes, noises, strangers or other sudden stimulation, appear to learn fear reactions more quickly than more placid infants.

Some common fears in children include being hit by a car or truck, war, not being able to breathe, fire or getting burned, being sent to the principal, falling from high places, burglars, animals, failure, criticism, getting lost, being alone, the dark, thunder and lightning, frightening media stories, imaginary creatures such as monsters and separation from parents. As children get older, social fears (such as being embarrassed or rejected) become more common, and fears of physical harm reduce.

How can parents help their children overcome fear? Children are most likely to be successful when they confront their fear, while at the same time learning a new way of coping with their anxiety. The key to overcoming fear is to help your child face the situation that provokes distress. Here are some guidelines.

1. **Discuss your child's fear or worry with them**
    Speak to your child about what it is she is afraid of. Some children find it very hard to describe specifically what worries them. Others can readily tell you what they are worried about, such as a scary noise, the dark or a monster in a cupboard. Unless you have a clear idea about the source of your child's distress it will be difficult to help her deal with the fear or worry.

2. **Avoid modelling unhelpful fearful reactions**
    Since children learn a great deal through observation, it is important to effectively manage your own anxieties and fears. This means avoiding becoming highly emotional or agitated when you confront things that make you feel uncomfortable. Indeed, some parents find that acting bravely when they are with their child in a situation of threat is a very powerful way of confronting their own fear.

3. **Model active coping rather than avoidance**
    Talk to your child about situations where you have felt awkward, embarrassed or fearful, and tell him how you overcame your fear. Many adults experience anxiety in social situations that involve meeting new people, and it may be helpful to discuss how you deal with this problem if your child is experiencing something similar.

4. **Praise your child for facing her fears**
    Praise is a very effective strategy for helping children tackle and confront feared situations. If your child has been very reluctant to invite other children home to play but one day makes the effort

to do so, offer praise and encouragement. However, be careful not to go overboard, because you might embarrass your child by drawing too much attention to her efforts.

5. **Give your child something to do when confronting feared situations**

Teach your child active coping strategies to handle the feared situation. For example, if your child becomes uptight before tests or exams, teaching him simple relaxation techniques can be useful. Much of the research on the treatment of fear shows that anxiety is reduced when individuals have some specific active coping strategy for confronting fear.

6. **Remain calm when your child is upset**

If your child is obviously becoming upset after having seen, touched or heard something she is afraid of, do your best to remain cheerful, relaxed and in control. You will only make the situation worse if you allow your child's distress to affect your own actions.

7. **Be firm but positive**

Sometimes children must tackle things they are afraid of, such as going to the dentist, receiving an injection or starting at a new school. At these times do not allow your child to manipulate you into letting him avoid the situation. The child should be made to confront the situation, despite having some anxiety.

8. **Talk to your child about situations of genuine threat or danger**

There are some situations that pose a genuine risk to children, such as riding bicycles on the road, crossing a busy street, open fires, poisonous snakes or spiders and being approached by strangers. Parents can often help children learn to cope with these situations by discussing them and laying down clear, specific ground rules.

9. **Enlist the help of other children**

Children often cope better with new and potentially frightening experiences if they are with other children of the same age. For example, if a child is anxious about starting school, a trip to the local school on a weekend with a child who already attends the school can be useful. The other child can tell your child about the school.

10. Decide whether to seek professional help

If your child develops a specific fear or is generally troubled by anxiety, you need to decide whether the fear reaction is sufficiently intense to justify seeking expert help. Generally speaking, if your child is genuinely phobic – the fear significantly interferes with her daily activities – or has a large number of specific fears, then it is worth seeking professional help. This help can be obtained by getting a referral to a clinical psychologist or psychiatrist who specialises in the management of children's anxiety problems. Generally speaking, treatments that involve children in actively learning to confront and deal with their anxieties are more effective than passive methods where a lot of talk takes place but little else happens.

Stomach aches and pains

A surprisingly large number of children suffer from recurring aches and pains of one kind or another. One of the most common of these complaints is the infamous stomach ache. It is known medically as recurrent abdominal pain (RAP). Pain that is severe enough to interfere with a child's usual activities occurs in 10–15 per cent of school-aged children. In the vast majority of cases, medical investigation fails to show any specific physical cause that can explain the pain. Many children eventually grow out of the pain, although up to one-third may experience pain for several years. Children suffering from RAP can experience considerable disruption to their normal lives, including quite intense episodes of distress. Parents often wonder whether the pain is real or put on, particularly when no physical cause can be found. In the vast majority of cases children do indeed experience pain.

The cause of recurring stomach aches is not known. There are many theories, but no one knows for sure why some children develop these problems and others do not. Some researchers suggest that the pain is a symptom of psychological distress (particularly anxiety), conflict in the family or parents' marital problems, however there is little firm evidence to support this. Other researchers suggest that such children may have some ill-defined physiological disturbance that makes them vulnerable to abdominal distress.

More recently, researchers have looked at the possibility that children may learn pain behaviours within their family. It is important to remember that pain is a subjective experience. Individuals' sensitivity to painful stimulation, their tolerance of pain and how they act when in pain are influenced by a whole variety of factors. For example, when one child accidentally hits his thumb with a hammer, he may wince, hold back tears, perhaps yell but continue with the task despite the injury. Another child might scream the house down, bellowing and sobbing with such intensity that his parents are convinced he must have broken a bone.

The things children do and say when in pain are referred to as 'pain behaviours'. It is through these behaviours, such as complaining, bracing, guarded movement, lying down, resting and so on that children communicate to others the amount and type of distress they are experiencing. Like other forms of behaviour, pain behaviours can be learned. Persistent pain can begin after a period of stomach upset or other illness where the child has associated being sick with attention, sympathy and care.

Complaining of pain often leads to lots of attention. It can also lead to sympathy, back and shoulder rubs, being allowed to stay home from school, reassurance, cuddles, not having to do the dishes, being offered painkillers and so on. This kind of response from parents is quite normal and appropriate for dealing with a child's acute pain. However, it is not always helpful for a child with chronic pain problems. The attention leads the child to complain more, not less.

Children also learn about pain through observation. Many children with recurring stomach pains have parents who themselves have a chronic pain problem (particularly headaches) or chronic illness. Children can learn a great deal through observation. If they see their parent frequently complaining of pain, lying down and resting, not being able to complete normal activities including housework, or getting attention and sympathy from other family members, they are more likely to experience pain. Many parents of children with recurring pain can unintentionally make the problem worse by giving too much attention when the child complains, excusing her from routine chores and activities such as going to school, or worrying and talking a great deal about the pain.

When children experience persistent pain, they have only a limited number of strategies to deal with it. They may tell Mum or Dad they feel sick and the parent might, in turn, tell the child to lie down and rest, give him a painkiller or take him to the doctor. Some children will try other tacks such as trying not to think about the pain, distracting themselves with another activity, placing a hot water bottle on their stomach, and so on.

More commonly, children complain and expect their parents to take their pain away. This of course is quite normal and appropriate if the child has a viral infection, has injured himself or is generally unwell. However, it is not always the best way for a child to deal with a chronic pain problem.

There are several things parents can do to help children with persistent pain learn to manage or cope with their pain. In many cases the pain will disappear. It is important for your child to be under medical supervision if you attempt any of the strategies discussed below.

1. Take your child to your doctor for a thorough medical examination

Some children who suffer from persistent pain have a specific physical problem that is causing the pain, and it is very important for them to have a thorough medical assessment. The doctor should take a detailed history of the problem and thoroughly examine your child. The doctor may also order laboratory tests or refer you to a paediatrician who specialises in gastrointestinal problems (a gastroenterologist). Physical causes for recurring pain can include constipation, worms, hernia, appendicitis, spinal cord tumour and lactose malabsorption. These need to be treated.

For a minority of these children the pain is a symptom of stress or other emotional or behavioural problems, so your doctor might also ask whether there are any other problems in the family or at school.

If the medical investigation shows that there is no medical cause for the pain, which is often the case, your doctor should advise you of this fact, which is often quite reassuring. You may be told not to worry and that your child will eventually grow out of the problem. Your doctor may also give you specific suggestions about not fussing over your child and advise you to concentrate your attention on times when your child is well.

2. **Discuss the problem with your child**

    Do not tell your child that she is imagining her pain or that it is 'in her head'. If your doctor does not discuss the problem with the child, explain to her that she is not seriously ill, that while the pain is uncomfortable it will eventually pass, and that she must learn to cope with the problem herself.

3. **Offer to help your child learn a new way of dealing with the pain**

    Explain that this will involve three things: keeping a pain diary, practising some special exercises to reduce the pain and being provided with some incentives for having fewer and fewer complaints.

FIGURE 12: PAIN DIARY

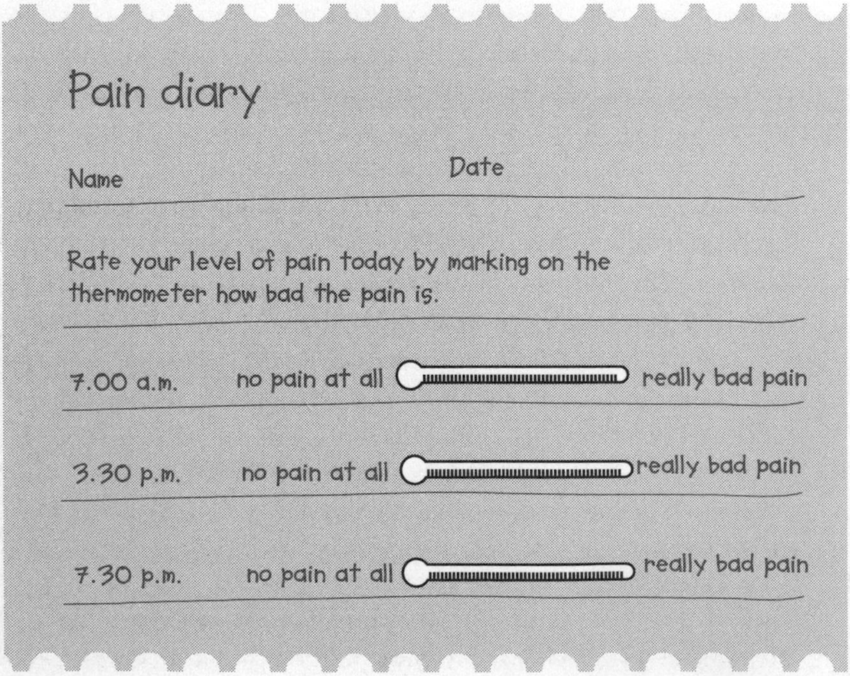

Pain diary

Name _____ Date _____

Rate your level of pain today by marking on the thermometer how bad the pain is.

7.00 a.m.   no pain at all ⊂▭▭▭▭▭▭▭▭⊃ really bad pain

3.30 p.m.   no pain at all ⊂▭▭▭▭▭▭▭▭⊃ really bad pain

7.30 p.m.   no pain at all ⊂▭▭▭▭▭▭▭⊃ really bad pain

4. **Introduce your child to the pain diary**

Figure 12 is an example of the kind of pain diary your child should complete three times a day. The diary is a 10-cm line in the shape of a thermometer, with one end corresponding to 'no pain at all' and the other to 'really bad pain'. The child marks the point on the line that corresponds to how much pain she is experiencing at the specific time. It is important that the ratings be done at the same time each day. This record is used throughout the programme to monitor your child's progress.

The diary should be kept in a convenient place, such as in the kitchen, so that it serves as a reminder to fill in the record.

You should also keep an independent record of your child's pain behaviour, similar to the one in Figure 13 (page 272). This record breaks each day into one-hour time blocks. If any of the behaviours occur during the hour, simply put a tick in the appropriate column. Don't bother to record every instance during the hour, just note whether or not the behaviour occurred.

5. **Help your child learn some coping skills**

Explain that from now on you want your child to try some new ways of dealing with the pain. There are several things that children can do when they are in pain, including using deep breathing and relaxation techniques, changing what they say to themselves when in pain, diverting their attention and using imagery. The best way for children to learn these skills is to practise them with you. Rather than insisting that the child use these skills, turn the exercise into an experiment. This involves suggesting that the child tries each one then decides for himself which ones work best for him.

6. **Relaxation techniques**

There are many different ways of learning to relax. We have found a method developed by Dr Tom Ollendick very helpful with school-aged children who have pain problems. Rather than trying to teach your child the technique yourself, you might be able to find a commercially produced audiotape that is suitable. You could also consider taking your child to a psychologist or other professional who offers relaxation training. If you tackle

FIGURE 13: PAIN OBSERVATION RECORD

Pain observation record

Name _____   Day _____   Date _____

Time	Pain complaint	Request for assistance	Crying	Vocal protest	Non-verbal pain behaviour	Rest	Non-interaction	Other
7–8 a.m.								
8–9 a.m.								
9–10 a.m.								
10–11 a.m.								
11–12 a.m.								
12–1 p.m.								
1–2 p.m.								
2–3 p.m.								
3–4 p.m.								
4–5 p.m.								
5–6 p.m.								
6–7 p.m.								
7–8 p.m.								
8–9 p.m.								

FIGURE 14: INSTRUCTION SHEET FOR PARENT'S PAIN OBSERVATION RECORD

Instruction sheet for parent's pain observation record

During the day, our child may exhibit behaviours as a result of being in pain. These pain behaviours could include any of the following.

Pain complaint (PC): This includes any instance of intelligible vocal protests about pain, such as 'I've got a sore tummy'. It does not include whining, crying or other protests that do not mention or refer directly to the experience of pain.

Requests for assistance (RA): This includes any requests for help or assistance as a consequence of being in pain, such as a request for medication, or for help to perform or complete a task.

Crying (CR): This category includes any crying due to the child being in pain.

Vocal protest (VP): This category includes any instance of intelligible vocal protests, displays of temper or oppositional behaviour such as refusing to comply with a request.

Non-verbal pain behaviours (NVPB): This category refers to any of the following:

> **Guarding** — abnormally stiff, interrupted or rigid movements while moving from one position to another.
>
> **Bracing** — a stationary position in which a limb supports another part of the body for a few seconds.
>
> **Rubbing** — rubbing or holding of the areas affected by the pain for a few seconds.
>
> **Grimacing** — facial expression of pain such as narrowed eyes, tightened lips or corners of mouth pulled back.
>
> **Sighing** — any obvious exaggerated exhalation of breath accompanied by shoulders rising then falling.

Resting (RST): This category includes resting on the bed other than at bedtime, or lying down anywhere else in the house without being engaged in an activity.

Non-interaction (NI): This category describes an absence of interactions with objects or persons.

Each time you observe any of these behaviours occuring during successive one-hour intervals, please place a tick in the appropriate column or columns on the recording sheet.

the task yourself, make a good-quality audiocassette recording of your own voice as you read the list of instructions in Appendices 2 and 3. It is very important to use a soothing, relaxing, calming tone of voice when making the recording. Perhaps a friend would be willing to help you here. The full list of instructions is given in Appendices 2 and 3 (see pages 315–21).

Relaxation training works best when your child practises it regularly, say once or twice a day for fifteen to twenty minutes.

Do the exercise with your child the first few times and offer praise for completing the practice session.

It often takes several practice sessions before a child learns to relax completely. Once the child has mastered the basic technique he should be encouraged to practise relaxing as soon as he feels a pain starting.

7. **Teach your child positive-thinking skills**
This involves teaching children things that they can say to themselves when they are in pain as an alternative to complaining. Some children in pain think negative thoughts. 'This is never going to go away.' 'Gosh this hurts.' 'Why is this happening to me?' 'What have I done to deserve this?' 'I hate this. I can't bear it.' These sorts of thoughts often make the pain seem worse. Positive thinking involves substituting different thoughts to deal with pain. Here are some examples of things children can be encouraged to say to themselves.

When they have no pain. 'I feel great. That's two days now.' 'It's working. I have not had a bad pain all morning.' 'Keep cool, stay relaxed and you'll beat it.'

When the pain starts. 'Stay cool. Don't get uptight.' 'Think positively.' 'Take a deep breath. Count back from ten.' 'What do I do next?' 'Hang in there. This will pass.' 'Just relax. Focus on slow, deep breaths.' 'Okay, find something to look at.' 'Just keep on going with what I'm doing.'

When the pain improves. 'Well done, I'm beating this.' 'Good work. It's starting to go.' 'I can't wait to tell Mum about this.'

When the pain worsens. 'Move slowly. This will pass.' 'It'll be over soon.' 'Keep trying one of my strategies.'

Figure 15 shows a summary of a coping strategy we have used to teach children with RAP to challenge and confront their pain.

8. **Deal with pain complaints by prompting your child to use self-coping strategies**
This involves changing the way you as a parent deal with complaints like 'Mummy, my tummy hurts' or 'Daddy, I feel sick.'

FIGURE 15: COPING STRATEGY FOR DEALING WITH PAIN

Coping strategy for dealing with pain

Step 1 Notice

A. Notice where the pain is.
B. Tell myself to take a deep breath.
C. Ask myself: What do I have to do next?

Step 2 Check

A. Is my pain 1 (a little pain), 2 (slight pain), 3 (fairly bad pain) or 4 (really bad pain)?
B. What happens to my pain now.

Step 3 Relax

A. Look closely at something nearby.
B. Relax my muscles.
C. Is my pain 1, 2, 3 or 4?
D. Check to see if the pain has eased.

Step 4 Reward

A. Say to myself: I am doing well.
B. Remind myself that the pain will go away because I am in control.
C. If I have no more pain, leave out the next step.

Step 5 Imagine

A. Imagine eating the rest of my pain away.
B. Is my pain 1, 2, 3 or 4?

Step 6 Repeat

A. Repeat steps 2, 3, 4 and 5 as needed.

When your child approaches, suggest he try one of his strategies. 'Okay. Now's the time. Remember what we talked about. Why don't you try one of the exercises I showed you?'

9. **If the child complies, offer praise and encouragement for getting started**
'That's the boy, Dean, you're dealing with it yourself.'

10. **If the child continues to complain or refuses to practise, suggest a specific exercise to try**
Become more specific in your suggestion. 'How about listening to the relaxation tape first to see if that helps?'

275

11. **If complaining continues, describe the problem then withdraw all attention**

    Let the child know that complaining simply does not help. 'Talking about it will not help your pain. It's over to you.' Walk away, ignoring all further protests.

12. **If your child acts as though she is in pain but doesn't complain to you, then ignore her completely**

    If you see your child bracing her stomach, walking in a guarded way or grimacing, ignore this behaviour.

13. **Do not give your child any medication to relieve pain unless it is under medical supervision**

    There is little evidence to show that painkillers are effective in relieving recurrent abdominal pain in the long run.

14. **Give your child plenty of attention when she is well**

    The idea here is to praise frequently and give positive attention to your child when she does not complain of pain and is engaged in normal activities.

15. **Establish some incentives for 'well' behaviour**

    Use a chart similar to the one in Figure 16 to reward your child for pain-free days. Each day the child goes without any pain he can earn a sticker, star, smiley face or points. Start off by setting a goal such as three pain-free days for a back-up reward. Gradually increase the requirement to four, five, six and seven days before the reward can be earned. Review the chart before bedtime each night and offer praise and encouragement for the child's efforts.

16. **Closely monitor your child's symptoms**

    Make sure you don't treat all pain complaints in this way. Children with RAP also get influenza, measles, mumps and viruses and have accidents. These problems need prompt medical attention and different remedies. You need to distinguish between these kinds of complaints and RAP.

FIGURE 16: STRATEGY FOR DEALING WITH PAIN – RECORD FORM

Strategy for dealing with pain – record form

Name   Month beginning

_____   _____

Week   Date

_____   _____

	Monday	Tuesday	Wednesday	Thursday	Friday	Saturday	Sunday
Morning 7 a.m.– 12 noon							
Afternoon 12 noon– 5 p.m.							
Evening 5 p.m.– 10 p.m.							
Total							

Place a sticker, a smiley face or agreed points in the appropriate box for each time period without pain.

Thumb (and finger) sucking

'Sarah, will you take your hand out of your mouth?' This is the exasperated plea of a parent who has just discovered her seven-year-old with her thumb in her mouth for the fourth time that morning, sucking furiously while her index finger is shoved up her right nostril. Thumb-sucking is a very common behaviour in infants and young children and indeed can occur in a foetus in the womb. It occurs in almost all normal infants and then decreases through the preschool years. About 10 per cent of six- to twelve-year-olds continue to suck their thumb or fingers. Thumb-sucking, because it occurs so frequently and declines with age, is not a serious problem and is not generally an indication of emotional or behavioural problems. However, it can become a source of friction and conflict between parents and children. In about 2 per cent of older children, the behaviour is clearly excessive and occurs whenever the child's hands are not otherwise being used. It can occur both during the day and while the child is asleep.

Parents of preschool children should not be overly concerned about thumb-sucking, even if they find the behaviour aesthetically displeasing, particularly when entertaining visitors. If, however, the behaviour occurs very frequently, it can cause dental problems (severe malocclusion of the teeth) that require treatment in older children.

Thumb-sucking in older children is often a habit they have developed and it is not generally a sign of emotional disturbance, although some disturbed youngsters may suck their thumb, fingers, hands or arms.

Parents can reduce their child's thumb-sucking in several ways. One of the most effective is a technique known as habit reversal. If your child is sucking very frequently, or is developing buck teeth, or the thumb-sucking is preventing your child from participating in other normal activities, it is reasonable to help your child overcome this habit. Here are some guidelines.

1. **Keep track of how often the behaviour occurs**
    Instead of trying to note down every time your child sucks his thumb throughout the day, select a one-hour time period in which the behaviour occurs frequently. Use a monitoring system similar to the one in Figure 17 (page 281). Every five minutes, look at your child for five seconds and simply note down in the appropriate column whether or not he is sucking. Keep this record for a week. During this baseline period, continue to use

your normal method of dealing with the problem. Your child should not know that you are monitoring his behaviour.

2. **Hold a discussion with your child to introduce the programme**

   After the one-week baseline, explain to your child that you would like her to stop sucking her thumb. Tell her that you will help her learn to stop. Explain why you think it is important that she overcome the problem. You can mention the effects on teeth as well as aesthetic reasons such as it looks awful, is unhygienic, and so on. Keep the explanation brief.

3. **Explain the incentives for good performance**

   Initially the child can earn a sticker on a chart for each five minutes without thumb-sucking. The sticker can be whatever the child likes: a star, smiley face, a quickly drawn picture, or for older children, points or ticks. Show the child a chart similar to the one in Figure 18 (page 282). Explain that you will set a timer for five minutes, and if she has not sucked her thumb or finger when the buzzer goes, she can earn a sticker. If the child manages ten or better, a small back-up reward can be given. Gradually increase the amount of time the child has to last before she can earn a sticker.

4. **Suggest something the child can do during high-risk times**

   The key is to find something else the child can do with his hands. Children who suck their thumbs a lot often do it when they are bored and not meaningfully involved in an activity. Try to find activities that involve the hands. If the child is watching television, which is often a high-risk time, he might interlock his fingers or clasp his hands together to prevent sucking whenever he feels the urge to put his hand near his mouth.

5. **Introduce the child to habit reversal**

   Each time you see your child thumb-sucking, she will be required to practise the correct behaviour repeatedly for a minute. When you observe your child thumb-sucking, say, 'No, take your hand away from your mouth now. Do your exercises for one minute.' The exercise consists of repeatedly and slowly putting the offending thumb to (but not in) her mouth and then slowly lowering her hand from her mouth, then interlocking the fingers of one hand with the fingers of the other and placing them in her lap. The fingers should be interlocked tightly for twenty seconds. This exercise should be repeated five times. You should, if necessary, guide your child through the movements, ignoring protests. Once the exercise has finished, reset the clock for five minutes. In other words, each time your child sucks her thumb she must wait a further five minutes before she can earn a sticker. When you notice your child thumb-sucking, speak matter-of-factly. Do not praise your child for doing the exercises.

6. **Have a trial run with your child**
Demonstrate exactly what he will have to do if he sucks his thumb. Answer any questions he may have. During the first few days, the programme should only operate during the selected one-hour period until the child has mastered the goal of sixty minutes without sucking.

7. **Remind the child of the rules**
Before you start, briefly remind the child of the rules.

8. **Catch your child doing the right thing**
Offer encouragement frequently during the first hour while the child refrains from thumb-sucking while engaged in an activity. 'That's seven minutes now you've gone without sucking your thumb. Well done.' This helps focus the child's attention on her successes.

9. **When thumb-sucking occurs, introduce the habit-reversal procedure**
This must be done immediately and decisively every time the behaviour occurs.

10. **Explain to your child that from now on he will have to last longer periods to earn back-up rewards**
Explain to your child that she must remember not to suck her thumb all day from now on. Divide the time your child is at home into thirty-minute time blocks, using a chart similar to the one in Figure 18 (page 282). If thumb-sucking is also a problem at school, you might consider discussing the problem with the child's teacher with a view to setting up a home–school programme that also involves the teacher. If this is the case, refer

to the guidelines for dealing with problems at school on pages 212–17. Continue the programme, using praise and rewards for the absence of thumb-sucking, and engagement in activities and habit reversal as a consequence for episodes of thumb-sucking.

11. **Phase the child off the programme**

Once the child is able to go three days without thumb-sucking, arrange a special treat such as taking him out for a meal or to a special activity in recognition of his efforts. After this, stop using the chart, but praise the child occasionally (then less and less frequently) for solving his own problem.

FIGURE 17: BASELINE RECORD OF THUMB-SUCKING

Baseline record of thumb-sucking

Time	Date						
6 p.m.	10/6						
5 minutes	✓						
10 minutes							
15 minutes	✓						
20 minutes	✓						
25 minutes	✓						
30 minutes							
35 minutes	✓						
40 minutes							
45 minutes	✓						
50 minutes	✓						
55 minutes	✓						
60 minutes	✓						
Total	9						
Percentage	75						

Fill in the date and the time you begin monitoring, and place a tick in the appropriate box if thumb-sucking is occurring at the time.

FIGURE 18: THUMB-SUCKING FORM FOR TREATMENT MONITORING

Thumb-sucking form for treatment monitoring

Name _____ Date _____ Day _____

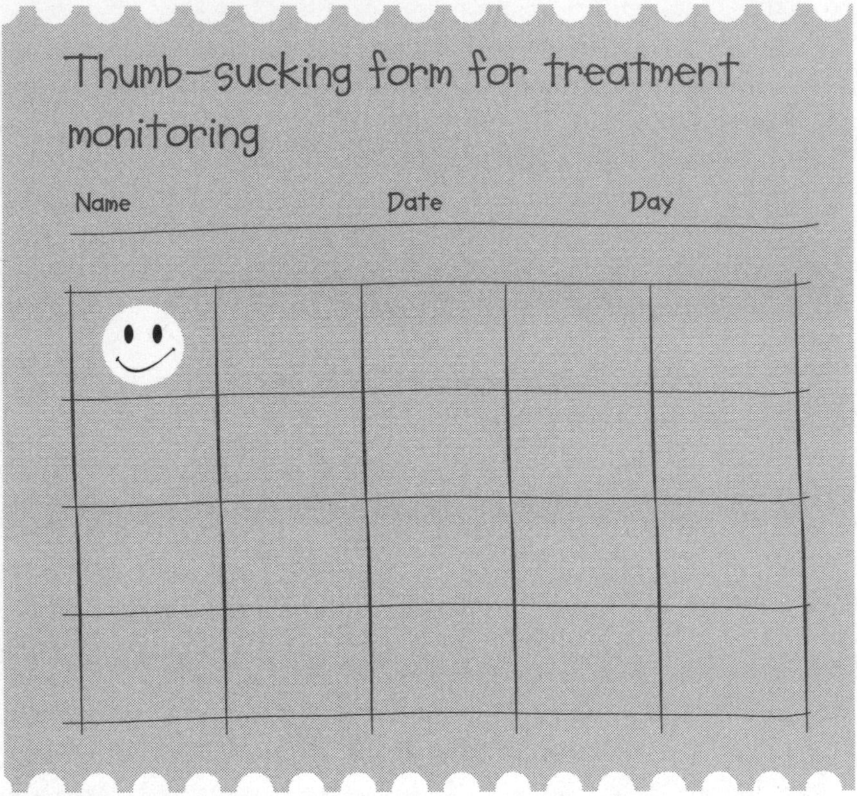

For each 30-minute interval in which thumb-sucking does not occur, place a sticker or a smiley face in a square.

Some children also suck their thumb in bed at night to help themselves get to sleep. Night-time thumb-sucking can be dealt with by putting a bitter-tasting substance on her thumb before she goes to bed. On the first few nights, tell the child that after she is in bed and has fallen asleep you will check on her every thirty minutes until you go to bed, and that if she is not sucking when you come in, you will place a sticker on a chart in her bedroom. If the child lasts the whole night without sucking, a surprise treat can be put under her pillow in the morning.

Parents need to decide for themselves whether the time and effort involved in stopping a child from thumb-sucking is worth it. Because most children eventually grow out of the habit without assistance, some parents may be prepared to endure the problem.

However, if you do decide to try to reduce the problem, follow the programme guidelines carefully and consistently.

Avoid hassling, criticising or continually giving instructions to children who thumb-suck. Sometimes the extra attention they receive can make the problem worse. Furthermore, children can become quite frustrated and irritated when attention is repeatedly but inconsistently drawn to the problem.

Bedwetting

Many children who are toilet trained during the day continue to wet their beds at night until the age of seven or eight. Bedwetting, or nocturnal enuresis, is a condition where a child has not learned voluntary night-time control over his bladder. Approximately 5 per cent of ten-year-olds and 2 per cent of twelve- to fourteen-year-olds wet the bed. In most cases there is no physical cause for the bedwetting. Nevertheless, enuretic children tend to have smaller bladder capacities than non-enuretic children. Bedwetting often seems to run in families and many bedwetters have one parent who wet the bed as a child, suggesting a genetic component. Many bedwetters are very heavy sleepers and are difficult to wake at night.

Children who continue to wet the bed throughout primary school are often embarrassed by their problem. Sleeping over at other children's houses or going on school camps creates considerable anxiety. Parents also become understandably worried about their child's problem. Family problems such as conflict can be a consequence of the bedwetting rather than a cause, and once the child stops wetting the bed other problems often disappear.

Children do not wet the bed because they are lazy, stupid, sick or defiant, and there is little evidence to show that bedwetting is related to allergies, disturbed family patterns or psychiatric disturbance. Some children wet the bed every night, while others wet once or twice a week but then experience periods of dryness for a week or longer. When children have learned to stay dry at night then start to wet again, it can be a sign of stress or anxiety. Urinating more often can be a sign of increased stress. The birth of a sibling, separation and divorce, remarriage or the death of a family member are all events that can increase episodes of bedwetting.

Bedwetting can be successfully treated in over 90 per cent of cases, although up to 40 per cent of children will start to wet the bed again and require further treatment. There are several successful treatments, all of which require parental involvement. The most successful methods are the urine alarm device, dry-bed training and retention-control training. In general, parents should seek professional advice to confirm the diagnosis and to help tackle the problem in the most appropriate manner. Here are some guidelines.

1. **Consult your family doctor**
    Your child should undergo a thorough medical examination to make sure there is no specific physical cause for the problem, and so your doctor can make the correct diagnosis.

2. **Get a referral to a competent professional**
    If your doctor suggests a referral to a paediatrician, psychologist or psychiatrist, make sure you find out whether this person has specific interests, skills and experience in dealing with enuresis, and ask what approach they take to treatment. Professional training does not guarantee that the person you are referred to has the necessary expertise to provide competent treatment for urinary incontinence problems. It is important that the person has specific experience and training in the use of behavioural techniques.

3. **Consider the treatment options**
    Following are the most commonly used treatments for enuresis.
    *   **The bell-and-pad device** is the most widely used form of treatment. A urine-sensitive pad connected to a buzzer or bell is placed on the child's bed. When the child wets, the urine completes a circuit and the alarm sounds, waking the child. The child is then expected to get up and go to the toilet to complete their urination. The basic idea behind this treatment is that if the bell or buzzer that wakes the child is repeatedly paired with the sensations associated with a full bladder, the child will eventually learn to wake up and inhibit urination. Over time, the child learns to wake up when his bladder is

full instead of to the alarm. The alarm device is typically kept on the child's bed until fourteen consecutive dry nights have been achieved.

This method has a good success rate, with more than 80 per cent of children stopping wetting. However, some children (approximately 30 per cent) relapse within the next few months, requiring a further period of treatment. This second treatment is usually successful.

Parents have an important role to play in this treatment. Be prepared for a few disturbed nights yourself because the alarm will often wake parents, who need to make sure the child wakes up and goes to the toilet. You will also be asked to keep track of the child's dry nights using some kind of behaviour chart. Give praise and positive attention for successes.

- **Dry-bed-and-cleanliness training** is often used together with the urine alarm device. It involves the child repeatedly practising the correct toileting behaviour before going to sleep (lying in bed, waking up and then running to the toilet) and when the child wets at night. The child is also expected to take responsibility for any accidents by removing dirty sheets, placing them in the washing machine, remaking the bed, resetting the alarm, and so on. Again, give praise and positive attention for successes. Parents sometimes find it difficult to get a half-awake child to go through these routines, and some children protest about being forced to do so. The advantage of the combined treatment, however, is that the child is taught proper cleanliness routines and is expected to take some responsibility for dealing with the problem. Dry-bed training can also be a successful treatment and tends to have a lower relapse rate.

- **Bladder-retention training** is a technique that aims to eliminate bedwetting by increasing a child's bladder capacity. The child is asked to drink fluids and to hold on for longer periods during the day before they urinate (no longer then one to two hours). This strategy is intended to expand bladder capacity and so reduce the need for night-time urination. This procedure on its own is successful with less than 50 per cent of bedwetters, but it is sometimes used together with the urine alarm device and dry-bed training.

- **Control training** involves the child learning better control over her muscles. She is asked to stop and start the urine flow three to five times when using the toilet.
- **Medication** is prescribed for some children to help eliminate bedwetting. The most popular drug used in the treatment of bedwetting is imipramine hydrochloride, known by the brand name Tofranil, which is an anti-depressant drug that has the side effect of urine retention. Drug treatment on its own is rarely an effective long-term cure because the majority of children relapse as soon as they come off the medication.

Some children respond to fairly simple methods, such as using a star chart with a back-up reward for dry nights. However, if your child has a longstanding bedwetting problem and wets almost every night, this strategy is not likely to be as effective as other methods.

There is little evidence to show that other forms of therapy, such as family therapy, play therapy or individual psychotherapy, are effective in eliminating bedwetting.

Various home remedies have been tried over the years, many of which are ineffective and some positively harmful. Parents who scold or spank their child for bedwetting often only make the child feel more anxious and inadequate. Some parents try to shame the child by hanging wet sheets out of their bedroom windows. Other strategies, such as making the child sleep on her back, or trying to stop her sleeping on her back, or buying a hard mattress, are quite unsuccessful.

It is generally better to seek professional assistance with bedwetting, and modern treatment methods are usually quite successful.

Issues relating to helping children solve problems

Encouraging children to be more independent

As children move through their primary school years towards puberty, they become more able to do things for themselves. They may wish to have more privacy, spend more time with friends, talk on the telephone, listen to loud music and express their opinions more forcefully. Their appearance starts to become more important to them, and arguments may develop over hairstyles, use of make-up and the style of clothing they wish to wear. Children's desires for more independence are quite normal and should not generally be viewed as problems. They need not be a major source of friction if they are handled sensibly. Nevertheless, parents can come into conflict with children over their desire to become more independent.

Parents can avoid many of the traumas with teenagers if they prepare themselves and their children for the task of taking increased responsibility. The groundwork for preparing children for the teenage years is laid during the later primary school years. This involves gradually allowing children more freedom to make their own decisions in some areas while keeping firm control in others.

Children at this age are generally capable of contributing to family decisions. Children still need rules to be enforced consistently but at the same time they need to be encouraged to express their ideas, opinions, feelings and views in appropriate ways. Older children often want to listen to and participate in adult conversations. This should be encouraged. Here are some ideas for encouraging children to become responsibly independent.

1. Give your child more responsible tasks

Like any skill, children learn to behave responsibly through practice and experience. There are many ways parents can gradually encourage more responsible behaviour. For example, a child may be given the job of being the 'light checker' or family conservationist, whose job it is to turn out lights that are not being used, thereby conserving electricity. Children can be involved in responsible chores such as helping clean the yard, planning activities for children who will be visiting, and helping serve and entertain adult guests. The best way to tell whether a child is ready for increased responsibility is to look for signs that they are interested in more responsibility. For example, they may ask to help or may enquire how a particular task is done. The key is to move at the child's pace. Don't rush or overburden your child.

2. **Praise your child for completing responsible tasks**

   When your child rises to the occasion and undertakes new responsibilities, offer praise and attention, particularly in the early stages. Offer a specific comment on the parts of the task the child did well, even if they needed your help for some aspects of it.

3. **Pay attention to responsible, kind or thoughtful behaviour that occurs without reminders**

   When children take the initiative and act responsibly of their own accord, praise and positive attention will encourage them to do so more often. If your child acts responsibly during a crisis or important situation, such as knowing what to do if another child is hurt in the playground or remembering what to do if she gets lost in a department store; or shows initiative, such as volunteering to stand for election at school, initiating a plan to start a new school newsletter, helping with deliveries for a community voluntary organisation; and so on, these efforts should be met with your approval.

4. **Help your child learn the skills involved in carrying out responsible tasks**

   Children often need help in carrying out responsible tasks. Some children will offer to take on things they are not ready for or tasks that are a little too ambitious. Suggesting a more modest plan may be necessary to prevent your child becoming discouraged. One or two specific suggestions are better than a lecture or numerous ideas on how to carry out the task.

5. **Ask your child for his opinion about issues that affect him**

   Another aspect of becoming more independent involves your child learning appropriate ways to express his ideas and opinions about matters that interest him. You can play an important role here by asking your child for his opinion on events at school, items of news or current events. 'Brian, what do you think about . . .?' He initially may have very little to say, or may respond with 'I don't know' or 'What do you think, Dad?' As your child moves towards his late primary school years and senses that you are genuinely interested in his opinions, listen to them and take them into account when deciding important family matters. This way your child will often become better able to express his views more clearly, logically and concisely.

Do not feel you have to agree with what your child says. It is okay for family members to have differences of opinion, providing they are expressed constructively.

6. **Allow your child to make more decisions for herself**

Another important part of children becoming less dependent on their parents involves learning to make decisions. Good decision making involves identifying alternative courses of action, weighing them up and choosing which course to pursue. Preadolescent children often find this difficult because they struggle to take into account all relevant pieces of information. For example, they tend to see things from their own perspective. Despite this limitation, children are quite capable of making some decisions for themselves, and the more practice they get the better they become.

Children are often confronted with dilemmas or choices before they are ready to make them. For example, many children have their first cigarette before reaching high school, and many teenagers have sex before they are legally able to consent.

Children should be encouraged to make simple choices first, such as how to spend their pocket money, whom to invite to their birthday party, what gift to choose as a birthday present, which chores to complete in what order, which homework tasks to tackle first. There are many other decisions that parents try to influence, and quite rightly so, until their children reach adolescence, such as when the children should be indoors, where they go after school and with whom, what clothes they are allowed to wear, what time they go to bed, what television programmes they are permitted to watch, when they are allowed to date, and which school they attend. In each of these areas it is irresponsible to expect children to be capable of making informed decisions.

The degree of freedom and choice children should be allowed and at what age is a controversial topic. There are no hard and fast rules here because children of the same age can differ quite considerably in maturity and capabilities. Giving children free reign too soon can be just as damaging and irresponsible as being overly controlling and not allowing a child any choice at all. In general, it is better to introduce more and more opportunities for decision making over a period of years, rather than to wait until a child reaches a specific age and then giving him all freedom at once. By approaching the task gradually and slowly, children have time to get used to the increased responsibility and trust, and to become more skilled at making responsible choices. Throughout this process, parents should be prepared to restrict then reinstate freedoms at a later time should the child act irresponsibly.

Helping children solve their own problems

One of the most important life skills young people can learn is the capacity to solve problems for themselves. Throughout their lives they will need this ability if they are to have successful, productive and happy lives. Problems that children are capable of solving come in many shapes and forms. They range from dealing with conflicts with siblings and peers, to handling disappointments and frustrations, to applying knowledge to work out the solution to a mental task. This skill can be developed in children through a combination of practice, observation, learning a few basic skills and feedback.

Some parents actively discourage their children from becoming independent problem solvers by trying to solve all their child's problems for them. This can be done in subtle ways when parents deal with children's questions about problems they confront, and by always giving them the answer to the problem rather than the tools they need to solve the problem for themselves.

Not all children are ready to learn problem-solving skills at the same time, and some will progress slowly. It takes many years for individuals to become skilled problem solvers. The sooner they start the better. Here are some guidelines.

1. **Create opportunities for your child to observe family problem solving**

   The basics of effective problem solving are best introduced by letting your child experience the process. Calling a family meeting to discuss an issue or dilemma can be a useful introduction. Start on a problem that is relatively straightforward and not emotionally charged, for example deciding on where to spend a summer holiday.

2. **Encourage your child to contribute to problem-solving discussions**

   When your child expresses an opinion on a possible course of action or solution to a problem, use encouraging comments. 'That's a good idea.' 'Yes, that's one possibility. Can you think of any others?'

3. **Prompt your child to come up with his own solutions**

   Children who run into problems over homework or conflicts with friends often want their parents to solve the problem for them. When this happens, prompt the child to express her own view on how the problem might be resolved. 'Is there anything else you might say to Mandy when she tries to copy your work in class?'

4. **Teach your child the basics of problem solving**

   The basic steps in problem solving are: defining the problem clearly, generating alternative solutions to the problem (brainstorming), weighing up the alternatives, choosing the best solution, implementing the solution and evaluating the outcome. When your child asks you to solve a problem he is capable of dealing with himself, remind him of each step one at a time. Get out a piece of paper. Ask your child to write down each heading.

   Put the responsibility back on to your child. For example, you might say, 'I know this is important to you, but I can't solve the problem for you. Let's do some brainstorming and see what we can come up with. Okay?'

Promoting children's self-esteem

Self-esteem refers to a person's view of themselves. Children with healthy self-esteem are likely to be happy, cooperative, successful at school and able to make friends easily. Positive self-esteem is caused by children thinking and believing good things about themselves.

Low self-esteem can be caused by parents making unfavourable comparisons with siblings, lack of self-care and hygiene, lack of regular exercise (and thus being overweight), physical or emotional abuse, and hearing frequent arguments and conflict between parents.

Here are some ideas for promoting healthy self-esteem in your child.

1. **Make your family a safe and secure place**
   Children feel more secure when their lives are predictable and don't change much from one day to the next.

2. **Encourage your child to be active**
   Encourage lots of active play that burns up energy. Spend time with your child in activities that will keep him active and healthy, such as running, skipping, jumping, chasing and hopping. These are activities that are fun and that children enjoy.

3. **Give your child plenty of affection**
   Children feel good about themselves when they know they are loved. Plenty of hugs, kisses and cuddles make children feel wanted and valued.

4. **Tell your child you care**
   Children appreciate being told that they are loved. Sometimes choosing a quiet moment, such as putting a child to bed, can work well.

5. **Encourage your child to set goals for herself**
   Your child will develop self-confidence when she sets goals for herself and shows herself that she can achieve what she sets out to do. Helping your child set goals often follows a discussion about a particular issue, such as schoolwork, sports, music or pocket money. It can involve simply asking her what she intends to do. 'So, what do you want to do about that?' 'What time are you

after in your swimming?' 'How many books do you think you can read this week?'

6. **Help your child learn to be a good friend**

    Having good friends has a major impact on a child's self-esteem. Friendships are important to children but they do not always know how to look after them. In incidental conversation, discuss what being a good friend means in specific situations. This may include allowing their friend to choose what games or activities they would like to do, sharing toys, speaking nicely to them and so on.

7. **Encourage your child to evaluate or reflect on his accomplishments**

    Encouraging your child to look back on something he has done or accomplished can be a useful way to help him form more accurate views of his strengths and weaknesses. For example, if your child is proudly showing you a painting he has just produced, ask him to tell you about it and how he feels about it. Encourage your child to think of things he does well. Tell him it is okay to make mistakes. To encourage your child to feel good about his accomplishments, prompt him to give himself some praise for his efforts. 'Tell me what you like about your painting.' 'You got a B-minus last time for your social studies project and an A this time. What do you think about that?'

8. **Encourage your child to express her ideas**

    Sharing opinions, ideas, thoughts and hopes teaches your child to express herself. This skill can be developed by listening to what your child has to say, summarising what you think she said and asking her a question or two about the issue she raised.

9. **Encourage laughter**

    Laugher is an emotional release. Children who feel good about themselves laugh spontaneously, develop a sense of humour and learn to tell jokes. Encourage this skill by listening and enjoying your child's stories and laughing at his jokes.

10. **Let your child make decisions**

    Your child will feel more self-confident when he has opportunities to make decisions for himself. Where it is appropriate and safe, let your child make decisions for himself. Children can make decisions about what they would like to play, whom they want to play with (within limits), what music they enjoy listening to and what games or sports they would like to play. Young children should not decide about issues such as their bedtime, dinnertime, what television programmes they are allowed to watch or what clothes they are going to wear on a school day. Involve your child in family decision making such as deciding house rules.

Conclusions

The primary school years are extremely important to children's self-esteem and their developing sense of who they are. Experiences at school and with peers help children figure out their strengths and weaknesses compared to other children of the same age. By the end of the primary school years the foundations have been laid for children to make a successful transition to the teenage years. However, by age eleven or twelve, children can vary enormously physically, socially and emotionally. Some twelve-year-olds can behave and have the interests of children much younger then they are, while others behave and look more like young teenagers. Primary school children have a greater capacity than preschoolers to solve problems for themselves, and they expect to have their opinion considered. Despite these developing abilities and the greater importance of peers and friends, all primary school children still need the firm guidance and emotional support of their parents.

PART THREE

constructive parenting

TACKLING THE TASK

CHAPTER 8

Putting a parenting plan into action

This chapter deals with how to put into action the parenting advice covered in earlier chapters. The best way to ensure that your plan is successful is to take the time to prepare both your child and yourself so that you can carry it out consistently. No strategy will work if you rush into it, without properly considering what will be involved. You will quickly become discouraged and will more than likely give up. Follow the steps below.

Working out a parenting strategy

Choosing where to begin

This is often the hardest step, particularly if your child has several problems or issues that need to be worked on. Most strategies for dealing with specific problems work best when you work on trying to improve the positive aspects of your relationship with your child at the same time. Begin with a problem that you are likely to be able to solve. This does not mean choosing a trivial or unimportant issue. Select one or two problems or issues to work on.

Check to make sure that the changes you would like to see in your child's or your own behaviour are fair and reasonable. Ask yourself: do you want to change your child's behaviour for your own convenience or would your child really benefit from the change?

Carefully read the guidelines dealing with your child's specific problem to make sure you understand what is required and that you have the time, energy and commitment to follow the plan consistently.

Do not tackle a problem on your own if you are very worried about your child and feel the problem requires professional help. For those problems that may have a physical cause contact your family physician for advice.

Taking a baseline and keeping track

A baseline record is a measure of how often the problem behaviour occurs over a specific time, usually seven to ten days. There are two main types of records that many parents find useful: a behaviour diary and a duration record.

A behaviour diary involves counting the number of times a specific behaviour occurs during the day and recording this information on a chart. An example of a behaviour diary appears in Figure 19 (page 300). Mrs Jameson used this record to get a clear idea of how frequently her son, Daniel, threw tantrums each day.

You will notice that each time Daniel screamed, shouted or threw himself on the ground, his mother wrote down the time it occurred, where the child was, what happened just before the outburst and what she did about it. This type of information is often very revealing for parents. You might find that the behaviour is occurring much more frequently than you thought, or that in fact it is not really a problem at all. You can also get an idea of the times of the day and the activities or other events that seem to trigger outbursts. Finally, you can see for yourself how consistently you deal with the problem. In Mrs Jameson's case it was clear that in the week concerned she tried six different methods of handling the problem. The other important purpose of a baseline is that it enables you to evaluate whether or not your parenting plan is working.

A duration record involves simply timing how long a behaviour lasts. This is of interest for recording behaviours such as how long a child cries after being put to bed, how long it takes a child to get ready for school and how long a child spends on her homework or chores. An example of a duration record appears in Figure 20 (page 301). The Bedford family used this record to assess how long their daughter Mary cried when put into her cot at night.

Another useful way of recording how often a behaviour occurs, especially when it occurs often – say, more than several times an hour – is a time sample record like the one in Figure 21 (page 302). Simply divide the child's day into time periods – for example, sixty, thirty, fifteen minutes – and place a ✓ in the box corresponding to the time interval when the behaviour occurred.

Information from both these records is easier to interpret if the data are presented as a simple graph like the one in Figure 22 (page 304). To plot the data, simply locate the column corresponding to the day concerned, then move up the column until you reach the number of times the behaviour occurred and place a circle or cross on the graph at that point. After a few days of recording, join the lines.

Getting yourself in a positive frame of mind

Once you have decided to tackle a problem that has been concerning you, get yourself in a positive frame of mind. Remind yourself about the need for positive thinking before you begin. It is easy to get discouraged in the early stages of putting a parenting plan into action. Your expectations have to be realistic. Remind yourself that it will take time to solve this problem.

Working out a parenting plan

The next step is to select the parenting guidelines appropriate to the problem at hand. Read each step carefully. It is often helpful to write down the steps on a checklist like the one in Figure 23 (page 308). This will serve as a quick reminder of what you need to do. For the first few weeks of the programme, or until you have learned what to do, note down whether or not you carried out each step. Just record 'yes', 'no', or 'not applicable' (if the step was not appropriate on that occasion). Simply add up the yes's, divide by the number of yes's and no's, and multiply by 100 to get a measure of how accurately you carried out the plan. You should be aiming for 100 per cent accuracy.

FIGURE 19: BEHAVIOUR DIARY

Behaviour diary

Problem event	When and where did it occur?	What occurred prior to the event?	What occurred following the event?	Other comments
Shouting	7.30 a.m. TV room	Told to get dressed for school	Let him watch TV a little longer	
Crying	8.00 a.m. TV room	TV turned off, told to get dressed	Made him go and get dressed	Rotten morning
Hitting fists on floor	8.05 a.m. Bedroom	Sent to room	Ignored him	

List the problem behaviours, when and where they occurred, and what happened before and after the event.

FIGURE 20: DURATION RECORD

Duration record

Date	Successive episodes																														Total
	1	2	3	4	5	6	7	8	9	10	11	12	13	14	15	16	17	18	19	20	21	22	23	24	25	26	27	28	29	30	31	
14/11	30 min	25 min	32 min	10 min	15 min																											1 hr, 52 min

For each separate occurrence of the target behaviour, record how long it lasted in seconds, minutes or hours. Total the times at the end of each day.

FIGURE 21: TIME SAMPLE RECORD

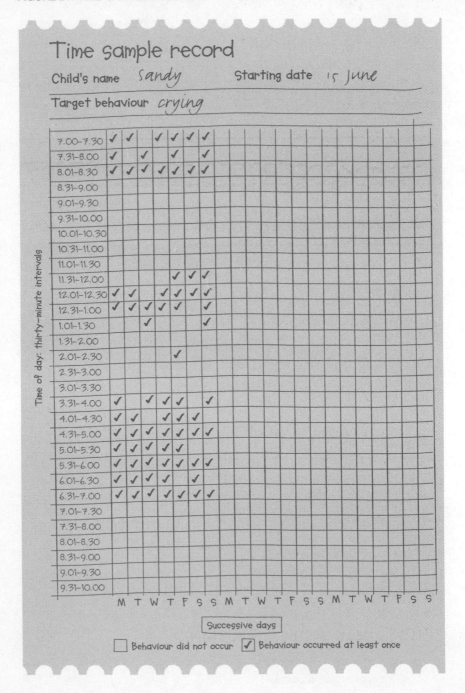

Putting a plan into action

The most important ingredient for success in changing children's behaviour is laying the foundation or groundwork properly. Take particular note of the sections in the guides that tell you the advance preparations you need to make, particularly those that involve discussing the problem and the plan with your chid. Once this has been done, put the plan into action for a trial period. Usually seven to ten days is enough. At the end of the trial period, if good progress is being made and things have been working smoothly, decide whether to continue as is or to make minor changes in your plan.

Monitoring progress and troubleshooting

Monitor your child's progress closely in the first few weeks. Keep your baseline record going and continue to graph the information so you can assess whether you have achieved your goals. If you are experiencing problems, first check to make sure that you have been following the guidelines properly. If you have been but your partner has not, you will need to discuss the issue with them and try to reach agreement on how best to deal with the problem.

Tackling other problems

Once you have successfully tackled one problem, you may decide to deal with others. The main guide here is to not take on too much at once. Changing children's behaviour, and indeed your own, is often most successful when the task is tackled gradually. If you rush into making too many changes at once, your child may feel overwhelmed, and gains achieved in one area may be lost in others. Many of the principles of constructive parenting can be successfully applied when dealing with problems not specifically discussed in this book. Be creative and develop your own solutions to other problems.

When to seek professional advice

If your child suffers from any of the following problems, consider seeking professional advice.

FIGURE 22: BEHAVIOUR GRAPH

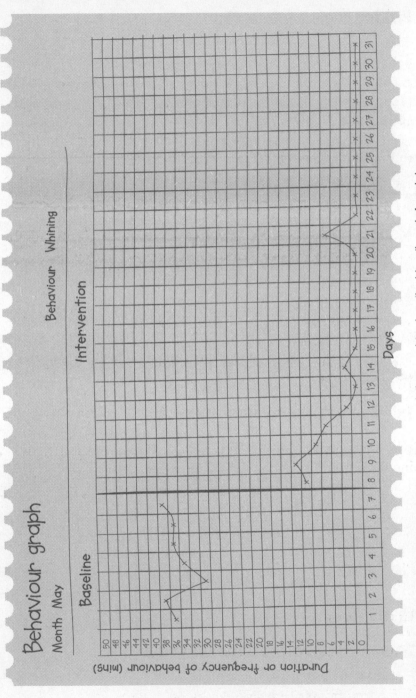

Plot the number of times the behaviour occurs each day by placing a cross in the appropriate column, then join up the marks for each day

304

Depression

Some children, particularly in the later primary school years, may suffer from depression. Some of the symptoms of depression include being persistently unhappy and miserable, withdrawn, sullen, not sleeping well, crying or becoming upset very easily, talking about harming oneself, having difficulty concentrating, or a recent change for the worse in school performance.

Serious antisocial behaviour

Children with extreme and persistent conduct problems often need professional help. If your child has persistent and extreme difficulties in following normal social rules or adult authority, is violent or very aggressive with other children, has repeated and persistent rage outbursts, lights fires, is repeatedly insolent, cheeky or rude, has been truanting from school or stealing, consider seeking professional assistance.

Concentration difficulties, impulsive behaviour and hyperactivity

Some children have real difficulties concentrating for any length of time. These children are disorganised and easily distracted. Children who have significant problems with concentration may be suffering from attention deficit hyperactivity disorder (ADHD). Children with ADHD usually have trouble concentrating (especially when doing schoolwork), and their behaviour may cause problems at school and at home. ADHD makes it hard work to concentrate, stay still and be quiet. Your child may have ADHD if they have difficulties both at school and at home and have had at least six of the listed behaviours in either of the following groups.

Inattention
The child often

- misses details or makes careless mistakes in schoolwork or other activities
- has trouble organising tasks and activities

- loses things needed for tasks or activities, such as toys, school assignments, pencils or books
- has trouble sticking to tasks or play activities
- does not seem to listen when spoken to directly
- does not follow through instructions that he is able to understand
- does not finish tasks, such as school activities or chores at home
- tries to get out of doing things that need a lot of thought and concentration
- is easily distracted or
- is forgetful in daily activities.

Hyperactivity/Impulsivity
The child often

- fidgets with hands or feet, or squirms in his seat
- leaves his seat in the classroom when he should be seated
- runs about or climbs excessively (more than most others his age)
- has trouble playing or working quietly
- is continually 'on the go'
- talks 'all the time'
- blurts out answers before the questions have been completed
- has difficulty waiting for his turn or
- butts into conversations or games.

In addition to the above points

- the child's behaviour is different from that of most other children of about the same age
- the behaviour happens in more than one place, for example at home and school
- the behaviour has lasted for more than six months
- the behaviour pattern started before the child was seven years old
- the child has no other major health or development problems and

- the behaviour is causing problems with school work, friends and daily living.

The behaviour pattern must be interfering with the child's ability to get on with her life, to learn or fit in with her world. If the child's behaviour is only a problem for the parents but the child is managing well at school, then it is usually not ADHD. Parents who believe their child might be suffering from ADHD should speak to their family doctor and have the child professionally assessed.

Unusual or bizarre behaviour

A small number of children engage in behaviour that is clearly unusual compared to that of their peers. These behaviours include hallucinations (such as hearing voices that no one else can hear), bizarre beliefs or delusions (such as believing that they are on a special mission from God), obsessions (such as recurring distressing thoughts over which they have no control), or compulsions (such as rituals they have to perform in order to avoid considerable anxiety).

Traumatic experiences

If your child has had an extremely distressing experience such as sexual abuse, witnessing a violent crime or the death of a parent or sibling, or has been in an accident or a natural disaster, she may suffer from a condition called post-traumatic stress. Symptoms include having vivid and distressing flashbacks to the event, recurring nightmares, marked anxiety, depression and recurring thoughts about the event.

Persistent anxiety or fear

If your child generally appears nervous, anxious, panicky or fearful in many different situations, consider referral to a specialist.

These are just a few examples of behaviours that are outside the normal range of problems experienced in most families. If you are in doubt and the problem does not go away, get an independent professional opinion.

FIGURE 23: PARENTING CHECKLIST

Parenting checklist

Situation: Fighting over toys

Steps to be completed	Date:												
	Time:												
1. Gain child's attention.													
2. Give a 'stop' instruction.													
3. Describe the correct behaviour (what the child should do).													
4. Wait five seconds.													
5. Repeat the instruction once if necessary.													
6. Speak up and praise if the child obeys the request.													
7. If the problem continues, describe what is wrong and introduce an immediate natural consequence (such as removal of the troublesome toy); explain why you are doing it.													
8. If the child disobeys or throws a tantrum, describe what the child has done wrong again and take the child immediately to quiet time.													
9. If the problem continues, put the child in time out immediately with a brief explanation.													
10. Remove the child from time out when the child has been quiet for the assigned time.													
Number of steps completed													

Whenever this situation occurs, record yes, no, or N/A (not applicable) for each of the steps.

A final word

We have covered a wide range of issues and problems relating to promoting children's development and dealing with children's behaviour. Some of you may feel that many of the things you are doing as parents contribute to your child's difficulty. In my experience this is rarely the case. The vast majority of parents I have worked with over the years are doing many positive and effective things with their children; they care for their children and want to do what is in their child's best interests. The solutions to many common difficulties often involve relatively minor changes or adjustments to the things that parents are already doing. For example, praising good behaviour a little more often, using a different discipline tactic a little more consistently, or simply observing your children more closely so that you become more aware of what they are doing, can produce dramatic and lasting improvements in some children's behaviour.

The basic message in this book is an optimistic one. The vast majority of children's adjustment and behavioural difficulties can be prevented or dealt with by parents and children working together towards a common goal. Many serious problems can be substantially improved so that a child does not have to endure a life of unhappiness. More minor problems, which are often part of children's normal development, can be tackled in a straightforward way using commonsense parenting. Remember, at times all children whine, complain, protest, have disagreements with their parents and become upset. The way we deal with these issues does, however, influence whether the problems continue, worsen or improve as the child grows older.

In concluding, I hope you have found this exploration of parenting useful in undertaking the most important job of all: raising healthy, well-adjusted children.

APPENDIX 1

Dietary guidelines for children

A child requires a variety of foods in the diet to promote growth, health and wellbeing. Daily selection of foods from the five food groups helps to ensure the provision of a nutritionally adequate diet.

The five food groups

Food group	Minimum number of servings for young children	Key nutrients	Some foods to choose
Breads, cereal, rice, pasta	4 1 serving = ½–1 slice bread = ¼–1 cup cooked pasta/rice	Carbohydrate Thiamine Niacin	Wholegrain/ wholemeal/ white bread, cereal, pasta, rice, muffins, crackers, bagels
Fruit and vegetables	5–7 1 serving = 1 child's handful of fruit and vegetables (choose a variety of colours)	Vitamin A Vitamin C Folate	Apples, apricots, bananas, cantaloupes, pears, plums, broccoli, carrots, capsicum, cauliflower, corn, green beans, peas, potato, tomato, zucchini

Food group	Minimum number of servings for young children	Key nutrients	Some foods to choose
Poultry, fish, meat and meat alternatives	1–2 1 serving = 60–120 g meat = 60–120 g fish = 1–2 eggs = ¼–½ cup pulses = ¼–1/3 cup nuts*	Protein Iron Niacin	Beef, veal, pork, ham, lamb, chicken, turkey, fish, soya beans, chick peas, lentils, eggs, nuts*
Milk[1], yoghurt, cheese	3 1 serving = 250 mL milk = 40 g cheese = 200 g yoghurt	Protein Calcium Riboflavin	Milk, yoghurt, cheese, custard, milk puddings
Extra foods	1–2 1 serving = 2 sweet biscuits = 1 small muffin = 1 bag chips	Carbohydrate Fat	Sweet biscuits, cakes, chips, chocolate

Serving sizes are approximate and will vary according to the age and size of the child.

+ Low-fat varieties not to be used for children under the age of two.

* Not to be given to children under five.

Note: Children aged one to six years old should limit their intake of fruit juice to 150 mL per day, and for seven- to eighteen-year-olds to 240–360 mL per day.

Sample menus

For children aged eighteen months to three years	For children aged three–five years
Breakfast Cereal: 1 Weetbix or ½ cup porridge and milk Toast: ½ slice with butter or margarine, peanut paste, vegemite, honey, jam Milk: 20 mL whole milk, to drink	*Breakfast* Cereal: 1½ Weetbix or ¾ cup porridge and milk Toast: ½–1 slice with butter or margarine with 1 egg scrambled, boiled or poached Milk: 150 mL whole milk, to drink
Mid-morning Milk or juice and some fruit and one cracker with vegemite	*Mid-morning* Milk or juice, and one banana or one apple and two plain biscuits
Lunch Sandwich: one slice bread with butter or margarine with cheese, peanut paste, ½ cup yoghurt and/or fruit	*Lunch* Sandwich: 1–2 slices bread with butter or margarine with cheese, peanut paste, cottage cheese and tomato, ⅓ cup yoghurt, ⅓ cup custard and/or fruit
Mid-afternoon Milk, ½ banana and one plain biscuit	*Mid-afternoon* Milk or water, and ½ slice fruit cake
Dinner Minced or chopped meat, flaked or crumbed fish or vegetarian dish including pulses 1 small boiled or mashed potato and ⅓ cup vegetables Milk pudding	*Dinner* Small crumbed and grilled leg of chicken or one grilled sausage or ½ cup savoury mince or fish fillet in sauce 1 small baked potato or ½ cup pasta and ⅓ cup vegetables or a small salad ⅓ cup ice cream and/or fruit
Supper Milk to drink	*Supper* Milk to drink

Note: Use butter and margarine sparingly

For children aged five–eight years	For children aged eight to teens
Breakfast Cereal: 1⅓ Weetbix or ¾ cup porridge or ¾ cup cornflakes and milk Toast: 1 slice with butter or margarine, and 1 slice cheese or ¼ cup baked beans or 1 egg Milk and/or juice to drink	*Breakfast* Cereal: 2 Weetbix or 1 cup porridge or 1 cup cornflakes and milk Toast: 1 slice with butter or margarine, and cheese or ½ cup baked beans or 1 egg Milk and/or juice, and tea or coffee
Mid-morning Milk or juice, 1 fruit and 1 biscuit	*Mid-morning* Juice, 1 fruit and 1 packet nuts and raisins
Lunch Sandwich: 2 slices bread with butter or margarine with ham, cheese, peanut paste, chopped egg or meat paste Small salad or raw carrot, tomato and celery 1 piece fruit or 2 tablespoons dried fruit and/or ½ carton yoghurt	*Lunch* Sandwich or roll (wholemeal or grain) with butter or margarine with ham, cheese, cottage cheese, peanut paste, meat paste or egg Salad with carrot, celery and capsicum 1 piece fresh fruit, dried fruit, nuts, cheese or yoghurt
Mid-afternoon Milk or juice and 2 crackers with cottage cheese or yoghurt and 1 small packet chips	*Mid-afternoon* Fruit or sandwich or crackers and low-fat cheese or cereal or yoghurt, and 1 glass milk
Dinner Meat, grilled rissole/burger, fish fillet 2 small boiled, mashed or baked potatoes, or ¾ cup pasta/rice ½ cup vegetables or a salad, or a made-up dish such as pizza, fish pie, cottage pie, pasta or lasagne Fruit plus ½ cup custard, ½ cup yoghurt or 2 scoops frozen yoghurt	*Dinner* Meat, fish, vegetarian dish 2–3 small boiled, mashed, baked or roasted potatoes, or ¾ cup pasta or rice ½ cup vegetables (include at least 2 types), or a made-up dish such as pizza, fish pie, cottage pie, pasta or lasagne Fruit pie plus ½ cup custard, 2 scoops ice-cream or ¾ cup yoghurt

For children aged five–eight years	For children aged eight to teens
Supper	*Supper*
Milk or Milo	Milk or Milo
	(Older children may enjoy a bowl of cereal or toast or a sandwich)

Prepared by Dr Clare Wall, Senior Lecturer, Institute of Food Nutrition and Human Health, Massey University, New Zealand. Reproduced with permission.

APPENDIX 2

Relaxation training with children aged 6–10

Rationale

Sometimes we all feel kind of tense or nervous. When you feel nervous your muscles get all tight and tense and it is hard to pay attention to what you are supposed to be doing. For example, some people feel nervous before they take a test or feel tense when they are meeting someone new. Can you give some examples of when you have felt tense? [Allow child to respond.] We're going to learn how to make ourselves feel nice and relaxed instead of tight and tense. We'll learn how to tell when our muscles feel tense and how to make them feel relaxed. [If any muscles are sore on a particular day and tensing them hurts, be sure to stop the child tensing those muscles; just relax them.]

Hands and arms

Pretend you have a whole lemon in your left hand. Now squeeze it hard. Try to squeeze all the juice out. Feel the tightness in your hand and arm as you squeeze. Now drop the lemon. Notice how your muscles feel when they are relaxed. Take another lemon and squeeze it. Try to squeeze this one harder than you did the first one. That's right. Really hard. Now drop your lemon and relax. See how much better your hand and arm feel when they are relaxed. Once again, take a lemon in your left hand and squeeze all the juice out. Don't leave a single drop. Squeeze hard. Good. Now relax and let the lemon fall from your hand. [Repeat the process for the right hand and arm.]

Arms and shoulders

Pretend you are a furry, lazy cat. You want to stretch. Stretch your arms out in front of you. Raise them up high over your head. Way back. Feel the pull in your shoulders. Stretch higher. Now just let your arms drop back to your side. Okay, kitten, stretch again. Stretch your arms out in front of you. Raise them over your head. Pull them back, way back. Pull hard. Now let them drop quickly. Good. Notice how your shoulders feel more relaxed. This time let's have a great big stretch. Try to touch the ceiling. Stretch your arms way out in front of you. Notice the tension and pull in your arms and shoulders. Hold tight now. Great. Let them drop very quickly and feel how good it is to be relaxed. It feels good to be warm and lazy.

Shoulders and neck

Now pretend you are a turtle. You're sitting out on a rock by a nice, peaceful pond, just relaxing in the warm sun. It feels nice and warm and safe here. Oh oh! You sense danger. Pull your head into your house. Try to pull your shoulders up to your ears and push your head down into your shoulders. Hold in tight. It isn't easy to be a turtle in a shell. The danger is past now. You can come out into the warm sunshine, and, once again, you can relax and feel the warm sunshine. Watch out now! More danger. Hurry, pull your head back into your house and hold it tight. You have to be closed in tight to protect yourself. Okay, you can relax now. Bring your head out and let your shoulders relax. Notice how much better it feels to be relaxed than to be all tight. One more time now. Danger! Pull your head in. Push your shoulders way up to your ears and hold tight. Don't let even a tiny piece of your head show outside your shell. Hold it. Feel the tenseness in your neck and shoulders. Okay, you can come out now. It's safe again. Relax and feel comfortable in your safety. There's no more danger. Nothing to worry about. Nothing to be afraid of. You feel good.

Jaw

You have a giant jawbreaker bubblegum in your mouth. It's very hard to chew. Bite down on it. Hard! Let your neck muscles help you. Now relax. Just let your jaw drop. Okay, let's tackle that jawbreaker again now. Bite down. Hard! Try to squeeze it out between your teeth. That's good. You're really tearing that gum up. Now relax again. Just let your jaw drop off your face. It feels so good just to let go and not have to fight that bubble gum. Okay, one more time. We're really going to tear it up this time. Bite down. Hard as you can. Harder. Oh, you're really working hard. Good. Now relax. Try to relax your whole body. You've beaten the bubble gum. Let yourself go as loose as you can.

Face and nose

Here comes a pesky old fly. He has landed on your nose. Try to get him off without using your hands. That's right, wrinkle up your nose. Make as many wrinkles in your nose as you can. Scrunch your nose up really hard. Good. You've chased him away. Now you can relax your nose. Oops, here he comes back again. Shoo him off. Wrinkle it up hard. Hold it just as tight as you can. Okay, he flew away. You can relax your face. Notice that when you scrunch up your nose your cheeks and your mouth and your forehead and your eyes all help you, they get tight, too. So when you relax your nose, your whole face relaxes too, and that feels good. Oh oh! That old fly has come back, but this time he's on your forehead. Make lots of wrinkles. Try to catch him between all those wrinkles. Hold it tight, now. Okay, you can let go. He's gone for good. Now you can just relax. Let your face go smooth, no wrinkles anywhere. Your face feels nice and smooth and relaxed.

Stomach

Hey! Here comes a cute baby elephant. But he's not watching where he's going. He doesn't see you lying there in the grass, and he's about to step on your stomach. Don't move. You don't have time to get out of the way. Just get ready for him. Make your stomach very hard. Tighten up your stomach muscles really tight. Hold it. It looks like he is going the other way. You can relax now. Let your stomach go soft. Let it be as relaxed as you can. That feels so much better. Oops, he's coming this way again. Get ready. Tighten up your stomach. Really hard. If he steps on you when your stomach is hard, it won't hurt. Make your stomach into a rock. Okay, he's moving away again. You can relax now. Settle down, get comfortable and relax. Notice the difference between a tight stomach and a relaxed one. That's how we want it to feel: nice and loose and relaxed. You won't believe this, but this time he's really coming your way and not turning around. He's headed straight for you. Tighten up. Tighten hard. Here he comes. This is really it. You've got to hold on tight. He's stepping on you. He's stepped over you. Now he's gone for good. You can relax completely. You're safe. Everything is okay, and you can feel nice and relaxed.

Legs and feet

Now pretend that you are standing barefoot in a big, fat mud puddle. Squish your toes down deep into the mud. Try to get your feet down to the bottom of the mud puddle. You'll probably need your legs to help you push. Push down, spread your toes apart and feel the mud squish up between your toes. Now step out of the mud puddle. Relax your feet. Let your toes go loose and feel how nice that is. It feels good to be relaxed. Back into the mud puddle. Squish your toes down. Let your leg muscles help you push your feet down. Push your feet. Hard! Try to squeeze that mud puddle dry. Okay, come back out now. Relax your feet, relax your legs, relax your toes. It feels so good to be relaxed. No tenseness anywhere. You feel kind of warm and tingly.

Source: Ollendick, T.H., 1981, *Relaxation training instructions*, Department of Psychology, Virginia Polytechnic and State University. Reproduced with permission from the author.

APPENDIX 3

Relaxation training with children aged 11–13

Hands and arms

Make a fist with your left hand. Squeeze it hard. Feel the tightness in your hand and arm as you squeeze. Now let your hand go and relax. See how much better your hand and arm feel when they are relaxed. Once again, make a fist with your left hand and squeeze hard. Good. Now relax and let your hand go. [Repeat the process for the right hand and arm.]

Arms and shoulders

Stretch your arms out in front of you. Raise them high up over your head. Way back. Feel the pull in your shoulders. Stretch higher. Now just let your arms drop back to your side. Okay, now; let's stretch again. Stretch your arms out in front of you. Raise them over your head. Pull them back, way back. Pull hard. Now let them drop quickly. Good. Notice how your shoulders feel more relaxed. This time let's have a great big stretch. Try to touch the ceiling. Stretch your arms way out in front of you. Raise them way up high over your head. Push them way, way back. Notice the tension and pull in your arms and shoulders. Hold tight now. Great. Let them drop very quickly and feel how good it is to be relaxed. It feels good and warm and lazy.

Shoulders and neck

Try to pull your shoulders up to your ears and push your head down into your shoulders. Hold in tight. Okay, now relax and feel the warmth. Again, pull your shoulders up to your ears and push your head down into your shoulders. Do it tightly. Okay, you can relax now. Bring your head out and let your shoulders relax. Notice how much better it feels to be relaxed than to be all tight. One more time now. Push your head down and your shoulders way up to your ears. Hold it. Feel the tenseness in your neck and shoulders. Okay. You can relax now and feel comfortable. You feel good.

Jaw

Put your teeth together really hard. Let your neck muscles help you. Now relax. Just let your jaw hang loose. Notice how good it feels just to let your jaw drop. Okay, bite down again hard. That's good. Now relax again. Just let your jaw drop. It feels so good just to let go. Okay, one more time. Bite down. As hard as you can. Harder. Oh, you're really working hard. Good. Now relax. Try to relax your whole body. Let yourself go as loose as you can.

Face and nose

Wrinkle up your nose. Make as many wrinkles in your nose as you can. Scrunch your nose up really hard. Good. Now you can relax your nose. Now wrinkle up your nose again. Wrinkle it up hard. Hold it just as tight as you can. Okay, you can relax your face. Notice that when you scrunch up your nose that your cheeks and your mouth and your forehead all help you and they get tight, too. So when you relax your nose, your whole face relaxes too, and that feels good. Now make lots of wrinkles on your forehead. Hold it tight now. Okay, you can let go. Now you can just relax. Let your face go smooth. No wrinkles anywhere. Your face feels nice and smooth and relaxed.

Stomach

Now tighten up your stomach muscles really tight. Make your stomach really hard. Don't move. Hold it. You can relax now. Let your stomach go soft. Let it be as relaxed as you can. That feels so much better. Okay, again. Tighten your stomach really hard. Good. You can relax now. Kind of settle down, get comfortable and relax. Notice the difference between a tight stomach and a relaxed one. That's how we want it to feel. Nice and loose and relaxed. Okay. Once more. Tighten up. Tighten hard. Good. Now you can relax completely. You can feel nice and relaxed.

This time, try to pull your stomach in. Try to squeeze it against your backbone. Try to be as skinny as you can. Now relax. You don't have to be skinny now. Just relax and feel your stomach being warm and loose. Okay, squeeze in your stomach again. Make it touch your backbone. Get it really small and tight. Get as skinny as you can. Hold tight. You can relax now. Settle back and let your stomach come back out where it belongs. You can feel really good now. You've done well.

Legs and feet

Push your toes down on the floor really hard. You'll probably need your legs to help you push. Push down, spread your toes apart. Now relax your feet. Let your toes go loose and feel how nice that is. It feels good to be relaxed. Okay, now push your toes down. Let your leg muscles help you push your feet down. Push your feet. Hard. Okay, relax your feet, relax your legs, relax your toes. It feels so good to be relaxed. No tenseness anywhere. You feel kind of warm and tingly.

Source: Ollendick, T.H. & Cerny, J.A. 1981, *Relaxation instructions with children aged 11–13*, 1981, Department of Psychology, Virginia Polytechnic and State University. Reproduced with permission from the author.

APPENDIX 4

Reusable forms

Behaviour diary

Problem event	When and where did it occur?	What occurred prior to the event?	What occurred following the event?	Other comments

List the problem behaviours, when and where they occurred, and what happened before and after the event.

322

Duration record

Date	Successive episodes																															Total
	1	2	3	4	5	6	7	8	9	10	11	12	13	14	15	16	17	18	19	20	21	22	23	24	25	26	27	28	29	30	31	

For each separate occurrence of the target behaviour, record how long it lasted in seconds, minutes or hours. Total the times at the end of each day.

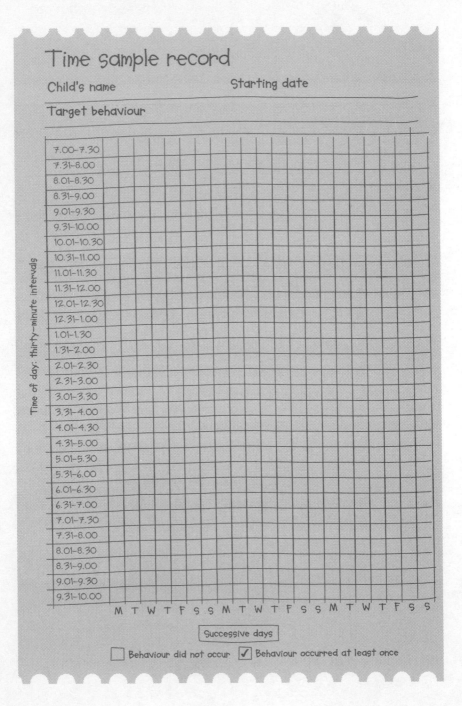

Time sample record

Child's name _____ Starting date _____

Target behaviour _____

Time of day: thirty-minute intervals		M	T	W	T	F	S	S	M	T	W	T	F	S	S	M	T	W	T	F	S	S
7.00–7.30																						
7.31–8.00																						
8.01–8.30																						
8.31–9.00																						
9.01–9.30																						
9.31–10.00																						
10.01–10.30																						
10.31–11.00																						
11.01–11.30																						
11.31–12.00																						
12.01–12.30																						
12.31–1.00																						
1.01–1.30																						
1.31–2.00																						
2.01–2.30																						
2.31–3.00																						
3.01–3.30																						
3.31–4.00																						
4.01–4.30																						
4.31–5.00																						
5.01–5.30																						
5.31–6.00																						
6.01–6.30																						
6.31–7.00																						
7.01–7.30																						
7.31–8.00																						
8.01–8.30																						
8.31–9.00																						
9.01–9.30																						
9.31–10.00																						

Successive days

☐ Behaviour did not occur   ☑ Behaviour occurred at least once

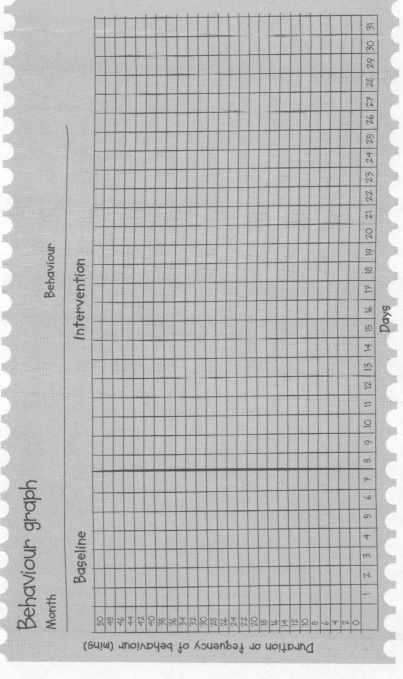

Behaviour graph

Month

Baseline

Intervention

Behaviour

Duration or fequency of behaviour (mins)

50
48
46
44
42
40
38
36
34
32
30
28
26
24
22
20
18
16
14
12
10
8
6
4
2
0

1 2 3 4 5 6 7 8 9 10 11 12 13 14 15 16 17 18 19 20 21 22 23 24 25 26 27 28 29 30 31

Days

Plot the number of times the behaviour occurs each day by placing a cross in the appropriate column, then join up the marks for each day

Parenting checklist

Situation _____

Steps to be completed	Date:												
	Time:												
Number of steps completed													

Whenever this situation occurs, record yes, no, or N/A (not applicable) for each of the steps.

ACKNOWLEDGEMENTS

This book is dedicated to my parents, Roy and Elaine Sanders, whose love and support have taught me the importance of family values and of good parenting throughout our lives. I would also particularly like to thank my wife, Trish, whose support and encouragement have been essential in completing this book, and our two children, Emma and Ben, who have been the most informed advocates and constructive critics of the constructive parenting approach, as they have experienced it first-hand within our family.

Many thousands of parents have participated in research projects undertaken by my research team at the Parenting and Family Support Centre, which is part of the School of Psychology at The University of Queensland. These parents and their children have helped me shape my ideas on how to raise healthy, well-adjusted children. I would like to especially thank those families who have devoted many hours, opened up their homes, and shared private reflections on themselves as parents and their children. This has allowed families to be observed, parents to be interviewed and much detailed information to be collected. This information provided us with essential feedback about what parents think and find useful.

I would also like to acknowledge the many colleagues and

students who have worked with me over the years and whose ideas and views have inspired and shaped my approach to parenting. These include my own supervisors and mentors Ted Glynn and Todd Risley, former students and colleagues Mark Dadds, Karen Turner, Carol Markie-Dadds and Alan Ralph.

Finally, I would like to thank the many health, education and welfare professionals who have used *Every Parent* in their work with families. These professional colleagues have provided me with invaluable insights into how *Every Parent* can be used as a useful clinical tool and resource in working with families.

INDEX